Mortal Dilemmas

What You Need to Know About Dying
Before You Are Dying

To Charlene & Dick, with thanks for all you have given to LPC and our denomination!

Sheryl L. Buckley

Sheryl L. Buckley, M.D., M.S.

Dedication

This book is dedicated to my parents, Marjorie Kitchen Buckley and William Faulkner Buckley, Sr. and to my pastor, the Reverend Doctor James C. Butler, who said to me, "You need to write this book."

Table of Contents

Acknowledgments vii

Introduction ix

Chapter 1: What's Wrong with Dying? 1

Chapter 2: The Mixed Blessings of Advance Directives 19

Chapter 3: Hospice and Palliative Care: Wonderful Blessings 39

Chapter 4: The Sanctity of Life. . .and Death? 61

Chapter 5: Pain—and Suffering? 99

Chapter 6: Growth at the End of Life 110

Chapter 7: Euthanasia and Physician-Assisted Suicide 120

Chapter 8: "Is This the Illness That Should Be *Allowed*
to Be Fatal?" 147

Chapter 9: "The Rules" According to Dr. Buckley 160

Afterword 165

End Notes 167

References 177

Appendix 189

Index 191

Acknowledgments

No work like this is the product of a single person. I have benefitted from generous help at many points along the pathway of bringing this book to birth. Professors Carol Donley and Damaris Peters-Pike of Hiram College read early drafts and encouraged me to continue the project. Carol also acted as my mentor when I first began teaching at Hiram. Minister-friends who also read parts of drafts and offered their critiques were the Reverends Kitty Borchert, Barbara Ray Davis, and Howard Ratcliff and the Reverend Doctors James C. Butler and Malcolm Peel. Dear friends who read all or part of the manuscript and shared their reactions (and sometimes their own stories which they graciously allowed me to use) include Coreen Cool, Karen Hottel, Brian Hodgekinson, Ken Hook (who read this while he knew he was dying from cancer), and Ginny Mayhew. My cherished God-mother, Betty Herrmann, also gave me the benefit of her perspective on the manuscript from a member of my parents' generation. I also owe a debt of gratitude to my students in the Weekend College at Hiram College, where I have taught this material several times, for their candid reactions which helped me to sharpen many points before I first started to write this work. One class agreed to take individual chapters home and critique them (after their final grades were turned in to the Registrar); their thoughtful analyses were extraordinarily helpful to me. They also shared many of their own stories with me and some of them are included in this book. Thanks to the Hospice of the Western Reserve, Cleveland, Ohio, who kindly gave me permission to reproduce their document, "Preparing for the Conversation," (see Appendix) which is part of an excellent free publication called *Courage in Conversation*. Finally, I must thank the patients from whom I learned so much, some of whose episodes of illness are recounted. I have changed details to protect their privacy but it was a privilege to practice medicine among them for thirty-two and a half years.

I am very grateful for the expert editing and overall guidance my editor, Katherine Harper provided. She was invaluable since this is my first book; every suggestion she made improved the work. Talented graphic designer-cousins Jenn and Ken Visocky-O'Grady graciously designed the cover art work. Another talented cousin reproduced the graphs in Figure 1 from my class notes in the Master's Administrative Medicine Program at the University of Wisconsin at Madison where I first learned about them in David A. Kindig, M.D., Ph.D.'s class. David Everett, Hiram College Librarian, was enormously helpful when I discovered that all of my library research skills were from pre-computer days and woefully out-of-date. He tirelessly produced copies of articles and other pertinent information. Chris Faiver, Ph.D., an experienced author, not only served as a project advisor but also functioned as my tech guru when I could not make the computer do what I wanted it to. Without his help the book would still be hand-written notes. Thanks to Tim Leonhart and Tim Snider and their team at Bookmasters for being supportive and handling all the details of the printing process, a complete mystery to first-time authors, so skillfully. If I have overlooked anyone who deserves to be mentioned, I apologize.

Introduction

"Y OUR FATHER HAS NOT REGAINED CONSCIOUSNESS. HOWEVER, HE IS NOW breathing on his own. He has not triggered the ventilator for several hours, so it is time to pull out the breathing tube. If he tires in a few hours and cannot breathe on his own, what do you want me to do?"

Standing at my father's bedside in the Intensive Care Unit, facing a pulmonary doctor I had only met two days before—and toward whom I had formed an unexplained but visceral dislike—I could hardly believe my ears. *What did I want him to do?* I briefly considered giving him my honest answer: "I want you to get out your magic wand, tap my dad on the shoulder and make him as healthy as he was about ten years ago, that's what I want. And if you can do it, you stupid S.O.B., why haven't you done so already? What in God's name are you waiting for?"

Then my eight years of medical school, internship and residency training and 20 years in practice as an anesthesiologist kicked in. This diatribe, I realized, although it accurately reflected my wishes, would not be endorsed by my profession's canons of behavior. Nor would my desire to grab the doctor by the lapels of his white lab coat and shake him the way a terrier shakes a rat. More importantly, neither of these would improve matters for my father. Although it took more self-control than anything ever had thus far in my life, I took a deep breath and replied, "It does not matter what I want. Mr. Buckley has left an Advance Directive. In it, he states that he does not want to be permanently maintained on machines. If he cannot breathe on his own, then we will respect his wishes and allow him to die."

This conversation occurred during the half-hour morning ICU visiting window for families. We returned for the 2:00–2:30 visit, at which point Dad seemed to be breathing all right. But later that same afternoon, the phone rang. There is a terrible dread associated with telephones when a loved one is in the hospital, especially when that person is critically ill.

Every time it rings, your heart just lurches. This message was the one our family dreaded: "Mr. Buckley has taken a turn for the worse."

My mother and I flew out the door, desperately calling my brothers' cell phones as we headed toward the hospital. We were veterans at this by now and knew that when you are in a real hurry, you bypass the parking garage and use the Emergency Room lot. We also knew the shortest route through the corridors to the ICU. Mom and I ignored protocol, bursting through the double doors without stopping at the call box to ask permission. An ICU resident turned toward us at the door to Dad's cubicle. His face was serious. "I'm sorry," he said. "Mr. Buckley has just taken his last breath."

He was correct. We stood at Dad's side as the cardiac monitor's beeps took on an increasingly irregular rhythm. One of my brothers made it into the room before the line went flat; the other, and the minister from our church, arrived just minutes later. William Buckley Sr. died on April 10, 1993, according to the wishes expressed in his Advance Directive.

Fast-forward eight years. Now it was my mother who was dying. Unlike my father, who had left us quickly after a dramatic final illness, Mom was at home under hospice care. Like many senior citizens, she had a number of chronic medical problems, which were being well-managed by a group of expert physicians. An adult-onset diabetic, she had responded well to the program her endocrinologist had devised. She had struggled for 25 years with a focal abscess in one kidney which kept resulting in kidney stones. She had experienced episodes of congestive heart failure but was competently managed by a wonderful cardiologist. Then she came down with a severe case of shingles and learned that she was among the small number of people whose pain never goes away. Her neurologist worked long and hard to find ways to make her as comfortable as possible and was very aggressive in treating her pain, which was truly disabling. In only a short time, my mother had become a member of the group now called the "frail elderly."

In what proved to be the last year of her life, she was hospitalized twice for her urinary infection and managed by an infectious disease specialist who ordered multiple intravenous antibiotics. Both times she found it a miserable experience. She was so weak that she required help to reach a bedside commode, but, as people with this problem know, urgency is one symptom of the infection, and she frequently wet her bed before someone arrived to assist her. She found this to be humiliating, frustrating and physically chilling. Lying in a wet bed is no fun. The first hospitalization ran from December 18th until January 15th, so she also forfeited all of the holiday festivities and decorations she so enjoyed. When she had to be readmitted in April for the same infection, she was profoundly discouraged. Again, despite multiple antibiotics and oversight by a specialist, it was almost three weeks before she was discharged.

She simply drifted downhill after that. There was no dramatic incident as there had been with my father. Although getting her to her doctor was an expedition and she now had to be pushed to his office in a wheelchair, I took her there twice because I was concerned that she was not regaining her strength and mental acuity. He did a conscientious work-up, looking for problems that might not have been identified or interactions among her many medications, to no avail. Between the pain from the shingles and her overall condition, a trip to the hospital for a CAT scan was an endurance challenge. She became so debilitated that a nursing home seemed the only way to provide the round-the-clock assistance and care she required.

Then a friend of my brother's asked if we had considered hospice. *Hospice???* I thought. Was she dying? Was that what the downhill course over the summer amounted to?

I called Mom's primary physician, who already knew that we were reluctantly considering nursing home placement, and asked him about a hospice evaluation. He was uncertain whether that course was necessary but agreed that investigating it was a good idea. "If they don't think she's dying, they won't admit her," he told me. The nurse came the next morning and talked with Mom and me for a long time. Then she drew up the necessary paperwork and admitted her to hospice.

Under the hospice philosophy, the comfort of the dying patient is paramount, so Mom's nurse immediately showed me how to make her more comfortable and simplify her medication. For the next seven weeks, the diabetic diet she had followed so faithfully for years was abandoned and she could have anything that tempted her to eat. Her friends and family came to call as they were able; we kept no "visiting hours." My mother, Marjorie Buckley, died peacefully in her own home, surrounded by her children and her beloved pets, on October 23, 2001.

Neither of my parents' deaths was easy on them, or on the family members who survived them. Reflecting on their two very different experiences was part of my motivation for writing this book.

We are all profoundly marked by the deaths we witness. Most people can remember losing a loved one at least once in their own lifetime. My own case is somewhat different, because I had the privilege of practicing anesthesiology for more than three decades. Some of my patients were in various stages of dying when they came under my care, so I had the opportunity to look at dying from an "outside" perspective. In addition, for about 20 years I chaired hospital ethics committees. The most divisive and difficult problems, often about end-of-life issues, landed at our door begging for some form of resolution, so I acquired a fund of stories from that experience.

For the past several years, I have enjoyed the opportunity to teach in The Weekend College at Hiram College in Hiram, Ohio. One of my longest-running courses is called "Contemporary Moral Problems." It examines issues in medical ethics such as abortion, euthanasia and physician-assisted suicide, genetic engineering, the use of humans and animals in research, and new reproductive technologies. Teaching that course has allowed me to resurrect my undergraduate philosophy major and spurred me to read the bioethical literature seriously and extensively. This study resulted in my creating a second course, "Euthanasia and Physician-Assisted Suicide," preparation for which led me to *The Troubled Dream of Life: In Search of a Peaceful Death* by Daniel Callahan, a philosopher and co-founder of The Hastings Center, a major bioethical think-tank in New York. His thoughts have profoundly influenced my own thinking and resonated strongly with some of my experiences practicing medicine and dealing with dying patients and their families.

Chapter 1 of this book deals with the question of why dying seems to be so hard in 21st-century America. Although it has never been pleasant, it seems to many observers that the experience is actually more difficult, not easier, today, despite modern medicine. Why is that so? What can be done to identify and fix the problems? Is technology part of the problem? Bioethicists, particularly those interested in the role of narrative in ethics, have alerted us to the power of language and metaphors, images that shape our thinking. One of the most common metaphors applied to medical practice by doctors and patients alike is the military. We talk regularly and easily about "batteries" of tests, "arsenals" of "weapons" like antibiotics, and "waging war" on disease. This common metaphor, however, has some unintended consequences that deserve exploration.

Chapter 2 discusses Advance Directives, of which "living wills" are one example. Despite their limitations, these are enormously helpful to patients, their families, and medical practitioners. They deserve to be more widely used even though they are not a perfect tool. When they were first proposed in 1969, the hope was that all adults would write one and end the problem of patients being given unwanted care at the end of life. Dying would be simplified and occur on each person's own terms. More than 30 years later, estimates say that only about 15–25 percent of adults has an Advance Directive. The chapter will explore the reasons— personal, logistical, medical and legal—why so few people have taken advantage of this valuable tool.

Chapter 3 discusses the relatively new end-of-life options of hospice and palliative care. I was appalled to discover how little I knew about either when my mother entered a hospice program, and I had been a doctor for almost 30 years! If I was that ignorant about hospice and what it offers to patients and their families, I know most other people are ignorant as well.

Chapter 4 looks at the widely-held notion that life is "sacred" and explores what that term means in both a religious and a secular context. Like many common ideas, the meaning of "sanctity of life" is rarely talked about. It is often trumpeted as the reason why abortion and euthanasia are, on the face of it, immoral. But a closer analysis of the phrase and the further ideas it implies shows that it is not a simple, self-evident idea at all. First we need to explore the idea that life, or at least human life, is sacred; then we need to ask what medical steps that sacredness impels us to take. Finally, we might ask if death, too, could be sacred.

Chapter 5 addresses the difficult issue of pain and suffering. We commonly speak of these two things as if they were inextricably related, but I do not think that is so. As a physician my responsibility is to manage physical pain so that no suffering takes place. Modern medicine has an array of tools to accomplish that end. Likewise, psychological suffering is very real and can be devastating. Psychiatrists are the medical professionals best equipped to help dying people manage their depression. Other suffering is essentially spiritual or existential in nature and religious professionals or other spiritual guides, not medical professionals, are the appropriate people to treat it.

Chapter 6 discusses the possibility that dying can be a time of important personal growth for a patient and his or her family. We don't commonly assume this to be true, and by no means is it inevitable. But I have seen it happen many times. Dying will always be a bitter experience in that it ruptures human relationships, but the possibility of significant personal growth through the dying process at least raises the possibility of making it bittersweet. Families used to know a lot about dying because it was so common and occurred almost always at home. We have lost that knowledge as a culture—except for hospice nurses, who have preserved, refined and expanded it. This chapter will share some of their findings and suggest sources for gaining even more information from their treasure house.

Chapter 7 looks at recent calls for those ultimate controls over death: euthanasia and physician-assisted suicide. Proponents of these actions often claim that legalization will prevent "unnecessary suffering," language that suggests that "necessary suffering" also exists. However, as Daniel Callahan has wisely noted, suffering has two facets: physical pain and a misery that is wholly psychological or spiritual in nature. Using euthanasia or physician-assisted suicide to remedy the latter is "a false answer, given by the wrong people."[1]

Chapter 8 asks a provocative question: "Is this the illness which should be allowed to be fatal?" Until I read this in Callahan's book, I must confess that personally, the subject had never crossed my mind. I certainly had assisted at surgeries performed on dying patients for the purpose of controlling their pain. None of the medical team had any illusions about "curing" the patient in those cases; we were simply trying to make dying less painful and their symptoms less intrusive. And the medical team sometimes debated whether we would want our relatives to undergo this type of surgery if they were dying. But the idea of deliberately evaluating an illness and asking if this illness at this time in a patient's life should be allowed to be the final one stunned me. All of my medical training had focused on fighting as long and as hard as medical knowledge, drugs and technology allowed us. To consider not fighting was revolutionary to me. Yet, when I compared my mother's death to my father's, I could see some merit to the idea. *Some* illness or trauma is going to be the final one; immortality is not an option. Callahan points out that when we choose to fight any one episode, we are also implicitly wagering that some future episode will allow for a more peaceful death, a gamble that we often lose. This chapter examines this question carefully since it is a novel one.

Chapter 9 presents "The Rules According to Doctor Buckley" as a way of summarizing the discussions in the book. One of the most important rules is the second one: "Plan ahead." It is possible to achieve a peaceful death, whatever that means to you, but it is highly unlikely to happen by accident. It can happen as the result of some hard thinking, some difficult and uncomfortable discussions, some paperwork, and a little luck. It is not realistic to plan on achieving a "perfect death;" humans simply cannot control our bodies, our technology, and all the events of dying to that degree. But it is not necessary to be passive either.

This book is an attempt to synthesize what I have learned from my own life experiences, my studies in philosophy, medical ethics and religion, and the stories I have heard from many sources over the years. My students at Hiram College have been extraordinarily generous in sharing their own experiences dealing with end-of-life issues with each other and with me. My pastor, James C. Butler of Lakewood Presbyterian Church in Lakewood, Ohio, encouraged me to teach a short version of my Hiram class as a church adult-education offering. The second time I did that, I was ably assisted by elder-care attorney Susan L. Evans, who also added much practical wisdom. My studies to become a Commissioned Lay Pastor in the Presbyterian Church have fed into this project, too.

I cannot provide a prescription for you for the end of your life. Our values are too varied and our life situations are too different for there to be appropriate "one size fits all" answers. But I do have some specific goals I hope to accomplish. The first is to introduce you to a very important and thoughtful book by Daniel Callahan. His book is excellent and can be read by motivated non-philosophers as I proved when I first taught my end-of-life issues class at my church. Forty-five Presbyterians of a variety of ages and educational backgrounds read and discussed the book and many of them told me what a profound impact it had upon them. However, they also said that without the discipline of weekly reading assignments and class discussion, they doubt they would have finished it. Most Americans prefer to be entertained and while I cannot speak too highly of Callahan's book, it is not entertaining reading.

I cannot improve upon Callahan's work, but I hope to act as a guide to those of you inspired to read it yourself and to highlight its most important points for those of you who do not read it. I also can add stories, and we humans do love stories. These narratives, gathered over my years of practicing medicine, chairing hospital ethics committees, and teaching at a liberal arts college, illustrate both how we can take control over some aspects of the ends of our lives and what can happen when we choose to let circumstances control us. I can also share with you the experiences I gained as a doctor being privileged to help care for patients, some of whom were dying, and what I learned first-hand about dying and death from the deaths of both of my parents, who were living with me when they died. Doctors learn about life daily from their patients, and I certainly learned from mine. I hope these stories inspire or provoke you into facing the reality that one day you, too, will die. Physical immortality is not an option. But you do have many choices about how your dying happens.

CHAPTER 1

What's Wrong with Dying?

IN ONE SENSE, THE ANSWER TO THIS CHAPTER'S TITLE IS SIMPLE: THE NEXT STEP after dying is being dead, and that is generally not regarded as a good thing. But some deeper reflection on the question reveals that a less flippant answer is called for. Death is the end of existence, or at least existence as we now know it. Some communities of faith believe that we move to a different type of existence. Other people believe that death is the doorway into another life in this world through reincarnation. Still others believe that death is a final, personal extinction. But whatever we believe about death, we know that it ruptures the most profound human relationships we have, both for the individual who dies and for those who knew and loved that person. Death is the end of a particular life story, whether it has been a life well-lived or squandered. And that has always been the bitter, painful reality of death.

But what's wrong with dying may also have a lot to do with the way we die today—the process of dying as much as the event of death itself. Some features of modern American dying conspire to make death somehow more difficult than it used to be.

First, death is less common today, and therefore when it occurs, it is unfamiliar and strange. Naively, we might say that unfamiliarity with death is an unalloyed good thing. Until about 1900, when roughly half of all children died before age two, death was an all-too-common part of almost every family's experience. Up to 25 percent of women died during childbirth or from complications of bearing children. In an era before antibiotics, both men and women died from infections which today we can usually cure. Most serious accidents resulted in death.

The smallest acquaintance with a family's genealogy in the 1700s and 1800s bears this out. One generation in my maternal grandmother's family consisted of Elizabeth Summerfield and William Cull, who emigrated from England and Wales to upstate New York in about 1850. They had 13 children, only six of whom survived to adulthood, typical numbers for the times. The Culls were unusual in that both Elizabeth and William lived into their late 80s, which represents a wonderful contribution of genetic hardiness to the family gene pool.

However, in other branches of the family tree I found the pattern of marriage, a couple of children, the death of their mother (often days to weeks after a birth), a prompt remarriage and more children with a second or even a third wife. In my father's family, Charles Faulkner (1731–1803) first married Hannah Morse and they had four children. Hannah died in 1765 and Charles promptly married Mary Bly; they had one more child, from whom I am descended. More recently my great-grandfather, William Harvey Faulkner (1845–1925) married Nancy Jennings and fathered four children by her. After her death in 1891, he married Rachel Moon and had a daughter with her who became my paternal grandmother.

This pattern only began to change in the 20th century. The average lifespan in the United States has doubled since 1900, meaning that it is possible for people to live into their 60s before first experiencing the death of a parent. Although death was certainly unwelcome in previous times, it was a familiar enough occurrence that everyone knew what they were expected to do and how they ought to behave. But because death today is a relatively rare event, many of us are at a loss as to how to react and what to say to offer support and comfort when it does occur.

My parents had lived in the same town for 50 years when they died. Both had been very active in our church and community, so visiting hours at the funeral home were well-attended. It was very meaningful to see how many peoples' lives my parents had touched: that people who were special to me were highly regarded by others, too. But some people were inarticulate when it came time to offer their respect and condolences to my brothers and me. Being a child of the '60s, I know how suspicious my generation was of what we labeled meaningless, rote formulations and customs: we thought "telling it like it is" was much more authentic. But the relative rarity of death compared to earlier times and the lack of culturally-accepted stock phrases for expressing grief, comfort and support left many visitors stumbling to find *any* words to say. Some of them literally settled for a hug and a pat without saying a word. I suspect that in earlier times, when death was a frequent event within a family and their community, people did not struggle so to find the appropriate words to speak. There were widely accepted funeral customs, including appropriate phrases of condolence and dictates about what clothing to wear and most people understood and abided by them.

Philosopher Daniel Callahan, in *The Troubled Dream of Life*, movingly describes a similar experience when one of his children died in infancy. "There was nothing more strained and awkward for my wife and me," he writes, "than trying to respond to those who did not know what to do, those who wanted to say something but had no vocabulary to speak of death, who wanted to give comfort but could do so in no forthright, strong way. More often than not, it was my wife and I who had to help them, to put them at ease as they struggled without success to find a way to talk with us."[2]

Mourning clothes and a black wreath on the door had the advantage of letting strangers and others who had not heard the news know that a death had recently occurred. The practical wisdom of these now-abandoned customs was dramatically borne home to me years ago when I ran into a friend whom I had known well in high school but had not seen for some time. I had just been named the Director of the Department of Anesthesiology in a local hospital and was very full of my personal good news. She was the first to say, "How are you?" and I proceeded to tell her exactly how wonderful I was. When I finally wound down and asked her how she was, she quietly replied that her husband had died the previous week after a long battle with cancer. I was mortified that I had overlooked her sadness and tiredness in the rush to share my news in a manner that now shamed me. Mourning clothes, however dated they might seem now, had the utilitarian advantage of alerting everyone about a person's status as bereaved. Some modern, widely-recognized social signal of bereavement would be very helpful.

Other once-common funeral customs are also now just distant memories. In a recent "Dear Abby" column in my local newspaper, the writer said: "I have a question that you've probably never been asked before. Is there a dress code regarding attire for a funeral? Most everyone has worn black at funerals I have attended. I don't particularly like black, however. I prefer bright colors, so that's what I have chosen to wear. Why is it that this so-called tradition is so entrenched that no one wants to break it? Wondering in Eau Claire, Wis." Abby's answer was "Dear Wondering: In the United States, black is generally considered the color of mourning. When someone attends a funeral, it is either to pay respect to the deceased or to show support for the grieving family. At a time such as this, it is considered improper to draw attention to yourself. That is the reason most people forgo bright colors and instead wear colors that are muted or subdued unless instructed otherwise."[3] Several things strike me about this exchange. The first is the questioner's apparent lack of familiarity with both the concept of mourning clothes for the family of the deceased and the idea that what a person wears to calling hours might have a specific function within the larger ritual of how one behaves at the time of a death. "Wondering" does not seem to realize that at one time there were widely-held public and private rituals for passing through this experience. The fact that the writer felt the question would be a unique one testifies to this deficit in knowledge about "so-called tradition." The point of visitation is either to pay one's respects to the deceased or to comfort and support the family, not to make a personal fashion statement. However, this goal seems lost on the writer.

Until the middle of the 20th century, deaths were also far more likely to occur in the home, as were births. Thus, in one sense, birth and death were common, household events. The daily routine, whatever it was, flowed on around the dying person. He or she was not separated from the family by a hospital or a nursing home. There were no externally imposed visiting hours to cope with, no restrictions on young children and pets, and friends as well as family could gather by the bedside. The dying person was fully a member of the family and community even as life ebbed away. Afterward, the body was washed and prepared for burial by family and friends, perhaps to be buried in a wooden coffin also fashioned by a family member. Visitation before the funeral took place in the home of the deceased or a relative, often in a formal parlor primarily used in this way. Today we still visit in a "funeral parlor" or "funeral home," but now we rent them for the occasion. In fact, I recently read that the change in the term "parlor" sometime in the 20th century was supposed to highlight the fact that no dead bodies had passed through the "living room!" Recently one family in my church decided to revert to the older way of handling death. Karen's mother, who lived with Karen and her family, died at home under hospice care. Her body was taken to a funeral home, embalmed, and then returned to the family home where the casket was placed in the "living room" and where visitation occurred. Her body stayed in her home overnight and was taken to our church for the funeral service the next morning.

Even the basic ingredients of funerals have changed, according to Thomas Lynch, a funeral director and poet. "Increasingly, the dead are dispatched to the crematory or grave without witness or rubric whilst the bereaved plan services to which everyone is invited except, notably, the one who has died. The event is 'life-affirming,' the music cheering, the bereaved all gracious and brave. 'Closure' may not be achieved, but it is proclaimed nonetheless. Such services deal with memories of the dead but refuse to deal with the dead themselves. It's like a baptism without the baby or a graduation without the graduates."[4] The latest funeral fashion is themed funerals, he says: golf bags, a rainbow trout jumping from a corner of the casket, or "Big Mama's Kitchen," complete with a faux stove, a kitchen table, and an apple pie.[5] However, he reminds us, the fundamental ingredients for a funeral really have not changed: "Someone who has quit breathing forever, some others to whom it matters, and someone else who stands between the living and the dead and says something like 'Behold, I show you a mystery.'"[6] He continues, "A good funeral is not about how much we spend or how much we save. Rather it is about what we do—to act out our faith, our hopes, our loves and our losses. Pastoral care is not about making death easier, or grief less keenly felt or funerals cheaper or more convenient. It is about bringing the power of faith to bear on the human experience of dying, death, and bereavement. And our faith is not for getting around grief or past it, but for getting through it. It is not for dodging our dead, but for bearing us up as we bear them to the grave or tomb or fire at the edge of which we give them back to God."[7]

The French historian Philippe Aries called the older way of dying "a tame death" and described it as "tolerable and familiar, affirmative of the bonds of community and social solidarity, expected with certainty and accepted without crippling fear."[8] Note that this description does not claim that death was welcomed. It was not, but it was accepted as a normal part of the life cycle. Contrast that with what Callahan has described as "the 'wild' death of technological medicine."[9] Death today overwhelmingly occurs in hospitals or nursing homes—about 80% of the time—often without the family in attendance. Death in an institution is impersonal, with the patient usually hooked up to IVs and machines and tubes. Often multiple medical specialists are involved, one per organ system, but they are frequently uncertain who is actually in charge of coordinating the patient's overall care. These factors conspire together so that death is hidden from our eyes: mysterious, frightening and impersonal in a way that simply was not true in earlier times. And we are not finding that change comfortable to live with. Today modern medicine has turned death from a fairly discrete event into a process that we are able to prolong but not ultimately prevent with the intensive application of technology and drugs. One of my patients a few years ago confided to me, "It's not death I fear. It's what's going to happen to me before I die."

Today, death also often occurs in the midst of a medical crisis with all the uncertainty the term implies. The patient is critically ill, as my father was, but will he recover or is he dying? Medical technology regularly, but not invariably, saves those who would have perished in earlier times. The paramedics restarted my father's heart while he was still lying on the kitchen floor of our house, and had he awakened and been neurologically intact, he would have been a Cardiopulmonary Resuscitation (CPR) success story, his life literally restored to him. But he did not regain consciousness. Would he ever wake up? Is the situation really hopeless or is more patience what's needed? There is often an enervating cycle of messages of hope when one organ system or other responds to some aspect of treatment, followed by despair as the medical bulletins report worsening test results.

Medically, the situation is often complex. Now that people live much longer lives, they usually have several chronic illnesses that complicate a life-threatening episode. Patients today are far more likely to be elderly or "old-old," an ungainly term we have invented to describe those of extreme age. Patients 100 years of age and above sometimes require surgery and often do surprisingly well despite their advanced age. But when patients with several chronic illnesses do not do well because of their multiple underlying abnormalities, they frequently become medical "train wrecks." Organ systems fail in a domino-like sequence, and the patient becomes more and more dependent on machines to sustain life functions. Usually, when they do survive, they are left with diminished ability to function; when they don't survive, it is only because all the technological possibilities have been exhausted.

Before antibiotics became common in the 1940s, infectious diseases killed indiscriminately. George Washington Vanderbilt was a grandson of Commodore Vanderbilt and the owner of Biltmore, the largest private house ever built in the United States, located outside Ashville, North Carolina. He died in 1915 from appendicitis and neither his wealth nor his social standing could do anything to save him. But death caused by overwhelming infection was usually at least quick and relatively painless. About the only deaths we experience today that are quick and painless are from massive, immediately lethal heart attacks or strokes.

All of these problems with modern dying are further aggravated when, as is frequently more common in our global economy, children and sometimes spouses live scattered around the globe. One of my friends from high school now lives in Colorado. When her mother was critically ill in Cleveland, she flew to be with her. After a few days the doctors pronounced her to be stabilized although still very ill, so my friend flew back West to her family and job. Three days later her mother's condition suddenly worsened and she returned to Cleveland. This scenario of emergency cross-country flights was repeated twice more. After the third pronouncement of "stabilization," my friend boarded another plane to Colorado, at which point her mother actually died. When the end finally comes in situations like this one, we are torn between feeling glad that the ordeal of dying is over and grief at the final earthly parting.

Even worse than these scenarios, Callahan points out, is the increasingly frequent story of an elderly person who dies after an extended stay in a nursing home, "long demented and cut off from human communication. [Their] children have lived with the particular hell of loving their parent, wishing they would die, blaming themselves for that wish, and dutifully paying painful visits."[10] Since current estimates are that 50 percent of persons over the age of 85 have some symptoms of Alzheimer's or other dementia and that same segment of the population is the fastest-growing in our country, this appalling scenario will become even more common in the future.

So perhaps it is true that how we die today is more difficult than in times gone by, even though the end result is the same painful reality it has always been. But are we as helpless as our ancestors in the face of dying? No, we certainly are not. Antibiotics and technology are wonderful tools. So are a number of powerful new ways in which we can face the problem. One is the medical option of hospice, which attempts to reclaim some of the features of Aries' "tame death." There are also Advance Directives such as living wills, which allow a person to specify certain types of medical treatment and support which, according to their circumstances, they do or do not want to receive. Most states allow a surrogate to be named to make decisions for a patient if he or she becomes unable to communicate.

People need to know that they have choices to make and that need to be considered before a medical crisis arises. The crisis itself will be difficult enough to handle; it will be immeasurably worse if people are suddenly faced with unfamiliar options and decisions when they are already overwhelmed with stress. A few years ago I was found to have a mass in my thyroid gland which had not been palpable five months earlier. Given the rapid growth of the mass, thyroid cancer was a possibility that needed to be explored. That process took about one month, and during that time most of my thoughts consisted of saying to myself, "I might have cancer. I might have cancer." I was simply in no position to do any high-quality thinking about other issues until my diagnosis was ascertained.

Facing the fact of one's eventual personal mortality, as difficult as that may be, allows an individual to begin to think about what their personal priorities are for their last days and then to take steps to help ensure that they have a measure of control over how events work out. Callahan suggests that we would all be well-served to do some serious personal thinking while we are well about how we would like to fashion our final illness. We cannot go back in time to recapture Aries' "tame death." But we can fashion what Callahan calls "a peaceful death."[11] Subsequent chapters of this book will discuss the most important steps to secure some control over dying. But there are still other problems to consider.

Callahan suggests that some difficulty with death results, not from the inevitable fact of death itself or even our prolonged dying process, but from certain concepts or paradigms about death that are widely held in American society. Perhaps if we could change those concepts, we might recapture some of the tameness that death once had and allow more people to die peacefully, on their own terms.

One problem, which as a medical professional myself I can see from both sides, is that doctors and other health care workers talk to each other using medical jargon. Like any discrete professional language, these special terms have a very precise meaning which allows us to be concise in sharing information with each other. But since non-medical people do not know our terms, if we use them with patients we can totally confuse the message we are trying to deliver. Although many health care providers conscientiously attempt to avoid using jargon, sometimes we forget. If patients do not question us about unfamiliar terms, terrible confusion can result. Years ago I saw a first-hand example of how this can happen.

At the time, I was practicing in a large community teaching hospital near a medical school. One of its premiere residency programs was in Obstetrics-Gynecology and most of our teaching faculty had appointments at the medical school as well as at our hospital. One day the Anesthesiology Department received a frantic call from the Delivery Room. A 14-year-old girl, totally lacking in prenatal care, had just been admitted in active labor. Still basically a child herself, she was panicked by her labor pains, and her blood pressure was desperately high. The obstetricians were suspicious that she had a life-threatening condition called severe pre-eclampsia, more common in very young mothers like this one and much more common in those who have come to term without seeing a doctor. An emergency Caesarean section was deemed necessary and the OB anesthesia personnel called for more help. I was one of several people who responded.

A live baby was delivered but, as is frequently the case without prenatal care, the infant did not weigh as much as it should have based on its fetal age and died later that evening. As I later heard the story, one of the obstetrical residents went to the young mother and told her that her baby had "expired." He then asked for her permission to do an autopsy to see what had been wrong. She signed the permission slip for the autopsy, which was scheduled for the next morning. When the team of attending and resident obstetricians made morning rounds, the young mother asked why no one had brought her baby to be fed and whether the "test results" from the autopsy were back yet. To their horror, the team realized that she had no idea that "expired" was a euphemism for "dead" or that an "autopsy" was the examination of a dead body. No one had meant to deceive her, but by using medical jargon, her doctor had inadvertently not communicated vital information to her. Often patients are either too intimidated to challenge doctors or nurses when they don't understand what we are saying or are simply too ill and too overwhelmed to care. Either situation can lead to a significant problem, as this story shows.

Sometimes words frighten even medical professionals. In her capstone project for the Master of Arts in Interdisciplinary Studies degree at Hiram College, Melinda Kapalin wrote about offering terminally ill children the opportunity to write something to leave as a legacy for their family. One of her interviews was with a bibliotherapist who works with dying children. She told Kapalin not to use the phrase "terminally ill" with respect to children. The therapist said that at her institution they were, by policy, not allowed to use that term; instead, the dying children were referred to as "life-challenged." The staff was not to use the word "terminal" for fear it would take away the children's hope.[12] If professionals who work with dying children cannot be honest about what is happening, what chance do the parents and children have for truthful communication? It is a sad reality that sometimes children do die. While we do not want to eradicate hope (more about this important word shortly), the reality is that, if we pretend that people are not or might not be dying, we also often prevent crucial kinds of communication, growth and healing which can occur even during the dying process. Research done with dying children has shown that all but the youngest children know what is going on, that they "have a strong desire to be heard and to have their questions answered honestly."[13]

There is a second, conceptual problem with medical language. Bio-ethicists, and particularly those who use narratives to engage problems and conflicts, have alerted medical practitioners like me to the power of language to shape our concepts. Years ago when doctors' tools were far more limited, death was identified as "the Great Enemy." After all, the average life expectancy in the United States was only about 45 years in

1900, so fewer people lived to what we now consider middle age; mothers, infants and children in particular died indiscriminately. Death was an all-too-common intruder in most families.

What do we do with enemies? We "wage war" against them. Think of the "war on cancer" we have been fighting for the last 40 years. In the medical arena, doctors and nurses and medical researchers are the "warriors" who "defend" sick patients against "marauding" diseases. We use "batteries" of tests and then pick from our "arsenal" of "weapons" to treat the illness, which we describe as patients "battling" their disease. Doctors write "orders" in patient charts and we expect them to be carried out with military precision.

To those in the know, the length of a doctor's white lab coat signals differences in status or rank as clearly as stripes on the sleeve of soldiers' and sailors' uniforms. In the institution where I did my internship and anesthesiology residency, the operating room had one dressing room for attending surgeons, another for resident surgeons, and yet a third for male OR staff. (Conveniently, at that time there were no female surgical residents.) Just as officers do not fraternize with enlisted personnel, apparently senior physicians do not change with their underlings. We describe cancer as "invading" our tissues; we "battle" other kinds of diseases. Our nation's chief medical officer is called the "Surgeon-General." There is even a startling similarity between boot camp and being admitted to the hospital. In both instances, the first thing that happens is that someone takes away your clothes (a quick statement about who is now in charge!). Other people control when and where you eat and sleep and wake and just about everything else that happens to you. You may not leave until you are "discharged."

Since death is conceptualized as the "Great Enemy," doctors are trained to experience the death of a patient, no matter how old or how injured, as a "defeat" at the hands of an implacable "foe." Just like soldiers in all times and places, doctors don't like losing. So what does a prudent military commander do when it becomes obvious that his force is going to lose this particular battle? Either he chooses a heroic (if also sometime foolhardy) no-holds-barred, take-no-prisoners assault on the enemy or he withdraws his troops to fight another battle on a different day. Doctors pursue both of these military strategies every day.

In some cases, we choose the "medical heroism" route. The patient may be dying, but by God, he or she will die with as many of their lab values within the normal range as humanly possible. I was taught to do that as an anesthesia resident learning how to care for patients in a surgical Intensive Care Unit. Until recently, patients dying of Alzheimer's disease who had stopped eating had nasogastric (nose-to-stomach) feeding tubes inserted or had feeding tubes surgically implanted. Then we tied their hands so that they could not pull the tube out. Note that this "win at all costs" strategy makes the patient's body the "battlefield" which bears the brunt of our medical warfare. And even when medical heroism carries the day and the patient survives this battle, death has only been "defeated" for this episode of illness. Some other day, the patient must become ill and lose that final "battle." The human mortality rate is still 100 percent. Death is not optional.

Doctors also follow the strategy of "prudent withdrawal" to save their "arsenal" for a different "battle" that they can "win"—in this case, another patient who might survive. When I was an intern it was common on morning rounds to walk up to the door of a dying patient's room and stop outside. "Let's not bother him," the senior doctor would say, and we would pass by without ever going in. We doctors felt we had nothing to offer, no "magic bullet," since we could not cure. We still could have offered the human comfort of our presence and we could have aggressively managed painful or disturbing symptoms even when we could not cure, but that seems to have been lost on us. "Victory" in the form of cure was our goal, not comfort. Anything less than "defeating the enemy" was valueless to us.

This, I believe, is the origin of those chilling words, "There is nothing more I can do." What the doctor is really saying is "I recognize and now admit that I cannot cure you." That is a different message from what is literally spoken. In fact, the doctor can do many things at this point, including referrals to hospice and palliative care and simple human caring. Patients tell doctors they truly value both our professional expertise and our compassion. Until the moment of death, there is always something that medicine can contribute to helping a patient achieve a peaceful death. Sadly, in the recent past the medicine-as-warfare metaphor blinded us to what we still did have to offer to our patients.

One of my dearest friends shared with me the story of her dying father's abandonment. Tom had been a vigorous man who operated industrial cranes for a construction company. He had been a patient of his doctor for many years when he was diagnosed with kidney cancer. His doctor delivered the diagnosis and pronounced his situation to be terminal. Then he went away. After a few days with no further visits, Tom finally asked the nurses when his doctor would come, and they told him that they, the nurses, would care for him from now on. There was "no need" for the doctor to come because Tom was dying. Like a prudent military commander, that physician was saving his "arsenal of weapons" for a battle he could win. Tom found this deeply distressing because he genuinely liked his doctor and missed the comfort he had always felt in their relationship.

Both my internship in 1972 and Tom's death in 1986 represent an older style of medical practice. I'm thankful to report that there have been changes. But modern medicine still has versions of this same story. Another friend of mine lost her lifelong best friend to breast cancer. Ashley was only 36 when she was diagnosed and, as a married woman who hoped to someday have children, she was determined to "fight" her disease with whatever "weapons" her surgeon, oncologist (medical doctors who specialize in treating cancers) and radiologist could provide. Unfortunately, their combined efforts were not enough. When her oncologist referred her to hospice care, her relationship both with him and the oncologic nurses who had been administering her chemotherapy was abruptly terminated. Ashley had enjoyed a warm and supportive relationship with this team, seeing the nurses several days a week while receiving chemotherapy and she missed them. She regretted the fact that there was not an opportunity to even say goodbye to these people who had been her "comrades-in-arms" during her fight.[14]

A more chilling story of medical abandonment appeared in a column in the *Cleveland Plain Dealer*. George, a retired machine designer and avid outdoorsman, became short of breath and tired. He visited his doctor, who ordered diagnostic tests. The results were sent to George in the mail: amyotrophic lateral sclerosis, better known as ALS or Lou Gehrig's disease. George knew that there was no cure for this progressive disease, so he placed an ad in his community newspaper to sell his canoe, outboard motor, and truck cap. A man named Greg called about the canoe. When told that George was selling because he had ALS, Greg asked what he was doing about it. "Nothing," George replied. "I'm dying. I'm going to a nursing home."[15]

Fortunately for George, Greg turned out to be the doctor-director of spinal cord injury rehabilitation at Cleveland's MetroHealth Medical Center. He sent a vendor of power wheelchairs as well as an RN case manager to see what could be done to help George and increase his mobility. George understood that his disease was going to be fatal. He was already significantly short of breath. But he wanted to be able to go outside and watch his German shepherd play. Therapists at MetroHealth aimed at increasing George's muscle strength and endurance. He went from being able to walk only 30 feet unaided to 200 feet. He no longer talked about going to a nursing home. He told Greg, "I feel 10 times better."[16]

But the unhappy consequences of using the medicine-as-warfare metaphor extend even beyond dying. The idea of "conquering disease" makes more sense when the illness is one from which a person recovers completely—as, for example, an infectious disease. When the episode is over, the disease is gone from the body completely. However, now that people live so much longer, they often acquire one or more chronic diseases, maladies that never "go away." Here, another limitation of the military metaphor becomes apparent. How does one "battle" high blood pressure or diabetes? The "enemy" in these cases will never be "defeated," or driven away. Instead, the patient must learn to live with and manage the disease to achieve the optimum possible health. The military metaphor has no terms for "living with" an enemy or "managing" an invader.[17] In fact, consorting with the enemy is considered to be treason! Yet patients must learn to consort with their chronic diseases.

Patients sometimes adopt other metaphors for certain episodes of illness. As Anne Hunsaker Hawkins has pointed out, patients sometimes describe a critical, life-threatening illness like a heart attack as a "rebirth" rather than a "battle."[18] These people emerge with a new set of priorities and a new commitment to diet, exercise, and other lifestyle changes that had been prescribed before the illness but previously ignored. They often reorganize their personal priorities, too, choosing to spend more time with family and friends and less at work. The changes are often so far-reaching that it is as if they were born anew. The medicine-as-warfare metaphor, however, has no language to describe the concept of rebirth.

The word "hope" is also a victim of the warfare metaphor. Hope in the medical context has been defined as "a wish for a future state of affairs."[19] Certainly when a doctor conveys a potentially fatal diagnosis to a patient, they both hope that the illness will be cured in the future. But that is not what always happens: there inevitably must be one illness which each of us does not survive. What does "hope" mean in the context of that illness? Is it legitimate to use that word with the dying? It all depends on what we (and the patient) take the term to mean.

According to Matthew Stolick, "hope" means different things to patients at different points in their illness. In the beginning, it is usually a wish for cure. During the treatment phase, hope may center on the power of equipment, technology, and the skills of physicians. But it may eventually switch from hope for a cure to hope for some prolongation of life as treatment proves to be ineffective. In the end, hope may become a wish for a peaceful death.[20] These goals are achievable even when a cure is not. Thus all "hope" is not lost, only "hope for a cure."

However, because physicians adhere to the military metaphor, they tend to think only of "hope for a cure." Many doctors feel that to tell patients that it appears they will die runs counter to the aphorism "Where there's life, there's hope." They therefore actively encourage patients to keep hoping for a cure even in the final stages of dying (which explains why some people die still receiving chemotherapy). When they finally use the terrible phrase "there is nothing more I can do," it usually signals that physician abandonment will follow shortly as it did so abruptly in Tom's and George's stories and in a softer way in Ashley's. By this point the patients may well be hoping for attainable goals such as some prolongation of life or being able to watch a dog at play or a peaceful death, so the pronouncement is particularly devastating. This physician attitude ignores the patient's legitimate hopes for future states of affairs other than being cured. As hospice and palliative care show so clearly, much can be done to benefit such "hopeless" patients. Cure may no longer be a possible goal, but control of symptoms, support and non-abandonment, and a peaceful death are hopes that can be addressed and often achieved— and that is not doing nothing!

The terminology of warfare has been borrowed by other areas besides medical practice. One of the first organizations dedicated to saving wildlife, "the Army of Bird-Defenders," was founded in 1873 by naturalist C. C. Haskins. Writing in the children's magazine *St. Nicholas*, Haskins "announced a plan for 'an army of defense, without guns' for birds, which would conduct a war of 'example and argument and facts, instead of powder.' The goal was 'perfect peace' for birds."[21] The use of military metaphors in medical practice similarly stresses unity of purpose, the focus on defeating disease and death, and the resolve to battle on until the engagement or the larger war is won. But metaphors sometimes have unintended consequences, and one of the painful consequences for dying patients and their families has been virtual abandonment by their physicians at a time when support was most needed. Yet, within the logic of the military metaphor, withdrawal makes perfect sense.

But is it still correct that death is "the Great Enemy"? Sometimes yes and sometimes no. From a purely biological standpoint, no person is immortal. However, death is a different threat to the integrity of a life story at different ages. When a child dies, we are always haunted by the lost potential, the "might have beens" of a life cut tragically short. What biography might that child have crafted had he or she lived? Similarly, when an adult dies, even in middle age, we are mindful of the many future experiences that they would otherwise have had. Perhaps the person who died had been patiently saving for retirement and postponing the activities they loved in favor of job and family during working years and was denied those opportunities by death. Perhaps they were anticipating the arrival of grandchildren and the chance to pass on knowledge to a new generation about the joys of fishing or how to tie a bowline. Death is always sad, even in old age, but there is an element of tragedy in the loss of people at the younger end of the age spectrum that is not present when an old person, who has had the chance to write a complete biography, dies. A person's place in his or her personal journey affects their perception of death as the enemy.

Note that chronological age is not an adequate surrogate for biographical completeness. In some European countries, for example, life-sustaining technology such as kidney dialysis is terminated on a fixed birthday, regardless of the patient's vigor. Some people at that age are still actively pursuing life projects; others are already profoundly demented and totally divorced from their environment. Age alone cannot make that discrimination. Thoughtful observers such as Callahan have argued that biographical completeness is a much more satisfactory standard. The younger the person, the more likely it is to be appropriate to fight death vigorously. But perhaps it should be an open, if not usually discussed, question how appropriate it is to fend off death as aging becomes very advanced. The military metaphor makes it very difficult for us to do this. Continuing to see death as always and in every circumstance the "Great Enemy" is a linguistic and also a conceptual mistake which needs to be modified today.

Another conceptual problem Callahan identifies is the place of death within medical practice. You might naïvely think that, because medical practice still regards death as an enemy, medical training focuses on death a great deal. Not so. Callahan notes that the classic *Cecil Textbook of Medicine* "refers directly in fewer than twenty-five of its twenty-three hundred pages to death (and only in five to pain)."[22] Modern medicine, at least in its theories, has been able to a certain extent to pretend that death is no longer under medicine's purview. Only life and a return to health are seen as the domain of the modern doctor. Death is outside the scope of scientific, theoretical medicine, if not (yet) clinical medicine where patients still inconveniently die. And we have been remarkably successful at succeeding with that self-deception with the aid of antibiotics and medical technology. This huge change over the last 50 years, Callahan says, leaves us "fundamentally uncertain whether death is to be accepted as a part of life or rejected as a repairable biological accident."[23]

All ideas result in consequences: some we anticipate and some are unintended, but they are always there. If we accept that death is indeed our ultimate fate as biological creatures, then we will have one set of attitudes toward death. They might include the idea that death should be fended off in childhood and adult life because the individual still has much living to do. But at some point, preferably well into whatever "old age" might be, a man or woman will develop an episode of illness or undergo a trauma sufficient to cause death. We must therefore prepare to face our own deaths with whatever resources—physical, emotional, and spiritual—we can muster. In this view, death could be seen as a part of routine medical practice, rather than a separate, relatively new medical specialty like hospice care or palliative medicine. But this is not the only viewpoint we could have. Indeed, it is currently the minority.

If, alternatively, we think that death is "a repairable biological accident," doctors are then logically the "repairpersons" who should be fending it off at all cost. We see the fruits of this mindset daily in hospitals around our country. A doctor who had worked to save an 87-year-old man mangled and left semi-comatose by a car crash told a researcher, "He's still hanging in there, going back for his umpteenth orthopedic procedure. The odds of him actually surviving are incredibly slim. But theoretically everything is reversible. So we just trudge along and see what happens." The researcher commented that this case sounded like one in which doctors and family members would later wonder, "Why in the world was he kept alive so long? Why was he given so much useless treatment?"[24] But this scenario is the perfectly logical outcome of conceiving of death as the "Great Enemy" or a "repairable biological accident." Each individual step in a scenario like this, Callahan, says, "was based on some hopeful medical possibility, with both the hope and the possibility stimulating each other to the point of folly."[25] As long as there is any possibility of survival, this conception argues for maximal possible treatment. It is like a captain going down with a sinking ship, except that in this case it is the patient, not the doctor, who will perish. It is the military metaphor playing itself out to its logical conclusion.

We in the United States now have laws that allow patients to reject unwanted treatment. A person facing long-term illness or death can opt out of the military metaphor even if his or her doctor does not. "Advance directives" is an umbrella term for several instruments that allow people to state in advance of an illness what kinds of treatments they do or do not want. These very important tools are the subject of the following chapter.

CHAPTER 2

The Mixed Blessings of Advance Directives

Our society has many ways for us to inform others of what we want if we are not able to tell them in person. Absentee ballots allow us to vote if we are out of town or otherwise unavailable on Election Day. Proxy forms enable us to cast a vote at a shareholder meeting we cannot attend. Traditional wills allow us to tell our executor how to divide our property after we die. Similarly, there are ways to tell families and health care providers what kinds of treatment we do and do not want in the event that we cannot speak to them directly.

"Advance directives" are legal documents. They can designate someone close to us as the person responsible for carrying out our health care wishes: the "durable power of attorney for health care" or "health care proxy." Laws governing advance directives vary from state to state; the state medical or bar association where you live can give you authoritative information about the statutes and forms for your particular state.

The term "living will" was first used by attorney Luis Kutner in 1969. A member of the Euthanasia Society of America, he published an article in the *Indiana Law Journal* entitled "Due Process of Euthanasia: The Living Will, a Proposal" in which he raised the possibility that patients unable to communicate during an illness could nevertheless make their wishes known, especially about forms of medical treatment they did not want, through a document created while they could communicate their desires.[26] Perhaps because of the word "euthanasia," an act that is still illegal in every

U.S. state, legislatures did not rush to enact laws enabling living wills. However, in 1976 California became the first state to pass a living will law.

Unlike a standard will, which passes on our wishes for what happens to our possessions at our death, a living will states our wishes for or refusal of certain types of medical treatment in the event that we are too sick or incapacitated to speak for ourselves directly; hence, the term "living will," for it becomes effective while the person is still alive. At the time these directives were conceived of, both doctors and patients had high hopes that living wills would make "death with dignity" possible and dying less problematic. Those hopes have not been adequately realized.

Too many people today do not have advance directives—only an estimated 14 to 25 percent of adults over the age of 18. It is still highly unusual for younger people to execute an advanced directive. Yet, the highly publicized end-of-life rights cases of Karen Ann Quinlan, Nancy Cruzan, and Terri Schiavo all involved young women who suddenly had a catastrophic illness. In the case of a severe accident, the law in most states already establishes the order of precedence for decision-making. Spouses are the first people who are empowered to speak; adult children are often next, then parents, siblings and any other relative who can be found. But even this legal order of precedence is problematic because often the patient has never expressed his or her wishes about medical care, both wanted and unwanted. Although the spouse or parent can legally speak, they have no idea what to say.

Over the years, as both patients and doctors have developed more experience using living wills to guide medical decision-making, other limitations in applying the documents have become apparent. The language in which living wills were originally drafted turned out in practice to be too vague. Terms like "heroic measures" were used to describe treatments that were unwanted, but it was often unclear what medical treatments were "heroic" in the patient's view and which were not. "Ordinary" and "extraordinary" were also frequently used but found to be confusing. A patient might think, for example, that a ventilator, a machine that does the work of pumping air into the lungs, is an "extraordinary" form of treatment, but as an anesthesiologist I used them in the operating room every single day, so to me they were perfectly "ordinary." Since living wills were invoked because the patients could not speak for themselves, it was functionally impossible to ask any questions about their specific opinions on ventilators at the point where doctors needed to know. Living wills also could not specify every possible medical scenario that might occur, so they resorted to very general statements, and it was sometimes difficult to ascertain whether a patient had ever envisioned the particular situation they were in.

When Do Not Resuscitate (DNR) orders became popular, they created quite a dilemma for Operating Room anesthesiologists. Many people feel that if they are already quite ill, they would not want to undergo the process of cardiopulmonary resuscitation (CPR) should their heart stop beating. This involves both breathing for the patient and pumping on his or her chest to circulate blood to the heart and brain while simultaneously trying to re-start the heart using electric shocks and various drugs. The technique can be life-saving when properly performed on someone whose cardiac arrest is discovered quickly by persons trained and equipped to provide CPR. Each year thousands of lives are saved by well-trained first responders and new, easy to use Automated Electrical Defibrillators (AEDs). However, the older the patient and the greater the number of underlying illnesses at the time his or her heart stops beating, the less likely the chance that the resuscitation will be successful. So some people choose to say that they do not want an attempt made at CPR.

But what about the situation where the arrest happens in the OR and is caused by either the anesthesia or a surgeon's tugging on a nerve which slows the heart so much that it stops? What would the patient want us to do in that case? Most patients never consider a scenario like this when requesting a DNR. They think only of a case in which their heart stops on its own, rather than one where medical treatment itself caused the arrest.

Anesthesiologists and hospitals responded to these directives in a variety of ways. Some institutions or Anesthesia Departments made a blanket policy that all DNR orders were temporarily suspended while the patient was in the OR and Recovery Room so that the doctors would be free to respond to a cardiac arrest. If a patient did not agree to this suspension, he or she was not permitted in the OR. Some doctors felt strongly that even to mention the fact that occasionally anesthesia or surgery causes cardiac arrests would so terrify patients that it was virtually immoral to do so. Some anesthesiologists felt that it was more appropriate to secure the patient's permission to suspend the DNR order temporarily.

Others thought it appropriate to explain the possibility of a medically-caused cardiac arrest during surgery, but to honor the patient's wishes even if medical therapy contributed to or directly caused the arrest.

Living wills also suffer from the fact that they always represent hypothetical choices about a situation in an imaginary future. To fill out a living will, we are asked to picture ourselves as terminally ill or unconscious. Most people have great difficulty imagining themselves in either of those extreme situations, so it is also difficult to imagine what kinds of treatment we would or would not want. "Even patients making contemporary decisions about contemporary illnesses are regularly daunted by the decisions' difficulty. They are human," C. E. Schneider has said. "We humans falter in gathering information, misunderstand and ignore what we gather, lack well-considered preferences to guide decisions, and rush headlong to choice."[27] All of these difficulties are aggravated by making decisions for an imaginary future that might not ever occur.

Yet another complication is that when a devastating disease is diagnosed, many people decide that treatment they never wanted to undergo suddenly looks much more appealing if it is the best chance for their survival. I cannot count the number of my medical colleagues over the years who said, when such a statement was purely theoretical, that they would never choose to undergo chemotherapy because of its unpleasant side effects. When they were diagnosed with cancer, however, suddenly the chemotherapy appeared much more attractive than it ever had before. Hypothetical choices are always difficult, but the only alternative is to wait until a crisis occurs and hope that your illness is such that you can make non-hypothetical choices for yourself in the midst of the crisis. Unfortunately, accidents, strokes and other illnesses often leave the victim unable to speak, so the opportunity to voice personal preferences has vanished, sometimes permanently.

Living wills also fail to live up to our early, perhaps naïve, expectations for another, more subtle reason. The first living wills often included the idea that they became effective when a person was terminally ill; many still use that language. About 2.5 million Americans die each year, the vast majority in two ways: approximately 500,000 people of cancer and another 625,000 of Congestive Heart Failure (CHF) and/or Chronic Obstructive Pulmonary Disease (COPD or emphysema).[28] The remaining deaths involve mainly the "frail elderly," who usually have more than one chronic disease. About half of these people have some form of dementia or other serious mental decline as a part of their last years. Scientists now estimate that about one-half of all persons will have signs of Alzheimer's disease by age 85, and that age group is the fastest-growing segment of the U.S. population today.

The final years of people in each of these groups differ markedly, as illustrated in Figure 1:

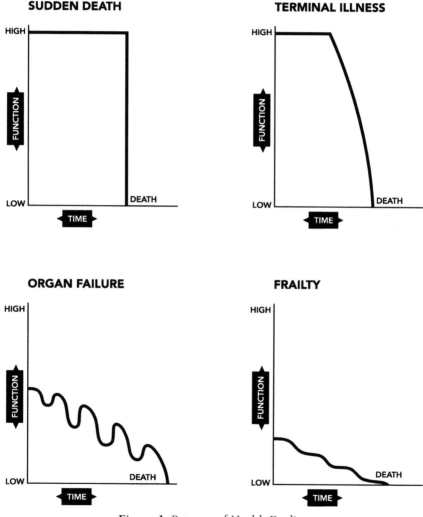

Figure 1 Patterns of Health Decline

The roughly 20 percent of those who die from cancer usually do so after many years of living with the fatal illness. Many people today achieve a remission of their cancer that lasts for five years or more; some unlucky souls are "cured" of one form of cancer only to eventually succumb to a different variety. Those who are so ill that they will soon die, however, enter a phase familiar to oncologists, which is marked by rapid, progressive, and irreversible decline. This is the group of patients we can most reliably label accurately as "terminally ill." Note, however, that they make up only 20 percent of annual deaths.

The final trajectory toward death is quite different for those with chronic heart and lung disease. Typically their initial illness is stabilized and they continue pretty much in their usual state of health for a while. Then they experience an acute exacerbation of their illness and are hospitalized, re-stabilized, and sent home. Most never quite recover the level of function, strength, and health they had before the episode began. Their illness consists of a series of episodes, each leaving them permanently more weakened and more debilitated, yet not "dying" by conventional standards. Lacking the rapidly descending pathway of a cancer death, doctors do not know when to apply the label "terminally ill" and thus to activate their living wills. In the SUPPORT study, The Study to Understand Prognoses and Preferences for Outcomes and Risk of Treatment, the largest study of death and dying ever done in the U.S., the day before they died, over 60 percent of CHF patients would have been estimated to live at least two months more.[29] While doctors on television never have difficulty knowing how long a patient will live, real-life doctors do. This uncertainty not only affects deciding when to apply advance directives but also referrals to hospice, as we will discuss in Chapter 3. What is clear from all the studies is that doctors consistently overestimate how long patients will live.[30]

Real, negative consequences flow from this consistent bias to overestimate remaining length of life. As biological creatures, it is true that we are headed toward death from the moment of our birth. But we don't live, at least today in America, as if that day is ever going to come. People who are told that they are dying, however, frequently make a new set of choices in light of that information. Those who have not yet made a conventional will disposing of their property will probably do so. If a difficult family relationship exists, they will likely work to set things right while they still can. There may be a life goal that they choose to achieve. Ashley, the 36-year-old breast cancer victim, and her husband had always wanted to go on a cruise. They did just that, about six weeks before she died.

By consistently overestimating how long patients might live, doctors collude with them, perhaps unintentionally but still surely, in postponing "getting their affairs in order," to use an old-fashioned term. By the time everyone finally has to acknowledge that dying is what's happening, the opportunity to order those affairs may be gone. I do not mean to suggest that doctors have high-quality crystal balls through which we know when a patient will die and choose deliberately not to share that information. But by joining in the death-denying culture in which we live, we do our patients a serious disservice. Better advice would be *to hope for the best while planning for the worst.*

The last and largest group of people has yet another type of final trajectory. The frail elderly, often rendered fragile by the accumulated assaults of several chronic diseases even when each is individually well-managed, already live at a much lower level of quality of life and functionality. Superimposed on their long period of chronic illnesses are episodes of acute illness. Alzheimer's and other forms of dementia, when combined with basic frailty, leave this large group of people in eventual chronic need of one-on-one assistance with activities of daily living such as bathing, toileting, dressing, eating, and taking medications on time. Early in their downward spiral, this assistance is typically provided by family and friends, but if they continue to survive, most of this group will require round-the-clock care in some venue or other. Death finally comes from what, in other circumstances, would be a fairly trivial problem: a urinary tract infection, pneumonia, influenza, a broken bone. In this group, with their chronic, underlying disease burdens and the toll taken on their bodies, a final trivial "assault" cannot be beaten back and death occurs. (Note the military metaphor at work!)

Again, deciding when in this downward trajectory the patient is "terminally ill" and their advance directive should be used is very unclear. Callahan has said that physiological dying is less and less important as the standard for making moral choices surrounding dying because if we wait until doctors are confident that the patient is indeed dying, they are already moribund.[31]

In an attempt to overcome some of the limitations of living wills, many states have now adopted Durable Power-of-Attorney (DPA) for Health Care statutes. These are different from the more-familiar general Durable Power-of-Attorney, which often gives a specific individual power over a person's finances. A DPA for Health Care only permits the named person to make health-care decisions in the event that the patient cannot speak for him- or herself. The DPA has one great advantage over the living will in that when the former needs to be used, it is for a specific medical situation, not a hypothetical one at some unknown time in the future. Living wills conceptually try to envision some things that might happen to us in the future and plan for them. In practice, that is a difficult task full of "what-ifs." The DPA, by contrast, is activated after a particular illness or accident. The choices are fewer because of the specificity of the situation. The person authorized to make decisions is not faced with an indefinite array but very specific options caused by the particular details of the illness. And the choices are not hypothetical, but real.

The statute presumes that the person named as the DPA knows from many conversations what types of treatment the patient does and does not want. Such conversations are, of course, quite uncomfortable to have. We live in a youth-worshipping, death-denying culture, so sitting down to discuss an illness so severe that the person might be unable to communicate is very hard. It is often extremely challenging to imagine ourselves in a situation of grave illness, especially when we are young and (at the moment) healthy. However, accidents strike people of all ages. Even young athletes occasionally die on the field or court from previously undiagnosed heart problems. So, hard as it is to have these conversations with a family member or trusted friend as a part of appointing them as your DPA, it is critical to do so.

My family was no different from most when it came time for these tough discussions. When I first moved back to my home town after graduating from medical school, I was able to have a series of conversations with my mother. From them, I gained a fuller sense of what her values and desires for health care were. My efforts to have similar conversations with my father met a stone wall. As the chair of a hospital ethics committee,

I knew first-hand the ugly situations that sometimes occurred when family members gathered by the bedside of a critically ill person and fought about what treatment should or should not be given when there was no previous guidance from the patient. Finally I asked my mother if she and my father were having "pillow talks" about his wishes in the event of a devastating illness. She told me that she, too, was having no luck prying any information out of him. However, a cousin in Buffalo whom he loved dearly had a series of strokes and was incapacitated by them. After visiting her, he came home and told me he was ready to create a living will for himself.

You have already heard in the Introduction to this book about my father's death in an ICU. Although it was difficult for him to face his own mortality and decide about wanted and unwanted treatment, he gave his family a wonderful gift by doing so. Every person who summons up the necessary bravery to face mortality and execute an advance directive gives his or her family this same awesome gift. When Dad's doctor asked me what I wanted to do should his breathing fail, I did not have to shoulder the responsibility for choosing what should happen. The words the doctor used to frame his question to me—"What do you want me to do?"—certainly seemed to shift the burden of choosing whether my father lived or died squarely onto my shoulders. But, thanks to my father's gift of an advance directive, I was able to ignore that poor choice of words and realize that the psychological and spiritual weight of this life-or-death decision rested where it belonged: on my father's own choice for himself. I did not have to choose not to reattach my father to a respirator. He had made his own choice, and that choice was that he did not want to be permanently maintained by a machine. My responsibility as his appointed DPA was to make sure that his doctor knew Dad had the appropriate forms stating his wishes and that we, his family, expected to see those decisions honored by his caregivers.

I cannot imagine, even after all my years practicing medicine, the burden of guilt and doubt I would have borne had I not known my father's wishes and instead had to make a life-or-death choice on his behalf. It was incredibly difficult to simply state that we were going to honor his wishes when I knew that his survival hung on the choice. It is a great service to your loved ones to take the responsibility upon yourself to state your own wishes rather than forcing an exquisitely painful choice upon them in a time of crisis.

Because advance directives are legal documents, each state has certain requirements about the number of witnesses required to verify a signature, who those witnesses can be (usually not family members or caregivers), whether the document must be notarized, etc. State-provided forms often rely heavily on medical terminology that may be unfamiliar to the person trying to execute the form. Many people engage a lawyer to help them execute their advance directives, thereby incurring some expense. Most lawyers are very uncomfortable in the role of medical advisor if asked to explain the range of choices. The ideal situation is to make an appointment with your doctor to ask medical questions and then meet with a lawyer, if desired, to execute the forms. (Some state bar associations have drafted instructions in lay terms designed to help people fill out the form without needing to engage an attorney. If your state does this, the instructions should be available on their web page.)

For some people, the sheer work involved in creating an advance directive serves as an excuse for not doing one. However, the most important step is not physically creating the documents but having the difficult conversations with family and friends that will allow advance directives, and especially durable powers-of-attorney, to accomplish their intended aim.

Most doctors find it hard to have frank conversations about dying and death with patients. In a case that once came to a hospital ethics committee I was chairing, the patient was a woman in her late 60s with ALS (amyotrophic lateral sclerosis), a neurological disease that eventually kills by paralyzing the muscles that control breathing. When those muscles fail, the only way to sustain life is by permanently connecting the patient to a respirator that breathes for him. Patients on ventilators require regular suctioning of the mucus that accumulates in the breathing passages. Their homes require a backup source of electricity to keep the respirator working in the event of a power failure. Although a very few families can manage to provide 24/7 care for a patient on a ventilator at home, most such patients live in specialized units in nursing homes where the sophisticated, round-the-clock care they require and back-up generators are always available.

Our patient was not at that stage yet, however. She was already paralyzed to the extent that she was bedridden and could only move one finger on one hand, open and shut her eyes, and breathe on her own. Because she could no longer chew or swallow, she was being fed by a tube surgically implanted into her stomach. She had been admitted to the hospital because of a stubborn urinary tract infection. While she was an inpatient, the nurses began to suspect that she was functionally blind in one eye. Because she could not turn the pages of a book, much less hold one, watching television and listening to the radio were her primary ways of passing time. An ophthalmology (eye) consultation was ordered and a mature cataract—that is, one ready to be removed—was diagnosed. By blinking her eyelids, the patient could respond to "Yes" or "No" questions. When cataract removal under local anesthesia and IV sedation was described to her, she quickly signaled "Yes." Being able to see the TV more clearly was of great value to her. However, when her family learned of the surgery, they were divided in their opinions about its risks and usefulness. Intra-family conflicts that cannot be resolved are primary sources of referrals to hospital ethics committees, and this dispute indeed landed at our door.

As a part of gathering information about the patient and her family, the committee talked with her primary-care doctor, an internist. He had been her physician for almost 20 years, and she had already been with him for several years when he diagnosed her ALS. As a pure aside in that conversation, one committee member asked him about her decision for or against permanent artificial ventilation when respiratory paralysis occurred. To our surprise, he said that they had never had that conversation! He knew that the day of making that choice was inevitably coming since ALS is progressive and there is no treatment, but he could never bring himself to broach the subject with her. He said it had been devastating enough to have to tell her about her diagnosis and that he could not bring himself to discuss the course of the disease with her at that time. In one sense, he was correct: immediately after conveying a terrible diagnosis is not the time to try to discuss all the ramifications of the disease process. But every time he saw her after that, her health was a little worse, so there never had seemed to be "a good time" to discuss with her the eventual respiratory paralysis and the life-or-death choice she would face at that juncture. A vital conversation had never taken place and her doctor had no idea of her wishes about permanent artificial ventilation.

Although the woman's disease was a terrible one, this story actually had a good outcome. First, the ethics committee was able to facilitate communication among her children, who finally decided to support their mother's wish to improve her vision by having the cataract surgery. Her surgery took place without problem and was quite successful, allowing her to enjoy TV again. More importantly, the committee asked her doctor what kind of support we could provide to him to help him have the difficult conversation about respiratory paralysis with a patient with whom he had come to feel very close over the many years of their professional relationship. He decided that it would be helpful to be accompanied by the hospital chaplain during the initial conversation, and ours was happy to participate.

More than one conversation was required, of course, especially since the patient could only respond by blinking. Nevertheless, the necessary information was shared, she reflected on her situation, and a decision was arrived at. Her choice was to reject permanent mechanical ventilation at the point where she could no longer breathe on her own. About three months after her discharge from the hospital, she was brought into our ER with respiratory distress. Because of the conversation accidentally facilitated by the circumstances surrounding her cataract removal, the doctors knew not to insert a breathing tube and simply administered morphine to relieve her sense of struggling to breathe. She quietly died about two hours later. This event occurred relatively early in my medical career, before hospice care was available. Had hospice care been available, she would not have had to be transported to the ER to be kept comfortable while dying.

If doctors find it difficult to have these types of conversations with their patients, ordinary people have an even harder time bringing up the subject. Death and dying are "downer" topics, and there are far more pleasant subjects to spend our increasingly sparse free time discussing. But if you want a chance at a dying process reflective of your values and choices, you must have these conversations.

Before going through the process of creating an advance directive—a legal document—you need to do some hard thinking about how you want the end of your life to be and what compromises with your desires you are willing to make. Most of us want to live in good health, to be physically active and mentally sharp, and to drop dead in an instant or die peacefully one night in our sleep. Sudden death is hard on the survivors, but easy on the one who dies, and most of us would sign up for this scenario if we could. But that is not how life works. We ordinarily don't get to choose in what form death will come to us (although a desire for exactly that choice is what is propelling the current push for the legalization of euthanasia and/or physician-assisted suicide, which we will discuss more in Chapter 7).

Think carefully. If you don't get your first choice, that sudden, painless final exit, what compromises are you willing to accept? What if your fate is cancer? Do you want to pursue every available type of therapy, whether surgery, chemotherapy or radiation? What about alternative treatments such as nutritional therapy, or a combination of traditional and alternative medicine? Would you be willing to travel to a national cancer center like Sloan-Kettering Medical Center in New York City or M. D. Anderson Hospital in Texas, or would it be more important to you to be near your home, family and friends, even at the "expense" of not pursuing state-of-the-art therapy? Would you want to have surgery not to cure, but to control pain? Would you consider experimental therapy whose value or outcome are not clear?

What I have described above is a very daunting task, but you are not finished yet. Now that you have worked out the hows and what-ifs of your death, you need to talk with your family or friends or both. Most of them are highly unlikely to be enthusiastic when you tell them about the need for these conversations, but their participation is crucial. It is imperative that people know your wishes in enough detail to be able to make the choices you would have made on your behalf. You need not only to share whatever specific wishes you have developed, but also enough of your overarching values so they can apply those values to a situation you never personally envisioned. It is absolutely critical that your health care proxy know your wishes well enough to truly "speak for you" if need be. Even if you do not take the final step of creating whatever types of advance directives are legal in your state of residence, these conversations provide crucial evidence of your wishes. Such conversations have sometimes held up as evidence in courts of law.

The person you choose to appoint as your DPA for health care may require some reflection. Ideally, it should be a close family member who lives nearby so that he or she can be physically present at the hospital on a regular basis to consult with the doctors caring for you. I say "ideally" because generally our family knows us and our deepest values best, and have known us for the longest time. Because they have the best insight into us as an individual, if choices that were not anticipated in the written forms need to be made, they are in the best position to figure out what we would have wanted.

However, not every family is like this. Today children and sometimes spouses live at great distances from each other and know each other only superficially. In dysfunctional families, siblings and parents may have no accurate idea of how their relations feel or what they value. In recent years, because the remarriage of widows and widowers often negatively affects pension benefits, older couples sometimes live together without being married. This partner may have the best current knowledge of the other's actual state of health and function, especially compared to children living on the other side of the world, but without health care proxy status, he or she has no legal standing at all. A similar situation occurs for many long-standing gay couples. They may have shared a life for years and, sadly, may be estranged from their birth families, yet within the doors of the hospital, one has no right to speak for the other without that piece of paper.

If, for whatever reason, you sense that none of your family is the best choice to speak for you, then you must give the power of proxy to the person best able to state your choices. If this person is not a family member, it is wise to tell your family at the time you make your choice. I have witnessed distressing shouting matches and more than one "swoon" when family members discovered that the health care proxy was a neighbor or friend. I have also seen the hospital attorney threatened with a lawsuit by family members who objected to the treatment called for in the advance directive, which the proxy had authorized appropriately. In one case I recall, the paperwork had been executed completely and correctly, the proxy had authorized choices fully consonant with the values expressed in the documents, and the attorney stood behind the process. He told the family that the documents were legal and the hospital would abide by them. Their threat of suit promptly collapsed. But I have heard stories of other institutions where the magic term "lawsuit" led the hospital attorney to advise the doctors to do as the family, rather than the health care proxy, asked.

Advance directive forms usually allow you to name two or three people to act for you in succession. Thus, you might name your spouse, then a child who lives nearby, and lastly a child who lives far away. In small families you may need to turn to non-family members as successors. I have a friend who is an only child. His father having already died, my friend was named as the proxy for his mother. There were no other family members. In their case, the family attorney, a relationship of long duration, was named as the next proxy in line. In other cases I know about, no one in the family felt capable of carrying out the patient's wishes of because of their own values, so that person turned to a friend who agreed to do so.

Advance directives can fail to achieve their intent when such family conflict exists. If you sense that your personal end-of-life choices are not ones that some family members can support, it is very important for you to talk with them. The goal is not to change their minds; our deepest values are very important to us and outright conversion from one moral or religious standpoint to another is rare. But your family does need to know that you have thought out your choices carefully, that your desires are important expressions of your own deepest values, and that you expect them to honor those choices, even if they would never make them for themselves. If you do not take care of this step, then some hospital ethics committee will attempt to do it for you down the road, except that then your family will be faced with crisis and far less able to consider the merits of any issue calmly and clearly.

While agreement, when it can be negotiated, is usually reluctant in these cases, family members are often able to understand your point of view and why you hold it for yourself. Even if they don't personally approve of your choices, they can unite behind honoring your wishes for your own care out of respect for you as a person. These people, at least, are prepared for controversy when your advance directive has to be activated. It will not be an additional shock to deal with for a group of people already in crisis. Doctors and hospitals are far less likely to cave in before threats of lawsuits by those opposing your choices if you have done the difficult but important work of making your wishes abundantly clear to those who will stand at your bedside. In particular, the person holding your health care proxy needs to know about your values and goals for the end of your life as much as is humanly possible, for they may be faced with making decisions in a scenario neither of you ever explicitly talked about or envisioned. At that point, only a rich and full sense of your priorities, values and goals will allow that person to make a choice consonant with your wishes.

I think you have a much better sense now of the size of the gift my father gave to his family, and especially to me as his health care proxy, by making his wishes known to us. We were fortunate that neither my mother nor my two brothers were in conflict over following Dad's desires at the end of his life, although my youngest brother struggled with knowing when it was the appropriate time to stop aggressive treatment.

If you do not tackle this daunting task of deciding how you would like your death to be and telling those you care for most about your choices, and if you cannot speak for yourself, you are by default going to get the type of care others think is appropriate for "a person in your condition." This may or may not be even close to the choices you would have made, but at the bedside, choices have to be made by someone. If it is not the patient or family, then it will be the doctor who decides based on his or her personal preferences and values.

Fortunately some wonderful tools exist to help facilitate the difficult discussions I have described. In 2000, journalist and commentator Bill Moyers (who, not incidentally, is an ordained Southern Baptist minister) hosted a wonderful Public Broadcasting series called *On Our Own Terms*. Now available as a set of four videos, the series discusses many different end-of-life scenarios through the stories of real people who are dying. Some deaths are well-managed; others just happen. The stories document hospice and palliative care teams in action in a variety of circumstances. I have the students in my euthanasia/physician-assisted suicide classes at Hiram College watch these videos each time I teach the course, and they have found them to be compelling and educational. (They are also very moving. I always give my students a "number of Kleenex rating" for each video and bring a big box of tissues to distribute.)

On Our Own Terms is a marvelous tool for educating yourself and your family about the many available choices at the end of life and for stimulating conversation about the stories you have witnessed and the choices that were made. The tapes are available for loan at many public libraries and can be purchased through the PBS web site.

A couple of years ago one student, a man in his 40s, came to me after the first class and asked if we could talk. He told me that he was fairly recently married to a woman in her 20s and that they had just discovered they were going to have a child. He realized that he and his wife needed to have conversations about end-of-life issues but was not sure how to get them started. He was also fairly sure that his wife would have a very difficult time following his wishes to limit care should she need to act on his behalf. I suggested that he watch the rest of the videos in class, share some of our reading materials with her, and then consider re-watching the videos at home with his wife. By the end of the class, I had also passed out a worksheet designed to help people think through the many decisions necessary before sitting down to write a living will or instruct a proxy decision-maker about their wishes and other materials designed to help get these difficult conversations going. (See Appendix.)

My student later e-mailed me to say that the Sunday after class ended he and his wife sat down to talk after church. Having seen the videos beforehand, they were starting from a common knowledge base, even though he had also had the benefit of the rest of the class. As they talked, using the worksheet as a guide, his wife initially resisted his choices. But with more conversation, she was able to say that, although she disagreed with his choices, she felt she would be able to honor them should she need to do so.

This was not an isolated incident: three other students in the same class were able to have the necessary discussions with their families as a result of what they experienced in class. In one case, the student herself was being treated for breast cancer but had done no advance planning with her family. Another student's husband was scheduled for a kidney transplant the next month but neither of them had executed an advance directive. A third student was a young woman who had never thought about end-of-life issues since the end of her own life seemed incredibly far away. Not only did she consider what she would want if she were unlucky enough to be in a serious accident and unable to speak for herself, but she identified a health care proxy, talked with that person extensively, and executed the necessary forms. She also asked two neighbors, an elderly widow and a young man about her own age, if they had advance directives. Neither did, so she shared her information from class and offered to have her attorney help them with the paperwork while he was assisting her.

Many hospice organizations have guides to discussing end of life issues. An excellent one is a kit called "Courage in Conversation: A Personal Guide to Advance Directives" published by the Hospice of the Western Reserve (*http://www.hospicewr.org*) in Cleveland, Ohio. Your state's hospice organizations may have similar materials as well as packets with forms for creating living wills and/or durable powers-of-attorney for health care.

It is important to revisit your advance directives every few years, perhaps once a decade. Just as changes in your life circumstances—for example, the birth of a grandchild—will lead you to revise your will, changes in your health status and what you value most at your current age may change. People who do this revisiting find it much less emotionally charged than the process of creating that first advance directive. All of your previous difficult thinking about choices can be reused, but filtered through your present circumstances. Some people find no need to make changes; others do. But it should not be surprising to find that end-of-life choices first made in one's 20s or 30s look quite different when they are revisited in one's 40s, 50s, 60s, or 70s.

Many hospitals will keep a copy of your advance directive with your previous patient records; it is then available at the hospital when needed. The person you appoint as your health care proxy should have a personal copy and be able to lay hands on it quickly. Your primary care doctor, assuming that you have an ongoing relationship, may be willing to keep a copy with your chart at their office. Some retirement communities distribute refrigerator magnets that state the location of the resident's advance directive or a vial containing the same information that can be rubber-banded to a specific shelf. Paramedics in those communities know exactly where to look. There is also a U.S. Living Will Registry where advance directives can be registered. These electronic documents are available 24/7 to any doctor or hospital anywhere in the country. Registration is free but must be done through a member health care provider or community partner. Your doctor or local hospital can tell you if they participate. This service is very helpful for persons who become ill or are injured while away from home.

Advance directives are not perfect tools, but what in this life is perfect? They give people the opportunity to think about their final illness and to make some choices about treatments they would or would not want to receive. The process of creating the document gives family members an opportunity to talk together about hard issues and also to realize how much they mean to each other. The importance and value of good communication is reinforced and practiced at a time when the family is not currently dealing with a crisis. They give to the appointed health care proxy the inestimable gift of not asking them to make life and death choices. Instead, their job is to see that the wishes of the patient are respected.

Some people, however, simply cannot or will not face the choices that executing an advance directive requires. They would prefer to leave the choices to their families when the time comes. If that is the best choice for you, it will be a great kindness to your family or proxy to tell them that you trust them to make the best decisions they can if they are ever called upon to make them. None of us is perfect; it may be that when the need arises, your proxy or your family find that they just can't do what they thought they could. All we can ask of each other is that we do our best.

While we are discussing advance directives, I want to mention Ethical Wills, too. This document allows us to pass on advice about values to our families.[32] It has no legal standing but is important nonetheless. Each Ethical Will is unique and there is no special format. Simply write down for your family something about your personal values, how they have shaped your actions, what you have learned from others, and what your hopes, dreams, disappointments, and blessings are. You should also include your personal ideas about the meaning of life and your spiritual or religious ideas. You might want to comment on beliefs you learned from others, especially older family members your heirs may not have known in person. You can also share thoughts about the most critical decisions in your life: why you made them, how you think about them now, what unfinished projects you are leaving behind, and what others might do in memory of you that would be especially consistent with your values and wishes.

Ethical Wills follow in the ancient tradition of passing on such advice to younger generations. In Chapter 49 of the Old Testament book of Genesis, Jacob tells each of his sons his role as head of one of the Twelve Tribes of Israel. In Deuteronomy 31, the 120-year-old patriarch Moses reveals to his people that he is dying and will "not go over this Jordan." He then delivers the moving exhortation, "Be strong and of a good courage, fear not, nor be afraid of them: for the Lord thy God, he it is that doth go with thee; he will not fail thee, nor forsake thee." In the Gospels of the New Testament, Jesus advises his disciples at length on their duties in the corporeal world and their place in the world beyond.

Ethical Wills should not be kept in a safe deposit box; they should be readily available so the information can be used as a part of the funeral or memorial service. A copy can be placed with your most-accessible copies of your living will, left with your designated durable power-of-attorney for health care or given to your family or spiritual advisor to keep.

CHAPTER 3

Hospice and Palliative Care: Wonderful Blessings

FOR THE HARD THINKING I HAVE JUST DESCRIBED TO BE HELPFUL, PEOPLE NEED TO know about the range of medical options available to them. One of the most important, relatively new choices at the end of life is hospice care. As you already know, my mother died at home under such a program. That was my first personal experience with hospice despite having practiced medicine for the previous 30 years. I discovered as we journeyed to her death together how woefully ignorant I was of all that hospice had to offer. Most people are even more ignorant. I want to start this chapter by telling you in more detail about the experiences described in this book's introduction. Our story is quite typical.

My mother's first significant health problem began in her teens, after a fall from a horse left her with multiple compression fractures of her lower spine. She healed quickly, as young people usually do, but was troubled by intermittent back pain for the rest of her life. Her second illness was an abscess deep within her right kidney that led to kidney stone formation. At the time of her first episode, in 1974, the only treatment available was open-kidney surgery. Three weeks after that ordeal, three more stones had developed in the same kidney! The doctor told her it was a classic good news/bad news moment. The good news was that he now knew why the formations were occurring. The bad news was that she had a focus of infection somewhere in the body of her right kidney. There was at that time no means of identifying where in the organ it was, and doctors naïvely thought that we would always be two generations of new antibiotics ahead of resistant bacteria, so the kidney was left in place. From time to time over the rest of her life she had to undergo periodic lithotripsy sessions, a procedure that breaks up stones within the kidney into pieces small enough to pass out of the body in the urine.

About 10 or 12 years after that, Mom had her first episode of congestive heart failure (CHF). By then she had also been diagnosed with adult-onset diabetes but she was very compliant about following her endocrinologist's plan for managing the disease and achieved good control of her blood sugar. As a part of the CHF workup, she had a cardiac catheterization, which revealed wide-open coronary arteries. "A racehorse would be proud to have those arteries!" her cardiologist said when he took me in to review the films with him. There was no obvious cause for heart failure. She responded promptly to treatment and remained symptom-free for several years before another episode occurred. After my father's death, while Mom and I were traveling together and sharing a room, I discovered that she had sleep apnea, a condition in which a person periodically stops breathing during the night. We were just learning then that chronic, untreated sleep apnea can cause CHF. While the symptoms of heart failure can be treated, the underlying damage to the heart muscle cannot be repaired, and she was left with a permanently weakened left ventricle that required her to sleep with Continuous Positive Airway Pressure (CPAP), a device that keeps the breathing passages open.

About six months after Dad died in 1993, Mom and I went to Toronto to see the stage musical *The Phantom of the Opera*. As we were getting into a cab to go to the theatre, the cabbie started to drive away before Mom had completely entered the vehicle. This threw her out the open door to the ground. Her immediate injuries were to her left knee and ankle and back, but what we did not know at the time was that she had also cracked her right hip, which only converted to an open fracture about six weeks later. The X-rays also revealed some osteoporosis, for which treatment was begun. Eventually her left knee and right hip healed enough so that she could walk around without a walker or a cane but she was never as mobile as before the accident.

At the time, our household consisted of three dogs, four cats, Mom, and me, and my anesthesiology practice at the hospital included overnight call. We needed help! We were blessed when God sent us an angel in human form named Coreen. She began with us as a short-term helper, but when it became apparent that my mother would never be able to shop for groceries or run errands again, Coreen became a permanent fixture.

In 1998 Mom, now 78, developed a painful rash that was diagnosed as shingles. Unfortunately she fell into the unlucky category of people whose pain from this disease never abates. She was also unlucky enough to have four damaged nerve roots rather than the usual one nerve root, and for the rest of her life she lived with constant pain. The turn of the new century gave her little cause to celebrate, for by then she was suffering from a host of chronic diseases: a smoldering infection in one kidney, diabetes, congestive heart failure, sleep apnea, osteoporosis, arthritis, and post-herpetic nerve pain refractory to treatment. The combination of these and the fact that any movement of her right arm caused intense nerve pain gradually led her to decrease her mobility. Relative disuse of her muscles further weakened them. Even so, she remained mentally sharp, interested in the world around her and an avid reader.

Fortunately for me, I was able to find a position as an anesthesiologist at an ambulatory surgery center where night call was not a requirement, so I could take on the role of household caregiver at night and on weekends. Without Coreen's devoted care, it would have been necessary to put Mom in an assisted living facility or a nursing home, which neither she nor I wanted. By the time Mom died, Coreen had become another daughter to her and one of my best friends. Of course, not everyone is able to afford in-home care on even a part-time basis, nor do family members always have the flexibility to find a different job that permits them to take on significant home-care responsibilities, so Mom and I were very fortunate all the way around.

In December of 2000, Coreen alerted me that Mom seemed generally weaker than usual. For the first time, she regularly required help getting out of her chair, although she could still walk to the toilet unaided. The change was gradual but real. By mid-month Mom required the assistance of two men to help her up four steps to attend an anniversary party. That night when we got home, I struggled to get her out of the car and up the single step from the garage into the house. She barely made it the length of the house to her first-floor bedroom. By the next day she was so weak she could not stand, and I called her doctor.

The diagnosis was a recurrence of her urinary tract infection (UTI) which led to a three-week hospitalization. The bacterium causing it—always the same one since 1974—was now resistant to every oral antibiotic, so an infectious-disease specialist was consulted and he eventually treated her with three different intravenous antibiotics. Unfortunately, the hospital was then going through staffing cuts, which meant that Mom really suffered. As anyone who has ever had a urinary tract infection knows, one of the symptoms is urgency, the sudden need to get to a toilet very quickly. Because of her extreme weakness, a common symptom of UTI in the elderly, she was not permitted to try to get out of bed alone. Insufficient help on her floor meant that there was usually a long wait once she rang her call bell, which led to wet sheets by the time someone came. My mother, as most adults would, found this to be humiliating and also chilling. By the time she was released in mid-January of 2001, I was at the point of hiring private-duty nurses to provide basic care for her and the Director of Nursing at the hospital and I were on a first-name basis due to my daily calls of complaint.

As is typical of the frail elderly, Mom never recovered her previous level of functioning. She now regularly required help to get up from her chair and Coreen walked with her to the bathroom door. Both Coreen and I were now worried about the brief time she had to leave Mom home alone while running errands or shopping.

Thus Mom was extremely discouraged when, only three months later, she began losing still more strength. It was another episode of the same UTI and required another hospitalization. This time the care was marginally better, but the food had not improved and the bed was far less comfortable than her own at home. To the relief of us all, this time she was released after "only" three weeks. Again, she never regained her previous level of functioning. (Doctors call this the saw-tooth downward pattern shown in Figure 1 in Chapter 2.) It now required both Coreen and me to get Mom to a doctor's appointment. She could no longer walk the length of our house, requiring a wheelchair for the twice-daily trip to and from her bedroom to the family room where she spent her days. When she started to need help getting up from the handicapped-level, higher toilet even with a rail mounted on the wall, I made an appointment with her internist for a fresh and full re-evaluation of her status.

My mom was very lucky to have been cared for by an array of fine, intelligent, and very caring physicians. She was extremely fortunate to have had such a dedicated team watching over her. Her internist and I carefully talked through what Coreen and I had observed and he reviewed all the studies done during the two hospitalizations so as not to duplicate any tests unnecessarily. He evaluated Mom quite thoroughly, looked at all her medications for drug interactions, and talked to her other doctors. In the end, he came to no definitive diagnosis other than that the cumulative toll of her medical problems was rising.

By mid-July Coreen was beginning to voice concern about her ability to take care of Mom by herself, and I reluctantly began to consider nursing home placement. As an anesthesiologist, I fully appreciated what an anesthetic nightmare my mother would be with all her diseases if she fell and broke a hip or an arm, and I certainly did not want that to happen. I had even gotten as far as selecting a local nursing home and arranging for her admission when I believe God sent us down another path.

On the day Mom was to be admitted, the nursing home called and said they could not take her until at least the following day. As anyone who has ever faced an overwhelming task knows, I had worked up my courage to face this move, and now suddenly it was not going to happen. I called my two brothers and told them, "I really think I could have done it today, but now, with another 24 hours to wait, I'm not sure I can do it tomorrow. What on earth am I going to do?" Both promised to think hard and fast about the dilemma and call me back. My youngest brother, Jeff, discussed our situation with a pharmacist friend, who said it sounded to him like we should be thinking not about a nursing home, but hospice.

The thought staggered me. Hospice, I was aware, was for dying people. It truly had never occurred to me that my mother might be dying. But I was desperate enough to call her doctor and ask for his opinion. He replied, "Well, I don't know whether she is dying, but call hospice and they will send a nurse to do an evaluation. If they don't think she is dying, they won't admit her." It was late afternoon of the Friday before Labor Day. Nevertheless, I called the organization he recommended and explained my mother's multiple diagnoses, no one of which was obviously in line to be fatal in the near term.

The holiday weekend notwithstanding, a wonderful nurse appeared on Saturday morning and joined us in the family room. She tried asking Mom questions about her present state of health and medical history. Mom seemed almost too weak to talk, so I gave most of the answers. After about two hours of evaluation, including looking over all her medications and helping me struggle to get her to the toilet twice, the nurse told me she felt Mom was indeed a hospice candidate. Her condition might not have been apparent to her primary doctor or her doctor-daughter, but it was no mystery to the hospice nurse. I distinctly remember feeling faint at that point. I was a physician living with a dying person and had not even recognized what was happening! In less than 24 hours I had conceptually traveled from nursing home to hospice. It was a jarring jump.

The nurse then explained to me how hospice worked and what the program would provide for Mom and the family. We did the paperwork to get her signed up. The nurse was not sure that Mom was competent to sign herself into hospice care, another surprise for me. Yes, she answered questions very slowly and incompletely, as if the effort to think was simply too great, but she had evolved to that state so gradually that it took seeing her through a stranger's eyes for me to notice how profoundly "slowed" she had become. Fortunately I held her health care proxy and had a copy at home, so I could make the necessary decisions.

Next the nurse did a physical assessment of our home. She strongly suggested putting the hospital bed (which they would provide) in the family room so that Mom would be directly in the flow of daily life. When I demurred that Mom had a "Sleep Number"™ mattress that was wonderful for her arthritic back, she assured me that not only would she provide an air mattress, but it would be filled with warmed air and have channels that would automatically inflate and deflate to keep Mom from getting bedsores. They would also provide three sets of custom-made sheets so that one set could be on the bed, one in the laundry, and one in reserve at all times. She also ordered a Hoyer lifter, a device that allows one person to safely move another person from a prone position to a chair across the room without either party being hurt. She suggested that an extra-wide wheelchair would make using the Hoyer easier and ordered one of those, too.

We went over Mom's medications and diet and the nurse explained that under hospice care, only those medications necessary for symptom control or pain relief would be continued. Hospice recommends giving patients whatever they want to eat. I learned that Mom would lose her interest in food as time went on, but that I should feel free to be creative in trying to tempt her, with the exception of steak or other foods that required a lot of chewing. Mom's face lit up when she learned that milk-shakes, a long-ago treat from her pre-diabetic days, were now an option.

The nurse explained that hospice would work with the doctor who knew Mom so well and that a hospice doctor could assist if there were special problems or issues the other physician did not feel adequate to handle. She also pointed out that hospice intended not only to care for Mom but also for the family who would be making the journey to her death with her. We would be one big team working together. To facilitate communications, one person needed to be designated to receive and pass on information. That person is called the "primary caregiver," although he or she need not be the person who does the actual giving of care. Since I was Mom's health care proxy and lived with her, I was the logical candidate.

The nurse encouraged me to tell my brothers that hospice was eager to address their questions or concerns, either about Mom and her care or their own feelings. She outlined the many different ways hospice stood ready to reach out to us: a primary care nurse who would visit us regularly and keep track of Mom's condition; an aide who would help bathe her several times a week; social workers; a lawyer to advise us on legal matters if needed; chaplains from a host of faiths; art therapists; and even volunteers to sit with Mom so she would not be alone when I needed to get a haircut or run an errand. I had round-the-clock telephone access to a hospice nurse at the central office who would have access to all of Mom's records and could advise or just support me. I was told to feel free to call. Later, when I did, I was amazed that the nurse knew all the latest details of Mom's situation, was aware of all the most recent treatment modifications we were trying, and was unfailingly a source of help and support for me.

I was relieved to learn that first day that the cost of hospice would be covered by Mom's health insurance. Because hospice is very "low-tech" compared to a hospital, it is comparatively inexpensive. Medicare and private insurance companies are delighted to pay for it. That helpful nurse explained that health insurance "trades" hospice and hospitalization benefits, so the patient does not technically have both at the same time. The emphasis with hospice is on home care because most people would prefer to die at home, but if necessary it can also be provided in a nursing home or acute-care hospital. Once insurance numbers and a signature are registered, hospice does all the paperwork, even the complicated forms associated with a hospice-to-hospital transfer and restoration of hospice benefits when the patient is discharged back into hospice care. If Mother developed symptoms that her team could not adequately control at home, we had access to an inpatient unit at the hospice where she could receive 24/7 care. The nurse also asked me if I was uncomfortable with the thought of Mom dying at home. If at any time I suspected that that would trouble me, she said, Mom's hospice nurse could arrange for her to be moved at the end to an inpatient setting.

Hospice does not cover every possible need, however. I learned that while Mom's primary nurse would come several times a week to evaluate her and coordinate her care, round-the-clock in-home care is not included. Hospice does provide a registry of trustworthy people who are available to serve for an additional fee. Eventually we did need someone to sit with Mom at night so that I could sleep at the other end of the house without worrying that I might not hear her call. Coreen, the angel you have already met, and another angel named Maggie did double-team work during the days: one of them was always with Mom while the other was shopping and running errands, which, amazingly, continue to be necessary even in the midst of dying.

When the intake nurse was finally ready to leave, I had a sudden failure of nerve. This was all just happening too fast. I had no idea how much of the conversation Mom had heard or understood. Did she know that hospice was a program for people who were dying? Did she understand that she had been judged to be dying? Did she have any idea of the commitment I had just made on her behalf? I told the nurse I was not quite ready to begin and she very kindly explained that my reaction was a common one. She would file the paperwork back at the office and whenever we were ready, we only had to call to activate the service.

By now Mom was so weak that, despite a handle on the edge of her bed to grasp as she sat up and a bedside commode right there, she needed help to stand up and pivot. She made six trips back and forth that night, proof (as if I needed more) that the UTI had come roaring back once again. By the last of these, she was too weak to stand up from the commode. I stood behind her, grasped her torso under her arms, and more or less threw her face-down on her bed. *This simply cannot go on*, I remember thinking. *Neither of us can continue like this.* So at 7:00 the Sunday morning of Labor Day weekend I called hospice for help.

Two hours later a truck backed up to the front door and a very kind deliveryman unloaded the bed, wheelchair, Hoyer lifter and several boxes of supplies. I was too preoccupied to have thought about moving the furniture in the family room to accommodate the bed, so he cheerfully pitched in and helped me. He assembled the bed, inflated the mattress and turned on the heater to start warming the air.

Next a male nurse arrived to check on us. He helped me get Mom out of her chair and onto the commode but said she was using far too much energy, so he called her doctor and got permission to put in a Foley catheter, a soft tube that constantly drains urine from the bladder into a collection bag. "Now she can save her limited energy for other things," he said. What a gift that was!

The nurse helped me get her into the clean, warm bed and noted some changes on her legs which he felt came from contaminated urine dribbling onto her skin. He called for an aide to come and give Mom a bed bath. A cheerful young lady arrived shortly and proved very competent. (Bed baths are a lot harder to do than they look, especially if your goal is to bathe the patient but not the bed!) When I apologized for intruding on her holiday Sunday, she said, "Honey, when you need a bath, you need a bath. It's no trouble at all." That attitude was unfailingly at the heart of every interaction we had with hospice. The nurse stopped by again later and showed me how to bandage Mom's leg to prevent further skin breakdown and to make sure we had her comfortably settled in her new, warm bed.

On Tuesday Mom's primary nurse came for her first visit. Joan was so kind and compassionate—another angel sent to help us in a difficult time.

When she came I was already at work at the ambulatory surgery center, so she and I interacted by phone. She kept me apprised of her assessments, shared any new ideas about how we could make Mom more comfortable, and praised Maggie's and Coreen's skill and dedication as caregivers. She assured me that they were exceptionally quick studies when she taught them something new and she certainly had a bag full of tricks to teach. Hospice nurses and aides are the front-line care givers to the dying and they have just about perfected the mechanics of patient care.

Joan also shared with me some of her conversations with my brother Jeff. Although he had first conveyed the suggestion of hospice to me, he agonized over whether that, rather than another hospitalization and round of multiple IV antibiotics, was the correct choice for Mom. He really struggled with the difference between being told that medicine has run out of options to cure a fatal disease like cancer and our situation, where no overtly fatal illness had been diagnosed. Joan allowed Jeff to talk, answered his questions, explained that reservations were common in ambiguous situations, and shared with him that she herself was then undergoing chemotherapy for breast cancer. This knowledge gave a new dimension to my respect for her and the job she was doing. She told Jeff that too many doctors and families wait until the patient is halfway through death's door before considering hospice and therefore miss out on much of the work to prepare for death that the program encourages patients and their families to do. She asked him, as she had asked me, if he was aware of any unresolved relationships, fears about dying, or spiritual issues that Mom needed to address is whatever time she had left. She alerted Jeff to hospice-facilitated support groups for families, including special summer camps for children who have experienced a recent death. She encouraged my brother to call her any time he needed support. Somehow this information seemed to lead Jeff to more peace with what had been essentially a one-person decision—my own.

Joan also taught me an important personal lesson during our journey together. She knew right from the start that I was a doctor, but steadfastly refused to fall into a nurse/doctor relationship with me. A couple of weeks in, she told me by phone that she had ordered a batch of liquid morphine to be delivered to the house. Mom had already been on narcotic skin patches for her shingles pain for years, so I was unclear why an additional drug might be necessary. Joan told me she wanted it available in the house before I needed it, so Mom would not have to wait for it to be delivered. If necessary, the liquid morphine could be placed under Mom's tongue and would work almost as fast as if it were given through a vein.

"How many milligrams do I give as a first dose?" I asked, falling into my physician mind-set.

Joan kindly but firmly replied, "Sheryl, what your Mom needs now is a daughter, not a doctor. I do not want to hear the word 'milligram' again. In hospice, we give a medication until we get the effect we want, so we don't worry about the size of the dose. But if it will make you feel better—and we want to help you, too—when you are thinking about administering morphine, call us and we will talk with you about the specific goal you are trying to achieve and how best to get there."

Joan was absolutely right: Mom had a great team of doctors and needed no more medical expertise. She needed a daughter. Letting go of the compulsion to oversee all the medical decisions that were being made freed up my energy to focus more fully on my mother and meeting whatever other, non-medical needs of hers I could. As her appetite flagged and then failed, I often made four or five different foods for a meal, hoping to find one that would taste good. When she enjoyed something enough to take more than a bite or two, I felt as if I had just won a marathon. Joan kept gently reminding me that a failing appetite was part of the body's preparation for death and not to take disinterest in food as a personal rejection or reflection on my attempts to find something to tempt her.

Twice during those weeks I called the hospice nurse in the middle of the night. One of the signs that death is imminent is a pattern of breathing called Cheyne-Stokes respirations, in which a person's breathing gradually slows down, stops for what seems an eternity, and then picks up more quickly than before. The cycle repeats over and over and often ends in death. One evening when I stopped by Mom's bed to say goodnight, I noticed that she seemed to have started Cheyne-Stokes breathing. I sat by her side until I was certain and then picked up the telephone. The night nurse agreed that the respirations were an ominous sign, but pointed out that Joan had visited only that morning and not observed anything that made her think death was close. Since Mom was resting quietly and not struggling to breathe, the nurse did not recommend that I do anything other than sit with her if I wanted to, and that is what I did. When I woke up the next morning, still holding her hand, Mom said rather brightly, "I'm starving! What's for breakfast?" This would be the last time she ate anything with evident relish, but that breakfast was a huge success.

A couple of weeks after that, Joan informed me during one of our phone calls that she was observing symptoms that suggested death was now just days away. She left some written information about physical changes we might notice and warned me that Mom might not want to eat at all. She suggested using ice chips and lemon-glycerin swabs to keep her lips and tongue moist and encouraged us to offer sips of water often but not to be surprised if she refused. She said we might also notice that Mom's hands and feet were becoming mottled and bluish and cool to the touch. All of these were signs of the body shutting down. Joan reminded us that when death occurred, we should not panic and call 911: rescue squads come to "rescue." She suggested that we think about whether it was important for my brothers and me to be in the room with Mom when she died and to plan for how we would assemble those who wanted to be there. If we needed moral support, she said, hospice would dispatch a nurse at any time, even in the middle of the night. She also explained that hospice would take care of all the paperwork required after death.

One Monday night seven weeks into our hospice journey, my mother's breathing became much more rapid and it seemed as if she no longer heard us when we spoke to her. Hospice nurses swear that hearing is the last sense to fail, so Joan had encouraged us never to say anything in front of Mom, even if she appeared to be comatose, that we would hesitate to say if she were wide awake. In fact, she encouraged us to talk to her even if this did not elicit a response. Both of my brothers came for the evening and so did a cousin who had lost his own mother the year before and who was in town for a business conference. I called my employers and told them I would not be in the next day. We ordered carry-out Chinese food and sat around Mom's bed telling stories about our joint family summer vacations and all the fun times we had shared. Jeff chose to stay overnight that night.

By midnight it was clear that something new was going on, and for the first time, Mom appeared to me to be uncomfortable. I called the hospice nurse and described what I was seeing, including rapid breathing. She instructed me to use the liquid morphine to slow Mom's respiration down to normal. "She sounds like she is working way too hard breathing, and that is not necessary," she said. As Joan had told me, she recommended an initial dose—but not in milligrams!—and told me how soon I should expect to see a response. Based on that, she suggested how soon I might decide that another dose was in order and said she would call back in an hour to see how we were doing. By that time, Mom's respiration had slowed from about 45 breaths a minute to 24. "Still too fast," said the nurse. "Keep going until we get it down to 12 to14 or till she seems quite comfortable." When she called back about an hour later Mom was indeed resting comfortably, no longer panting, but breathing quietly about 14 times a minute.

Joan arrived the next morning and met me face-to-face for the first time. She agreed that death was very near and asked what additional help she could give to Jeff and me since Mom was beyond any earthly help. We sat in the living room, talking quietly about Jeff's personal struggle with the decision not to re-hospitalize Mom and to follow the hospice route. Joan deftly and compassionately reminded him that death comes eventually to all of us, that Mom had lived a long life and had carried the burden of multiple diseases, and especially chronic pain, for a long time. She suggested that second-guessing was not likely to be helpful for any of us, and that Mom's imminent demise seven weeks after entering hospice care strongly suggested that her condition really had been untreatable. Just then Maggie called us to the family room. Before our eyes, Mom took a couple more breaths, turned very pale, and died.

We called my brother Bill and Jeff's wife, Christine. Minutes later Coreen arrived from a Mass being offered in her own mother's memory. We sat around my mother's body and told more stories and shared memories. Shortly thereafter Mom's hospice aide arrived as scheduled to bathe her. Joan suggested that the aide and Maggie wash Mom's body and I found myself suddenly eager to participate in this oldest of human rituals, lovingly preparing a body for burial. Without any sense of being rushed, we carefully washed and dried Mom's hair and body and changed the sheets one last time. It felt so fitting to provide this final physical service to the body that had housed my mother's spirit. Although my mother, brothers and I had been with my dad when he died, the nurses had hovered around waiting to prepare his body so that the bed could be readied for a new patient. This time there was no sense of pressure, no need to rush, no feeling of a state of crisis. Joan called Mom's doctor and the hospice office to inform them of her death and the funeral director to tell him we would let him know when to come to the house.

Christine and Mom's three youngest grandchildren arrived with a small bouquet they had picked in their back yard. The girls, ages eight, six, and three, were able to approach Mom's body in a quiet atmosphere and see first-hand that an expected death is not scary, just sad. Joan stayed until we were able to assure her that we were okay. She left and drove to Mom's doctor's office to have him sign the death certificate and then took it to the funeral home. Our minister arrived and gathered us around her body in prayer. When we were all ready, the funeral director came and took Mom's body away.

I mentally reviewed the events of the past few hours. Having thought that Mom's weeks under hospice care had prepared me for her death, I naïvely underestimated how strongly my medical mindset would try to reassert itself against all common sense. Pilots rehearse managing the crash they hope to never have. Doctors and nurses rehearse CPR and other complex but rarely done tasks. It embarrassed me a little to realize that, although Mom had slipped away without any struggle, my medical training had tried to reassert itself when she suddenly paled. In fact, I had nearly jumped up on the bed and started pumping on her chest to resuscitate her. I think Joan sensed my muscles tensing, because she firmly took my hands in hers and pulled them against her. What purpose would resuscitation have served, had I succeeded? Mom would have re-awakened to a life dominated by pain and weakness and had to face dying again at some future date. I now knew first-hand why, when hospice was first introduced in the early 1980s, families of patients who were not lucky enough to have outside support at the moment of death sometimes panicked and called the rescue squad. Instead, hospice suggests "rehearsing" the moment of death and emphasizes not panicking and staying away from the telephone unless it is to call them.

Later that evening, both of my brothers asked if I would be all right until morning and offered to spend the night with me if that would help.

I hadn't thought about this, but when I asked myself the question, I was grateful and a little surprised to say very honestly that, no, I was not at all troubled by being in the house where Mom had just died. Instead, I found I was overwhelmingly proud of what we had achieved together: we kept Mom in her own home, we kept her comfortable, and I, in particular, kept her at the center of my life while she was dying. I already missed her, and I still do today. But I was simultaneously grateful that she had laid down the burdens of disease and dis-ease she had carried for so long with few complaints. I was relieved that her pain was past and thankful for the lessons she had taught me about facing adversity with quiet courage and minimal whining. I was profoundly grateful for the physical services and comforting I had been privileged to provide for her—all those meals of which she took three or four bites, the evenings spent reading in the same room with her as she dozed, even for the first-time opportunity to wash her body after death and help prepare to lay it to rest. Her family had had the chance to tell her in words and in deeds how much they valued her life and to say good bye. All of this was intensely meaningful to me then. Years later, it remains so. In fact, I think it was the greatest single accomplishment of my life.

The hospice journey gave several other gifts to Mom's family and friends. Our Presbyterian church has for several years participated in a program of adult lay care called the Stephen Ministry. Both of my parents and I trained and served as Stephen Ministers. Two of my mother's oldest friends from the congregation, Jean and Luke, resurrected their training and began regular visits with Mom while she was under hospice care. In the beginning she was able to converse in a desultory fashion with them, perhaps somewhat distracted by the jamocha milkshakes they brought to her. Even as she was less and less able to converse they continued to come for short visits, always praying with her and anyone who wished to be included. Their last visit was the Saturday before she died. Although she was already well into her journey to death, she certainly did enjoy that final milkshake!

Because we had lived in one community for over half a century, Mom had a big circle of friends. She had been a stay-at-home mother while we were growing up, as was usual in the 1950s, so she spent many hours working at and for the church. By dying at home and not in a rule-bound institution, Mom was able to receive care from her friends—and so was I. People would call and ask if they could stop by while they were out running errands or shopping; Mom and I weren't going anywhere, so it was almost always possible. For the first few weeks under hospice care, she really seemed to enjoy these brief contacts with old friends, and they frequently arrived with food of some sort to share with us. I am much more appreciative now of what a gift it is to be allowed to visit and share like that, whether we are the visitors or those who are visited. We live our lives in communities, and both the community and the one who is dying need the sense of those interconnections as we prepare for death. Such a community is diminished by the loss of one of its members and everyone needs the time and space to acknowledge that reality. It is impossible to do that kind of visiting in a hospital setting, particularly in an ICU where patients receive hours of hands-on care every day. It's a fair trade-off to forego that kind of visitation when a person is ultimately going to recover and can receive visitors at home during their recovery, but it is a real and permanent loss when it cannot occur with one who is dying.

Another wonderful event had occurred the Sunday before Mom died. She and I were alone: Maggie and Coreen were enjoying a well-deserved weekend off and the evening aide had not yet arrived. Mom had been lying quietly with her eyes closed and I was reading in a chair beside her. Suddenly, her eyes flew open, she gasped and a look of utter joy suffused her face. "Auntie!" she said in a voice full of happiness. The hair on my arms immediately stood at attention because I knew who Auntie was—her beloved great-aunt Huldah Johnson, who had always lived with Mom's family. In fact, until her death when I was 15 years old, Auntie and I had shared a bedroom. Both Joan and one of our ministers had told me that dying persons often "see" or somehow experience the presence of "someone not alive," as hospice nurses and authors Maggie Callanan and Patricia Kelley term it in their wonderful book *Final Gifts*. Sometimes the visitor is said to be a deceased family member and sometimes a figure with religious significance such as Jesus or an angel but always a comforting, welcoming guide.[33]

Auntie referred to my mother as "Dollybird" during her childhood and occasionally even when she was a young woman. One famous family story is about an early visit by my dad to my mother's family home before their marriage. They had met at Hiram College during Freshman Orientation in 1938 and by the end of the week were dating. Dad came from a Baptist family in western New York, so when he arrived in college he did not smoke, drink, dance, or play cards. My mother's religious background was Episcopalian, so there was a bit of culture clash there. Mom had brought Dad home for a weekend in the "big city" (suburban Cleveland) and wanted him to take her to the rooftop restaurant-bar at a downtown hotel. Dad was not at all sure that a good Baptist should go to a place like that. Auntie fixed him with a steady stare. "Listen, Bill," she told him, in a schoolmarm tone that brooked no opposition, "Dollybird *wants* to go to the Allerton and *you* are going to take her." And that was that! In life and in death, Auntie was the perfect take-charge person to guide Mom home.

Having witnessed my mother's experience, there is no doubt in my mind that it was a joyful one for her. I can still see in my mind's eye the look of elation on her face and hear the eagerness in her voice. "Auntie" is the only word she said and she only said it once, but that happy look remained on her face for a long time and when it faded, it was replaced by a half-smile that was still there when I went to bed that night. I have no idea whether my father had a similar experience before he died. I hope so, since the hospice nurses who describe them so uniformly report that they are joyful and comforting. It was certainly a privilege to be present when Auntie came to visit Mom.

This was not to be our family's last experience with hospice. Just five weeks after Mom's death, her last surviving brother became acutely ill. He, too, had multiple chronic illnesses but was in stable condition until he developed pneumonia. Because of underlying lung disease, his doctors put him on a ventilator, expecting to withdraw it as soon as the antibiotics worked their magic. Uncle Ken seemed to rally nicely within 24 hours and the machine was removed, but by the next day it was apparent that things were not going well and it had to be replaced. He quickly spiraled down after that. His family was asked about his wishes for care and since he did not want to be permanently maintained by machines, they decided to opt for hospice. He was clearly too ill to be moved home at this point, so he received hospice care in the hospital.

This gave his family 24-hour access to him: there were no limits on the number of people who could visit at any one time. The entire focus was on keeping him comfortable and supporting his family. Uncle Ken died a few days later, still hospitalized but having experienced all the benefits of hospice care.

So, if hospice care is this wonderful both for the patient and for the family, why is it not the "standard" or "usual" way for Americans to die? Based on my own story, I think one answer is ignorance. Too few people have heard of hospice at all. Many people who know something about it think it is limited to people with specific ailments. While hospice was first started in England by Dr. (later Dame) Cecily Saunders to remedy problems for people dying of cancer, the program has never been limited to those with a cancer diagnosis. One reason I have recounted my family's experience with hospice is to illustrate its role even for those without a terminal diagnosis. Another element of confusion may arise from the requirement of both Medicare and private insurance that the patient be judged to have six months or less to live. As I have mentioned before, it is simply not possible for doctors to predict how long any given patient will live. Even with cancer, all we can offer are statistical probabilities: a certain percentage of patients in a particular stage of a particular type of cancer will die in a particular time span. The great news for hospice patients is that if you live longer than six months, your doctor can simply recertify you for another six months. Only if you are deemed to no longer be dying from your disease are you removed from hospice care and returned to your previous insurance coverage. When you are eventually judged to be dying again, you can return to hospice care. Essentially, you cannot "outlive" your hospice benefit. This makes perfectly good sense when you realize that hospice is radically less expensive than care aimed at curing a serious disease like cancer. There is a real economic incentive for your insurance company or the federal government to favor hospice care over acute care. But because of the myth that you will be tossed out of hospice if you live "too long," many people do not ask for (or demand!) a referral until just days before their death. According to Kathleen M. Foley, M.D., the median length of hospice stay nationwide is 22 days. One-third of hospice patients die within seven days.[34] I once asked Mom's nurse Joan about the shortest time she had ever cared for a hospice patient, and she ruefully said, "That would be the lady who died as I was admitting her."

It is a tragedy when patients are referred to hospice and die within a few days for at least two reasons. First, this gives the program little or no chance to provide its full range of services. Joan was careful to address not only my mother's physical needs but her emotional and spiritual ones as well. Because she was already relatively uncommunicative when she entered hospice care, I was never entirely sure that Mom knew she was a hospice patient. We were fortunate to be longtime members of a local congregation and our minister tried diligently to talk to her about any unresolved spiritual issues she might have. Had he not been available, hospice was prepared to provide a chaplain of the appropriate faith. Joan had several conversations, perhaps some I don't even know about, with my brother Jeff, who was genuinely troubled by the decision to turn to hospice care rather than pursue another hospitalization. This type of outreach and personal support is an important and integral component of hospice care. In fact, the program follows up with the family at intervals for at least a year with a variety of written materials about the grieving process and suggestions of support groups. Special attention is paid to the needs of grieving children.

The second tragedy when patients are referred to hospice for a few days only is that the program's financial viability is jeopardized. As Mom's story illustrates so well, the first and the last few days on hospice require a lot of service. At the beginning, the admissions nurse educated me about what hospice did and did not provide. Our physical need for equipment was assessed and supplies and drugs were delivered. Over a holiday weekend everything was delivered and set up, a nurse visited twice, and an aide arrived to give Mom a bed bath. That was a lot of concentrated service for one patient. But hospices are paid at a flat rate, so much per day, regardless of whether a patient needs a full day's care or nothing at all. As the patient's death approaches, hospice again provides more intensive service and support to the family, and once it occurs hospice handles the necessary paperwork and removes the medical equipment it has provided. In order to survive financially, every hospice needs patient days between these care extremes—days where patient costs are less than they are paid for that day. Every year more hospices close than open because patient admissions come too late.[35]

Some patients may refuse hospice care due to their particular life story and self-image. Some people consider themselves "fighters" who have constantly battled overwhelming odds and always succeeded in beating them. For people like this, the passivity of hospice—with its focus on improving the quality of a patient's remaining days, not lengthening them—just does not fit. Fortunately, these people can now take advantage of another new medical specialty called palliative care. Although it can be defined several ways, Dr. Timothy Quill says that it involves "total care for patients whose disease is not responsive to curative treatment, and includes pain and symptom management as well as psychological, social, spiritual, and existential support for the patient and family."[36] Palliative care is a way for a patient and family to reap many of the benefits of hospice without having to eschew all attempts to prolong life. Sometimes patients with a disease that will likely prove fatal develop a symptom that must be managed before they become "eligible" for hospice care. Palliative care serves these patients by taking their symptoms seriously and committing to control them. Palliative care is a very new medical specialty. recently only 0.4% of the doctors practicing in Ohio were palliative care practitioners, so practically speaking, this treatment is usually only available in large cities. Nevertheless, hospice has already profoundly improved the options for dying patients and their families, and palliative care surely will do so in the future as it becomes more common. By late 2005 more than 2,000 physicians had been certified by the American Board of Hospice and Palliative Care and more than 10,000 nurses and nursing assistants by the Hospice and Palliative Care Nursing Association.[37]

If your doctor will not discuss hospice with you, then call the program yourself. The doctor's reluctance may have more to do with personal issues than with your condition. A few years ago, after earning a Master's degree in Administrative Medicine, I worked part-time as an assistant medical director for a health insurer. Mostly I reviewed anesthesia claims; however, on one particular day I was the first doctor to arrive and the utilization review nurses were desperate for help. "Please call this doctor in Iowa," one of them said. "See if he will talk to you because he won't talk to us and everyone is frantic." The story was that his patient, a woman in her late 50s, was dying from widely metastasized breast cancer in an ICU in a rural hospital with full resuscitation orders. She repeatedly pleaded with the nurses to discharge her because she wanted to die at home. But her doctor—an oncologist, a specialist in cancers—would not even discharge her from Intensive Care! No one, not the ICU nurses, not the hospital's utilization review nurses, not the insurance company's medical staff, and certainly not the patient, could understand why he insisted on keeping a dying woman in an ICU, some of the most expensive real estate in the hospital and appropriately reserved to serve those who will recover by virtue of its care.

I was reluctant to call him because I assumed the conversation would be confrontational, but the situation was dire and my heart went out to a woman who was not asking for a miracle but only to go home to die. So I phoned and introduced myself. He was no more cordial than I had anticipated, and he really bristled when I asked him why this patient was not on hospice care at home. "I don't *believe* in hospice!" he said furiously, and slammed down the phone.

Suddenly, the whole sad scenario made a warped kind of sense. In fact, I thought of two different possible explanations for his bizarre behavior. One was that this doctor was personally terrified of death and unable to deal with his own mortality or that of his patients in a rational way. He was treating his conflicts about death rather than his patient. Or perhaps he had simply and utterly bought into the military metaphor that sees every patient's death as a personal defeat. The only way he had of living with such defeat was to use every last ounce of medical prowess, even to the point of absurdity, so he could tell himself that he was vanquished by an unbeatable enemy. It was the Little Big Horn all over again, but he was Custer forcing his patient to be one of his troops. Neither scenario could excuse him for ignoring his patient's clearly, repeatedly expressed wishes. Sadly for her, she died the next day—still in the ICU.

Obviously I am a fan of hospice and palliative care. Hospice has profoundly reshaped the options for persons who are dying. Palliative care will only add to its range of services and the focus on comfort and symptom control. But I do not want to romanticize dying, either. My mom was fortunate in that her final illness was not inherently painful; not everyone is so lucky. Hospice does work to achieve satisfactory pain control, but many patients experience some pain and/or other troublesome symptoms. What hospice promises is that they will work with you, whatever that takes, until your symptoms are tolerable. Sometimes to achieve that goal a brief period of hospitalization is required to get the worst symptoms under control. Occasionally surgery or radiation is needed, not for cure but to control pain, and hospice will arrange for that.

But dying is always hard work, both for the dying person and his or her family. In a wonderful essay called "Sometimes Dying Still Stings," Dr. Greg Sachs shares the story of his father-in-law's death at home with the aid of hospice. Despite excellent end-of-life care, everyone in the family was suffering. "Al was being ripped from our midst and it hurt like hell," he writes, but "because some of the suffering is existential or spiritual, there may be limits to what we can achieve even with superb, multidisciplinary end-of-life medical care." As a geriatrician who also does hospice care, Sachs is now reluctant to use terms like "good death" because he does not want to make death seem too rosy or create unrealistic expectations of how easy it can be.[38]

Many more people need to know about hospice: that it is commonly available as an insurance benefit, that patients can initiate the discussion about hospice with their doctors, and that it is beneficial to enter care early because a person cannot outlive the hospice benefit. No program can remove the grief, loss, fear, and emotional suffering we feel at the approaching death of a loved one. Even those of us who profess faith in an afterlife, the resurrection of the body and the immortality of the soul, experience the day-to-day grief and sense of loss that follow death. Death ruptures the most profound human relationships and that rupture is always painful to endure. It is our fate, however, to endure it and hospice certainly helps both patients and their families to do so.

CHAPTER 4

The Sanctity of Life. . . and Death?

THAT HUMAN LIFE IS SACRED IS A WIDELY-HELD WESTERN THEOLOGICAL AND philosophical belief. Sometimes this claim expresses an overtly religious judgment and sometimes a secular one. Most commonly we use the word "sacred" in an explicitly religious context. In some communities of faith it is said that human lives are sacred because they are "a gift from God." Historically the sacred nature of human life is attributed to the claim that men and women were created "in the image of God" (Genesis 1:26). Clement of Alexandria, one of the early Church Fathers (ca. 150–220 CE) claimed that not only had God made every human being in His image but also that "since Christ's coming, His divinity fills all humans equally and deifies all humanity."[39]

This strong grounding of the sanctity of human life in the Judeo-Christian tradition found its politicization in the Anglo-American legal system. It is a part of the moral framework for the Declaration of Independence, which lists life as the first among the inalienable rights of "life, liberty and the pursuit of happiness." In healthcare it has been translated into the belief that under no circumstances should doctors act deliberately to end a human life. The American Medical Association's position on euthanasia issued in June 1994 and updated in June 1996 states: "Euthanasia is fundamentally incompatible with the physician's role as healer; would be difficult or impossible to control; and would pose serious social risks."[40]

Many of those who stand outside any community of faith also accept the idea that life is "sacred" in a non-religious sense, because they think it is intrinsically valuable, morally important in and of itself. Ronald Dworkin, in his marvelous book *Life's Dominion: An Argument about Abortion, Euthanasia and Individual Freedom*, explains that some things, like money, are "instrumentally valuable": tools or instruments to help people get something else they want. Cash or a credit card allows me to purchase food, clothing and shelter, all necessities of life. The paper from which the money is made or the plastic in the credit card do not makes them valuable, but rather the things that they allow me to buy. Other things are "subjectively valuable," seen as desirable by some people but not by others. Such things are often a matter of taste: *Fidelio* tickets would have a different subjective value for an opera lover and a football fanatic. But Dworkin says that something is "intrinsically valuable" if it is valuable in and of itself, independent of either its usefulness or the enjoyment it provides. Many Westerners feel that human life is intrinsically or innately valuable or sacred in just this way and that "it is intrinsically a bad thing, a kind of cosmic shame, when human life at any stage is deliberately extinguished."[41] Even people who do not believe that human life is sacred because it was created by God usually agree that it is intrinsically important; that is why we speak of "murdering," or unjustifiably taking another human being's life, but only of "killing" animals.

After all, none of us is a self-created being. At minimum, our lives are a biological gift from our parents. Many people think they are even more than that: a divine gift from God. Death, the end of our sacred or intrinsically valuable lives, is seen as an evil, and rightly so. Death severs our deepest and most important human relationships. It is devastating when it claims someone we know and love, and it is deeply distressing to us even when it claims the lives of people we do not know in far-away places, as tsunamis in Indonesia, earthquakes in Pakistan and nuclear disasters in Japan have recently reminded us. John Donne was correct: the bell tolls for us.

But does this sacred or innately valuable nature of human life mean that we are required *under all circumstances* to use technology to sustain a life even when the treatment cannot possibly effect a cure? To sharpen the point, are we morally required to honor the sanctity of human life by applying such technology when it only prolongs the process of dying? This is a new question. Previous generations never had to wrestle to find the morally appropriate answer because the technology that permits this life-extension simply did not exist. Our generation does have to find an answer, however, because not only does the technology exist, but in many cases its use has deformed, prolonged, and distorted dying, causing real suffering to the patient, the family, and the doctors and nurses. We need to do some hard thinking about the appropriate response to the widespread conviction that human life is sacred when it comes to the application of medical technology.

There are several ways to approach thinking this problem through. In the chapter that follows, I am going to explore a few of them in hopes that one or more will resonate in a way that helps you come to a personal position on the use of life-support technology.

As an anesthesiologist, I used ventilators to keep surgical patients breathing almost every day of my career. They were a wonderful addition to medicine's armamentarium—there's the military metaphor again!—when they were invented. By doing the work of breathing for the patient, ventilators permitted the use of powerful muscle relaxants that, in turn, allowed surgeons better access to body cavities by allowing muscles to be pulled out of the way easily. They also proved to be wonderful substitutes for normal lungs when a person was stricken with pneumonia, especially when both lungs were involved, until the antibiotics could work their magic against the bacteria or the body could rid itself of the virus. But none of the doctors developing this technology did so with the idea of its becoming a long-term substitute for a failing organ or a way to postpone dying. A lung transplant, for example, is a much better solution to failing lungs than permanent mechanical ventilation, because when the transplant works, the patient's lung disease is cured and essentially normal function is restored. A person permanently maintained on a ventilator requires skilled nursing care 24/7 and must usually live in a specialized nursing home. Their mobility is extremely limited by the necessity of electrical power to run the machine and the length of the tubing tethering them to it. But, as so frequently happens with technology in all fields, new uses its designers and developers never dreamed of were developed. So today we have people whose lives are maintained, sometimes for many years, by mechanical ventilators. Actor Christopher Reeve suffered a broken neck in a riding accident and was unable to breathe on his own for several years. He was maintained entirely on a ventilator until new surgical technology allowed him to breathe spontaneously for several hours a day.

So first we used medical technology as a bridge until a patient could be restored to health. Then we discovered how to use the same technology for long-term support of an organ system that had suffered a catastrophic assault but that lay within an otherwise healthy body, with the expectation that thorough healing would eventually occur. If it did not, then we hoped that a good quality of function still would be achieved since the damage was limited to one organ system. We now apply this same technology in a third way, however, and that is the most troublesome.

Today, we often mechanically support multi-organ system function in patients who are definitely or most likely dying. In this case, we are not using the technology as a temporary support to return a patient to health nor as long-term support for a single organ system, but literally to stave off death for just a while longer. This third, new use of life-support technology is the most common type to be stopped by choice because it has become clear to the patient or his or her family that it is not supporting any credible return to health. It is merely prolonging the process of dying.

Doctors sometimes refer to the use of medical life-support in such a situation as "futile." The common meaning of this term is "useless" or "ineffective"—but useless and ineffective against what? If a certain technology does not cure a disease, but prolongs life for another month, is it "futile?" If a treatment only works 25 percent of the time, is it futile? 10 percent? 1 percent? Is a feeding tube giving a profoundly demented person food and water "futile" because it will not improve their mental state or "useful" because it keeps the body alive for a while longer? Who gets to judge what "futility" means? Only doctors, from their technical, medical, "objective" standpoint? Only families, without regard to input from health care professionals and no matter how idiosyncratic their reasoning? And, most profoundly and therefore most difficult, what does "futile" mean in the scenario of only prolonging dying with no possibility of contributing to a cure?

When we turn to the history of medicine for guidance, we find that it is only recently, perhaps starting in the 18th century, that it was considered part of the duty of a physician to save life.[42] The Hippo-cratic writings contain an essay entitled "The Art" that warns against attempts to cure those who cannot be cured. Plato wrote in his great dialogue *The Republic* that Asklepios only used his healing arts on those who were generally healthy and of strong constitution: "[B]odies which disease had penetrated through and through he would not attempt to cure. . .The art of medicine was not intended for their good."[43] Today this cautious approach has been superseded by the custom of treating even when medical experience has collectively shown that such treat-ment has a very low probability of succeeding. ("But a miracle might happen, doctor!")

Once CPR was invented, hospitals quickly adopted a policy to try to resuscitate every patient who died there, regardless of how old or how desperately ill they were. I chaired a hospital ethics committee that wres-tled with the concept of Do Not Resuscitate (DNR) orders when they were first being discussed. Some members expressed strong moral feelings that we were required to try to bring back every newly-expired patient, even those who had just died of cancer! Now DNR orders have become com-monplace. Doctors have also been guilty of giving very mixed messages to patients and families, e.g., "The therapy in question cannot be of any benefit to you but I feel obligated as your physician to offer it."[44] Howard Brody argues in *The Healer's Power* that the term "futile" can only be used in reference to specified and appropriate goals of therapy for an individ-ual patient. He concludes that the legitimate and appropriate exercise of medical power ought to include the power to make judgments of futility, and that doctors have no obligation to provide futile therapies. He adds that if a physician judges that treatment is futile, patients and families should be allowed an opportunity to seek medical care from other pro-viders if they choose to do so.[45]

Most patients and their families and most health care providers, espe-cially individual doctors and nurses, do not want to receive or give futile treatment. Nor do they want in general to simply prolong dying when death is the inevitable outcome. It would be wonderful if some sort of red flag popped up when an illness truly becomes a fatal one. If we had a way to alert doctors, nurses, patients and families that a corner had been turned, decisions about removing "life support" technology before the actual pronouncement of death would be ever so much easier to make. But we do not have such red flags.

In a column the week after the death of Terri Schiavo, *Cleveland Plain Dealer* columnist Regina Brett wrote, "The struggle over her life convinced me that we're supposed to fight like hell to live until that moment comes when it's time to surrender. That moment will be different for each of us."[46] But how do those of us in practice recognize that moment, especially given the profession's probabilistic nature? Most patients do not realize how much of the clinical practice of medicine is based on probability statistics for large groups. I had practiced medicine for many years before I really understood this myself.

One question every patient facing surgery—especially an elective procedure—wants to know is his or her chance of dying. Not only are good statistics available today on the mortality rates for many types of surgeries, but in some cases doctor-by-doctor and hospital-by-hospital data exist. For a fairly high-risk procedure such as open heart surgery, the mortality rate might be 2.5 percent at a particular hospital. The oversight organizations to which the hospitals report their data examine the information very carefully, so it is generally reliable. (It can be difficult to interpret properly, however, because patients may differ markedly from hospital to hospital. For example, the mortality rate itself cannot take into account the difference between a well-nourished suburban population and a poor, inner-city population where disease is often accompanied by chronic malnutrition.)

But what an individual patient wants to know is not the general statistic that 2.5 percent of patients die within 30 days of having this surgery and therefore 97.5 percent live, but whether he or she will fall into the lucky or the unlucky group. No doctor can predict that with absolute accuracy. The best we can do is to describe some common characteristics of those patients who do die, and then tell this individual patient how many of those characteristics they share. The lower this number, the greater their chances of surviving. But I have seen high-risk patients sail through surgery and post-op recovery without a hitch. I have also seen patients die whom we all genuinely expected to live. So doctors cannot provide the very answer the patient wants to know. We can say with great accuracy how a large group of patients will behave but not how it will be for an individual patient.

Given this underlying uncertainty in clinical medical practice, it is therefore not surprising that it is also difficult to decide at exactly what point a patient moves from "desperately ill but potentially able to survive" to "irretrievably dying." Often when a patient gets to one or two days away from death we can finally see that this "battle" is one we are going to lose. (Note how medical language focuses on me, the doctor, as the loser, when the true casualty is the patient!) But if we wait until this late in the game to recognize this fact, the patient may already have undergone a prolonged period of intensive application of life-supporting technology, including many days in an ICU. If we truly want to lessen suffering, then we must make some decisions earlier in the process.

There is real suffering involved in being treated in a modern ICU, a place where too many people die. They are technological marvels, each bed space full of machinery and monitors and pumps. They also are busy 24 hours a day, so they are noisy at best and chaotic at worst when some type of crisis intervenes. In fact, patients who are not unconscious will develop "ICU psychosis" from lack of sleep and the absence of day-night cycles within about a week. Because of the intensive nature of the medical care being provided, family access must be limited. Putting up with the machines, monitors, pumps, noise, and sleeplessness is one thing if restored health is at the other end of the process. But if death is going to be the outcome, then to put a patient through the rigors of an ICU environment strikes me and many others in the medical profession as cruel. Death is far more peaceful when it occurs in a hospice environment than in a place where peace is a rare commodity. But the uncertainty about individual patients' outcomes makes defining the onset of dying difficult.

Language can also be subtly confusing when we talk about futility and other end-of-life issues. What does it mean to say that a patient has "no hope" of recovery? Do we literally mean that there has never in the entire case literature of medicine been a single patient in an identical condition who has survived? Most patients are not written up in the medical literature, so no one knows their stories other than their families and their doctors. No doctor has a "God's eye view" of all patients, even in the age of the Internet. Does "no hope" mean that within one individual doctor's experience, he or she has never seen a patient like this survive? What about other doctors, whose experience might be more extensive?

Does "no hope" mean that somehow the doctor has received a special message from God that there will not be a miraculous healing in this case? Newspapers trumpet "medical miracles" all the time; why shouldn't a desperate family pray for one and insist on treatment long enough so that it can occur? Or does "no hope" reflect a professional judgment that the odds of survival, based on the medical probabilities for similar patients equally about as sick, are too small to be acted upon? Any and all of these "translations" are possible and several can actually coexist. No wonder the situation is confusing, ambiguous, and anxiety-filled.

We are slowly accumulating research that gives more objective data. This helps somewhat but does not make our dilemma go away. Data require interpretation in order to work. Doctors, nurses, patients and families must use their own judgment to apply data to an individual situation, and we all understand data within the context of our values and perspectives. While the weight of data can help us modify our understanding of the likelihood or the odds in a given situation, we are still stuck in the situation of taking a gamble about how treatment will work for this particular patient.

Sharing food and water is one of the most symbol-laden human activities. We feed newborn infants, we share food with strangers and visitors as a sign of hospitality, and food and drink are a feature of almost every good party. The central ritual for the entire Christian church is the bread and wine meal of Holy Communion. Not to provide food and water feels different psychologically than not providing a ventilator or an antibiotic because of the symbolism of caring and connection expressed by the ordinary sharing of food and drink.

After it became common medical practice to place feeding tubes in severely demented persons who were not maintaining their weight despite hand feeding, researchers studied the outcome of tube feeding to see what actually happened when the tubes were inserted. (For obvious reasons, patients in this condition often cannot meaningfully consent to be research participants and families are reluctant to agree on their behalf, so research on severely ill or demented persons is fairly new.) In theory the tubes are placed to provide food and water, lessen the risk of aspiration pneumonia caused by food sneaking up the esophagus and falling into the breathing passages, and prolong life. But do feeding tubes actually meet these goals? They are known to cause several problems, such as diarrhea, which can create a net loss of fluid and cause skin breakdown. Tubes clog and sometimes need surgical replacement. Despite their delivering their contents directly to the stomach, bypassing the throat, aspiration can still occur because of reflux (backing up) of stomach contents into the esophagus and trachea. Careful studies of outcomes have not convincingly shown that tube-fed patients live longer than those who are fed by hand. "Difficulty with eating is a marker of severe dementia, which is a uniformly fatal disorder. Since eating is typically among the last activities of daily living to become impaired in persons with dementia, difficult in eating unfortunately signals that the person has entered the final phases of the illness."[47] This observation at least raises the possibility that feeding tubes at this point act only to prolong dying.

Yet another reason to insert feeding tubes is to promote the comfort of patients with advanced dementia. We can never know for certain whether they do, because it is almost impossible to obtain data on the subjective experiences of persons in this condition. We can, however, gather information from dying cancer or stroke patients who have lost the desire to eat and drink and are able to share their experiences with us. A growing hospice literature indicates that these patients do not experience more than a passing hunger and that any thirst can be managed with ice chips and mouth swabs.[48] Although we do not know with certainty, it seems logical that the subjective experience of the severely demented would be no worse than that of the lucid patients in terms of "suffering" from lack of food and water. In the dying, that purported suffering seems not to occur.

Many, many demented people pull at their tubes, even those that have been surgically implanted; often their arms must be tied down to prevent this. In fact, surgically-implanted tubes became popular because doctors hoped that they would be more secure than tubes passed through the nose and down the throat into the stomach which a patient can easily pull out. The experience of being tied down often results in agitation, however, and an attempt to "escape" the restraints, which may in turn lead to a need for sedative drugs. It is at least ironic that we end up tying demented people down in the name of honoring the sanctity of their lives.

Doctors are further tempted to use feeding tubes since the technology for implanting them has become so much easier. What once required abdominal surgery now is done with the aid of an endoscope passed through the mouth and esophagus into the stomach. The procedure requires only light sedation and local anesthesia, so the relative ease of performing it lures us into doing so. This minimally-invasive technology was actually developed by two doctors in 1979: Michael Gauderer, a pediatrician, and Jeff Ponsky, an early developer of endoscopy. They devised their "PEG tube" as a bridge technology to provide nutrition to infants and children until their underlying illness was treated. By 2005, Gauderer estimated "doctors insert about 300,000 new PEG tubes a year, and that roughly 225,000 of these new PEG tubes are for patients 65 and older."[49]

In 1986 the American Medical Association, in its ethical opinion "Withholding or Withdrawing Life-Prolonging Medical Treatment," concluded that "Life-prolonging medical treatment includes medication and artificially or technologically supplied respiration, nutrition or hydration."[50] In 1990 in the Nancy Cruzan case argued before the U.S. Supreme Court, five of the nine judges explicitly recognized that artificial nutrition and hydration are medical treatments, and the remaining four recognized that fact implicitly.[51] When patients can no longer maintain their nutrition and hydration through hand feeding, and medical technology must be used to implant a tube and to deliver food and water through a tube, food and water also become the type of medical treatment which patients or their health care proxies have the legal right to reject.

Although the medical and legal professions agree at the highest level that this is the appropriate way to think about feeding tubes, we all still are haunted by the symbolic meaning of providing food and drink to each other. That is one reason why the rhetoric in 2005 of "starving Terri Schiavo to death" was prominent among those advocating for the replacement of her feeding tube. Since we have moved death out of our homes and into institutions, hospice nurses represent the largest reservoir of first-hand knowledge about caring for the dying and how to make them most comfortable. Most of the rest of us are speaking purely hypothetically about what we *imagine* is going on. The hospice nursing literature uniformly insists that a part of the natural process of dying is loss of interest in food. My own mother certainly exemplified this: her appetite gradually faded away despite my desperate efforts to make the "right" dish that would tempt her appetite. A few days before they die, patients simply refuse food. They seem quite comfortable as long as their lips and mouths are kept moistened with ice chips or swabs. Throughout history dehydration at the end of life was the normal end of the dying process, so perhaps we should not be totally surprised that research suggests that it creates increased levels of natural opioids, narcotic-like substances produced in our bodies. These are apparently triggered by dehydration and act to keep the dying person comfortable.[52] As the bodily systems shut down during the process of dying, fluid moves out of the blood vessels and accumulates as edema or swelling in tissues. Intravenous fluids provided at this point do not keep the patient hydrated but only increase the amount of swelling and discomfort. Hospice nurses regularly counsel families not to worry and fuss over failing appetite and apparent lack of thirst.

Once all of this was common knowledge because every family cared for dying relatives at home. Today, most of us have no first-hand experience, so when we read comments like that of former House Majority Leader Tom DeLay about Terri Schiavo ("A young woman in Florida is being dehydrated and starved to death. For 58 long hours her mouth has been parched and her hunger pains have been throbbing. . .") we cannot say from our own experience that he is simply mistaken in his claims.[53] Mr. DeLay seemed to have confused the response of a normal, healthy body to dehydration and starvation, which is indeed uncomfortable, and the experience of the dying or lack of experiences of persons in a vegetative state. Anyone who has attempted to go on a weight-loss diet knows first-hand that within minutes of starting to diet, we become almost obsessed with the food we cannot have. The hungry among us or concentration camp survivors have reported that hunger pangs certainly are painful when food is not available. It becomes increasingly uncomfortable when we are thirsty and cannot get to water. But we should be very careful not to confuse these experiences of basically healthy bodies with the experiences of the dying, as hospice nurses regularly warn us. Daniel Callahan points out,

> *If an inability to take food and water by mouth is the ordinary concomitant of a terminal illness—as it has been since time immemorial—that*

71

should be understood as a symptom (not always certain, of course) of a terminal condition, one way the dying body shuts down its key systems. That circumstance was never, until recently, described as a patient's "starving" to death, which connotes a violent, painful death. . . . Indeed, the inability to take food and water itself helped to induce the final, usually gentle, coma. It led to a peaceful, not a violent, death.[54]

As a result of all these factors, nutritional status often does not improve with the use of feeding tubes.[55] Overall, research shows that "tube feeding seldom achieves the intended medical aims and that rather than prevent suffering, it can cause it."[56] The family, especially in a hospice setting with unlimited access to the patient, can continue to show both symbolic and practical care and love for the patient by offering ice chips and frequent mouth swabs without actually making the dying process more uncomfortable.

Another true story about medical futility demonstrates how slippery a concept it is. A 10-year-old girl was sadly diagnosed with a brain tumor of a cell type which could not be treated. The neurosurgeons declined to operate because it would be "futile" in terms of stopping the growth of the cancerous tumor and suggested comfort (hospice) care instead. Instead, the child's family took her out of state, where doctors operated twice, extending her life but not curing her. Meanwhile, the cancer continued to grow. She was returned to her home town and the first hospital. There she gradually sank into a coma as the tumor enlarged. When she could no longer breathe on her own, her family, certain that God would perform a miracle cure and backed by their fundamentalist pastor (and financed by private medical insurance), insisted that she have a tracheotomy and be put on a ventilator.

The cancer grew larger. The girl's eyes now bulged grotesquely from her head, pushed out by the enlarging tumor. She had repeated cardiac arrests. Finally, the pressure within her skull rose so high that blood no longer flowed to her brain. She showed no evidence of any cortical or brain-stem activity. She was dead according to brain-death criteria. But she was on a ventilator, so her chest continued to rise and fall and her heart to beat because it does so without needing direction from the brain. When her family was informed of her death, they chose not to believe it. With their pastor's encouragement, they waited "for God to decide."

From a medical perspective, this child was a corpse in a pediatric ICU bed. Other children whose lives could potentially be saved with intensive care were being turned away because the bed was not available. The family maintained a constant vigil at the bedside so that the ventilator could not be turned off in their absence. (This would have allowed the child to "be dead" based on the traditional sign of lack of breathing and absent heartbeat. Without the steady provision of oxygen, the heart will soon stop beating, so in less than five minutes the child would have then been dead even by the mother's definition.) The vision of needing security guards to restrain family members if the doctors acted unilaterally to terminate "life support" kept them from doing so. Finally the hospital offered a compromise: to allow the family to take their daughter (or her body, depending on one's perspective) home on life-support.

The "final end" came 14 months after brain death had been diagnosed. The girl's heart finally stopped beating. The paramedics could not resuscitate her, nor could the ER doctors where she was transported. A family friend told reporters that the mother took this as proof positive that her daughter was no longer alive, and that "She didn't decide. God decided."[57]

How should we understand this story, which is sad on so many levels? It is always sad when a young person dies because ordinarily they would have had years of life ahead and that future has been denied them. It is sad when a person dies after being gravely ill for so long: both the child and her family endured much suffering. It is sad because not only the family but the doctors, nurses, hospital bioethicists, and other staff had to struggle with so much moral and other conflict. It is sad because it leads us to health care injustice and that is a tremendous problem in America today. It is sad because it is confusing. Is this a story of technology used to its maximum limits to save one young life, and should we feel grateful for what it accomplished even though it could not cure? Is it a story of technology run amok and hope out of control disguised as religious doctrine, and ultimately a sorrowful one? The only mercy in this story is that for the final 14 months this child could not have suffered because the bodily organ in which the experience of suffering occurs, the brain, was beyond any function.

The newspaper article about this story did not say, but I am sure that the cost of prolonging this one child's life easily exceeded one million dollars and may well have been much more. Even so, it was "futile" because she was not cured. The costs were paid by the family's health insurance company, which we all know resulted in their raising everybody else's rates. Each person or company insured by that firm eventually helped to "pay" for the family's choices. Nowhere in this story or in the debate over Terri Schiavo's death was there a moral discussion about all the millions of Americans who do not have *any* health insurance. Many commentators saw no irony in advocating paying as much as it takes to keep one individual alive, yet not providing meaningful access to healthcare for millions of others.

If every human life is sacred, why aren't the lives of the uninsured so intrinsically valuable that we have a moral obligation to see to their health as vigorously as some politicians sought to save Terri Schiavo's, especially in the "culture of life" advocated by then-President George W. Bush? Should there be some limit on how much the preservation of one individual's life should cost? Does it make a difference if it is the individual who pays or society as a whole? Should there be some limit on how many dollars one individual's religious values should cost the rest of us? This is the subject for a different book so I will put it aside, but health care justice is a huge, looming problem that we are not addressing today.

All technology eventually becomes used in ways that its inventors never imagined; that simply seems to be the nature of the interface between technology and human ingenuity. Life-support technology has morphed from a temporary bridge to ongoing support of a single organ-system to a full-court press to postpone, but not eliminate, dying. But does the sanctity of life force us to go all the way down this path to include prolonging human dying by technological means? Albert H. Jonsen, an early, influential writer in American bioethics, in the 10th annual Paley Lecture in the series on Science and Society sponsored by Cornell Medical College, asked the question, "What does life support support?"

In addressing this question, Jonsen started by recalling the (then-recent) story of a young California woman, 22 weeks pregnant, who died as a result of a cerebral accident, a stroke. Since she unquestionably met all the standards for the legal definition of brain death in her home state, had she not been pregnant she would have been buried. But at the request of her husband, her corpse was kept alive using life-support technology for 64 days so that the fetus she was carrying would have an increased chance of survival. A healthy baby, a bit premature, was delivered by Caesarian section from a cadaver. Once the baby was delivered, "life-support" technology was turned off and the body was finally buried.[58]

This is an extreme case but does illustrate how far away from supporting "life" life-support technology can go. After relating this story, Dr. Jonsen asked, "Is quasi-total (quasi because we do not have technical support which replaces brain function as we do for heart, lung, kidney, and nutrition functions) or quasi-permanent support of continued life an obligation that can be demonstrated to fall on physicians and others responsible for the patient?"[59] His answer was that, no, doctors have no such obligation. "The meaning of life is a perennial philosophical question and will not be answered any better by modern bioethicists than by the Greeks, the Medievals, or the Enlightenment savants," he said. "We do have, however, a dimension of the problem they did not, namely, life totally or quasi-totally, and permanently or quasi-permanently, supported by machines. Yet, we will always return to the intuition that life is supported, not by any machines, however wonderful, but by the personal perceptions of one's history, by the love of one's family and friends, by engagement, however simple, in the ongoing currents of the social and natural world. Unless our life-support technology can support such life, it is empty of human significance."[60] Jonsen's is one version of what the sanctity of life obligates us to do.

The formal statements of various religious traditions are resources to which believers turn for answers. Is the death of a human being under all circumstances a moral evil that requires us to postpone death for even another day to honor the intrinsic value of human life? Some religious traditions would answer with an unequivocal yes. "Every instant of life, the rabbis teach us, is of incalculable worth. This is an inviolable principle of Jewish medical ethics. Jewish law sanctions medical treatment even if it will extend life only momentarily," according to Dr. Michael Kirsch.[61] However, other scholars from the same faith assert that "the Orthodox Jewish tradition, also commonly assumed to advocate any intervention which might prolong life, in fact rejects interventions that cause or prolong suffering" and that "many Orthodox Jewish thinkers regard the dying person in a special light and argue against 'impediments to dying' in the final year of life."[62]

Other religious traditions share similarly varied interpretations of human beings' moral obligations. After Terri Schiavo's death, Allen Verhey wrote an article for *The Christian Century* about several different Christian "pro-Terri" arguments. The first states that food and drink ought to be provided to a patient, even when no sign of consciousness exists: that "Terri might not count for much as the world counts, but she surely counts as among 'the least of these' in Jesus' parable (Matt. 25)."[63] That's one argument and it is one theologically conservative Christians sometimes make. Verhey's second argument, however, comes to the opposite conclusion: "Christians regard life as a good, to be sure, but not as a second god. . .They may refuse medical procedures that may lengthen their days but do nothing to make those days more apt for their tasks of reconciliation or fellowship. . . . Remembering Jesus and following him, we can hardly make our own survival the law of our own being."[64] The author points out that neither argument is new, both positions having been debated by Catholic and Protestant moral theologians for about 30 years. Even though these are two very different, opposing conclusions, they share some important common ground: the conviction that there is an important moral distinction between killing and allowing to die, a distinction that will be discussed at some length shortly. Verhey continues that the two arguments "disagree on whether withdrawing food and fluid is more like killing or more like letting die. They also disagree on how to describe and weigh the benefits and burdens (of continuing artificial feeding)."[65]

He continues by citing a third disagreement over how to see and describe and explain the action of removing the feeding tube: whether it should be considered a refusal to give food and drink or the simple withdrawal of medical technology.[66] Because of these disagreements, Verhey calls on churches to become "communities of moral discourse and discernment" where, "in memory of Jesus, Christians learn that life is a great gift but that death is not the greatest evil [and] the victory over death is finally a divine victory, not a technological victory."[67] He also calls on his readers to "appreciate ambiguity. There are situations where there are no right answers, no good answers, situations where goods collide and cannot all be chosen, where evils gather and cannot all be avoided. There may be situations—and I think there are such situations—in which it is morally appropriate to withhold medical procedures (including procedures for nutrition and hydration). That does not make death a good."[68]

In the same issue Dixon Sutherland of Stetson University, a Baptist-affiliated school in DeLand, Florida, is quoted as having said, "What churches should not do. . .is advocate for sustaining life the way Schiavo's parents and their supporters did. They're not erring on the side of life here; they're erring on the side of death defiance."[69] The United Methodist Church in 2004 approved a document on "faithful care" that "advised against 'romanticizing dying' and for accepting 'relief of suffering as a goal for care of dying persons rather than focusing on prolonging life.'" In 1991 the Episcopal Church at its general convention stated that "There is no moral obligation to prolong the act of dying by extraordinary means and at all costs if [a] dying person is ill and has no reasonable expectation of recovery."[70]

Roman Catholic Cardinal Theodore McCarrick of Washington, D.C. characterized the removal of Schiavo's feeding tube as a "form of euthanasia."[71] However, the editors of the lay Catholic–published *Commonweal* magazine disagreed, writing: "The mere prolongation of bodily functions where there is no hope of recovery and where the patient has no ability to realize human or personal goods is not obligatory."[72] The fact that the religious community does not speak to this issue with a single voice is one mark of how theologically and morally difficult end-of-life issues are.

Yet another sad outcome of the Schiavo case was that George Greer, the Florida county justice to whom the case was assigned by the usual judicial lottery and to whom it was remanded several times by higher courts, was advised by his Southern Baptist pastor to leave his congregation, despite the judge's reputation as a conservative Republican and conservative Christian. When petitioned by some Christians to ignore Florida law and the decisions of other courts, Judge Greer insisted that his highest obligation as a judge was to uphold the law.[73]

Persons who identify with a particular faith community should explore what obligations that tradition feels the sacred nature of human life implies. There is not just one "answer" to the question of what the sacredness of human life compels us to do medically, so you need to understand what your particular tradition says. What I can tell you for sure from my years of practicing medicine is that you don't want to begin having a discussion about your denomination's position for the first time at your loved one's bedside, when you are already deep in crisis. Instead, I beg you to invite your spiritual advisor over for dinner and find out right now what your tradition says about the morally-appropriate use of such technology. This gives you the chance to think about whether that position is one you can accept as binding for yourself or not. If the answers you hear do not strike you as appropriate choices for yourself and your family, you have some very hard thinking to do. Or you may find that you need to revise your advance directives as a result of this discussion or have a new conversation with your health care proxy now that you have a clearer understanding of what your faith tradition requires.

Not all people are affiliated with a specific religious tradition, however. A different, non-theological approach suggested by Daniel Callahan may be of benefit to those who do not claim a religious perspective. He proposes two imaginative tests. Philosophers often use such "thought experiments" in much the same way physical scientists use the laboratory to test a hypothesis and see where it leads. In what he calls the "historical mourning test," Callahan asks us to imagine a specific, devastating condition such as dementia, a case so severe that the demented person has not spoken aloud for a long time and gives no other evidence of having an inner life. He asks: "If such a person had died of a routine urinary-tract infection a century ago, it is unlikely that death would have been raged against as unfair, wrong or untimely. Such a death would, we know, have been accepted as the ordinary way in which a person in that state died, and understood as a blessing, a relief, and a release."[74] Does the fact that we now have an antibiotic to treat that infection make that same death a moral evil if we do not treat the person? Or should we still see that death as a relief and release from suffering? Callahan answers, "Death in such a situation falls within the range of a good coincidence of the biological inevitability of death in general and the timeliness of death for an individual. More time is not likely to offer a better life, but it will almost certainly increase the likelihood of a poor death."[75]

The second imaginative test he calls the "treatment invention test." In that test we are asked to imagine that we are living a century ago and suddenly faced with a person who cannot, through a devastating stroke or injury, swallow food or water given by mouth. Such people died rapidly from dehydration or from aspiration pneumonia caused by attempts to give them food and water orally. Callahan asks "if. . .we would have wished for the invention of artificial feeding for the sole purpose of keeping that person alive? Would we have pined for a technology that could suspend someone in an irreversible (PVS) state for five, or ten, or even thirty-seven years, as has happened in one case?"[76] If the answer we give is no, that we cannot imagine anyone longing for a way to keep such a person alive given their circumstances, then why should we feel obligated to do so now just because we have the technology to do so? Other possibilities exist now that we choose not to use. Surely no sane person hopes that nuclear weapons are ever used again, yet the technology and hundreds of bombs exist. At least in theory we have the technology to clone human beings, but I have yet to see a morally persuasive argument for doing so. We already have most of the genetic engineering skills to make "designer babies," but that does not mean we should do so. The mere possession of technology does not impel us, morally, to use it. We unfortunately are left with the responsibility for making difficult, sometimes excruciating choices.

Another approach to thinking about these thorny issues is to explore exactly what kind of evil death represents in human life. That it is an evil is unquestioned. It ruptures our most profound human relationships, and sometimes also leads to financial and physical hardships. It is hardly ever benign and unimportant. But despite believing in the sanctity of human life, our ancestors did not seem to think that death was a specifically moral evil whose presence called forth a moral response unless it came about by murder or negligence.[77] When death intervened in human life due to illness, whether to the newborn or the elderly, it was seen as the inevitable final act in the human drama. Everybody died at some point in the story, but as a biological necessity, not a moral failure to rescue.

St. Augustine was the first to argue that human death occurs not by the dictates of the natural world but because of Adam's fall. Pelagius and Julian, other early Church Fathers, were arguing at that time that human death was simply the nature of things and that no one person could bring death upon all humanity. Augustine countered with his theory of original sin based upon his interpretation of Genesis Chapters 1–3. He stated that human death is strictly a moral issue, that it "arose only after Adam's single act of disobedience, infecting every generation of the human race thereafter." The fifth century Church chose to accept Augustine's interpretation and labeled Pelagius and Julian as heretics.[78] Despite this belief having been adopted as official Catholic dogma, however, even believers have acted as if there were no individual, current moral responsibility for death as a biological event. This may have been based not so much on theology as the brutally practical reality that until roughly 50 years ago there was precious little doctors could do to fend off death in most circumstances. But modern medical technology has forced us to examine exactly what kind of evil death is in human life and how far we are morally obligated to treat when all we do is postpone that particular kind of evil. It makes a difference whether we conceptualize death as a biological evil that will eventually end the existence of every living creature or a moral evil against which we must struggle at all costs or in some other way.

Callahan argues cogently that the older understanding of death as an evil but not a moral one has been replaced by the current notion that death is a moral evil in human life and that human beings have a moral obligation to use medicine to combat death in every circumstance or dishonor "the sanctity of life." Thus, after Terri Schiavo's death we heard President Bush ask those who wanted to honor her life to work to build "a culture of life." The idea that the sanctity of life always forces us to action to honor that sanctity or intrinsic value leads to two conclusions:

1. For conservatives and supporters of (some so-called) "traditional religious values," if technology holds out any shred of hope of prolonging life, the sacred nature of life obliges us to use it, or at minimum, privileges the discussion in favor of its use.[79] To say no to any technological possibility of extending life, even if it cannot possibly cure, is to dishonor the sanctity of life and attempt to "play God" inappropriately.

2. For liberals, the erasure of the distinction between nature and human agency, equalizing the power of some diseases to kill us with human actions like stopping a respirator, seems to argue for the legitimacy of final and total control of human life through euthanasia and physician-assisted suicide—"autonomy triumphant, suffering banished, wasted dollars saved," as Callahan describes it. He says those who hold this

position are tyrannized by the idea that if they can act, they must. To refuse to act in the face of suffering is to be morally responsible for that suffering. If a particular disease is causing deaths and we do not fund the research to defeat it, we are responsible for the deaths that occur.[80]

We can be tyrannized by both of these ideas, and we are. Therefore, we need to analyze both of these positions very carefully to see if we morality forces us to be so extreme. We will turn to the issue of euthanasia and physician-assisted suicide in Chapter 7.

Does the idea of the sanctity of life really force us to accept the use of all medical technology even when its use cannot cure and so only serves to prolong the dying process? The actual results of this are often grueling for the patient to whom it is applied. Doctors and nurses caring for such patients have often, in my hearing, used the word "torture" to describe such use of technology when there is no reason to believe that it can restore the patient to health. But if we say no to its use, are we dishonoring the sacred nature of human life? If human life is sacred or intrinsically valuable, how are we to think about the role of death at the end of life? We need as a society to think about these difficult questions very carefully because a lot is riding on the conclusions we reach. And unfortunately, as our model of public discourse on a difficult moral issue, we have the 40-year "debate" on the morality of abortion. This has most often been conducted not constructively but by hurling epithets as if one side clearly owns the moral high ground on the issue.

The United States faced its national confusion about moral issues in the spring of 2005 during the excruciatingly public death of Terri Schiavo. A young woman in her late 20s when she had a cardiac arrest, she suffered extensive brain damage. Eventually she was diagnosed as being in the Permanent Vegetative State (PVS), a devastating situation where the lower brain stem still functions to automate some bodily functions like breathing but the cortex of the brain, where thought, speech, emotions, and all other human experiences reside, has been destroyed. This situation is sometimes described as "awake but unaware," because the person may have seeming periods of sleep and wakefulness but is completely unaware of his or her surroundings. Of course, normal people are never awake but unaware; even in sleep we are constantly monitoring our environment, which is why the ringing alarm clock or the scream of the smoke detector wakes us up. Whether the diagnosis of PVS was correct became a matter of bitter debate between Schiavo's husband and her parents, and court battles raged for years over whether the former could remove the feeding tube keeping her (or perhaps just her body) alive. Her husband, her legal spokesperson under Florida law because she had not executed an advance directive, said that his wife had stated that she did not wish to be permanently maintained by technological means. Despite the rhetoric, all of the courts uniformly accepted the diagnosis of PVS based on expert testimony and therefore authorized the removal of the feeding tube. Ultimately it was removed and Terri Schiavo died on March 31, 2005.

During the final days of this drama, we all heard rhetoric likening removing the feeding tube keeping Schiavo alive to murder, the unjustified killing of an innocent human being. Protesters outside the hospice where Terri was being cared for, some from anti-abortion organizations, held signs reading "Commute Terri's Death Sentence." A Florida state senator, reacting to the rejection of the second attempt to enact "Terri's Law" to legislatively authorize the reinsertion of the feeding tube, said, "We voted to end a life."[81] The extraordinary national publicity—the passage by the state legislature of a law specifically overturning a decision by a Florida court which had been appealed and upheld all the way to the Florida Supreme Court, the passage over Easter weekend of legislation to move the case to a Federal court, the President of the United States flying from Texas back to Washington, D.C. to sign it as soon as it passed—all speak powerfully to how far some politicians are willing to go to honor "the sanctity of life."

But was this response the morally correct one? The medically correct one? Are we required to use technology simply because it exists without regard to its effects in order to be morally responsible? Just because we can, do we have to? Why or why not? When? Because the Schiavo case was so protracted and because emotions were rubbed raw by rhetoric from both family camps and their advisors, let's set that particular case aside and examine a famous earlier case.

Nancy Cruzan was also a young woman, only 25. The victim of a single-vehicle auto accident, she was found lying face-down in a ditch with no heartbeat. Her heart was restarted by paramedics but she never "woke up." Eventually she was diagnosed as being in the Permanent Vegetative State. After seven years of daily visits to the Missouri nursing home where she was ultimately cared for, her parents, who were her legal guardians, petitioned the local court for permission to remove her feeding tube. Over time they had concluded that Nancy-the-person had died in the accident. Only Nancy-the-breathing-body was being kept alive. They recalled that when one of her grandmothers had died while on life-support, Cruzan had mentioned that she would not want to be kept alive by machines. At the time, no one in the family paid special attention to this remark. After all, Cruzan was a young woman in glowing health, and the family was coping with the grandmother's critical illness.

The court agreed to permit the removal of the feeding tube but the Missouri Attorney General appealed the decision because of the state's interest in preserving the life of one of its citizens. He also felt that insufficient evidence of Cruzan's wishes had been presented to allow the court to authorize such a drastic, permanent, and fatal act. Eventually the case reached the U.S. Supreme Court, which sent it back to the original court to be retried.

This time some friends of Cruzan's who had not testified at the first trial offered to describe conversations they had had with her at the time of her grandmother's death. Their friend, they agreed, had told them she would never like to be maintained like that, kept alive only artificially. The court decided that this additional evidence of the patient's wishes met the "clear and convincing" evidentiary standard that the state demanded and the U.S. Supreme Court had upheld as the state's right to demand. The trial court once again authorized the removal of the feeding tube and this time the Attorney General did not appeal. The tube was removed and Nancy Cruzan died a few days later. Was this a good decision by her family and the courts or was it moral mayhem at work? Sorting out the answer is not easy. And some of our difficulty is conceptual.

It would be easy if only we could demonize all medical technology, but we can't. Feeding tubes are an emotionally-charged issue but a good illustration of how technology can perplex us. A few years ago one of my cousins, a football coach in western New York who was in excellent health, discovered an enlarged lymph node in his neck. Unfortunately it was discovered to be a cancer that required surgery, chemotherapy, and radiation. Before Mike's treatments started, his doctors told him that they wanted to surgically insert a feeding tube because the side effects of his treatments would make swallowing painful and otherwise he would lose a lot of weight. They felt his general health would be better supported by keeping his nutrition normal. He had the tube inserted through his abdominal wall and for months used a large syringe to push in pureed food. When his treatments were over and his throat had recovered from the effects of radiation, the tube was removed. Fortunately, his therapy went well and he is now considered to be cured of cancer. Keeping his nutritional state normal enabled his body to heal from the effects of surgery, chemotherapy and radiation faster. In a case like this the feeding tube replaced the vital function of swallowing to deliver food into the stomach as a temporary bridge until health was restored and it was no longer needed.

Now think about Nancy Cruzan or Terri Schiavo and their feeding tubes. In both of those sad cases, the tube was not a temporary bridge. It was a permanent replacement for a vital function which would never recover. The doctors who first developed feeding tube technology never imagined that they would be used in this permanent fashion. One told the newspapers at the time of the Schiavo case that it "never entered our minds this would produce such a massive ethical dilemma."[82]

When technology can be applied as a bridge during the healing process, few people dispute its use. Most of us would welcome its application to us or a family member. When my uncle was first admitted to the hospital just five weeks after my mother's death, his doctor's assumption was that he would need a breathing tube and artificial ventilation for a day or so until the antibiotics had a chance to beat back the bacteria causing his pneumonia. His family readily agreed to the plan. Had things progressed according to plan, everyone would have been delighted when his health was restored by the timely application of sophisticated technology doing its life-saving work. But that was not the way his story played out. His initial response was so good that the breathing tube was removed the next day. But it quickly became apparent that his lungs were not going to be able to do their job without artificial support. Other organ systems began to show the ominous signs of the sequential failure so common in the elderly with multi-system chronic disease. In his case, artificial ventilation begun as a temporary bridge to restored health was replaced by artificial ventilation as an ongoing necessity.

Are those two different uses of the same technology morally equivalent? Because artificial ventilation was started, may it be stopped? If it is stopped, what kills the patient: the pneumonia, the underlying disease, or the human hand that turns off the ventilator? When I was in medical school we were taught that earlier generations had called pneumonia "the old man's friend" because it killed swiftly and relatively painlessly in the era before antibiotics. We now have both the power to use antibiotics and return some old men to their previous state of fairly good health and the power to use antibiotics to save a profoundly demented older person with Alzheimer's from "the old man's friend."

So how do we use powerful medical technology in morally appropriate ways, especially in a pluralistic society with many different, competing sources of value and little social agreement on thorny issues? Moral dilemmas are always accompanied by deep personal anguish because the stakes are always high, sometimes literally life or death. They arise precisely when "good reasons for mutually exclusive alternatives can be cited; if any one set of reasons is acted upon, outcomes desirable in some respects but undesirable in others will result. . .Although the moral reasons behind each alternative are good reasons, neither set of reasons clearly outweighs the other. Parties on both sides of dilemmatic disagreements thus can correctly present moral principles in support of their competing conclusions. Most moral dilemmas present a need to balance rival, ideal claims in untidy circumstances."[83] The claims are "rival" in that they cannot both be acted upon at the same time; only one alternative can be chosen. They are "ideal" in that rarely do the exact facts of a patient's situation precisely mirror or exemplify the moral principles. And the circumstances are almost always "untidy"—the patient can no longer speak but did not execute an advance directive and the family has no idea about wanted or unwanted care; the child with the durable power-of-attorney for health care is exploring the Amazon for a month and cannot be reached because her cell phone is dead; Dad's living will is in the safety deposit box and no one remembers where he hid the key or what the document states.

While there is no simple formula for dealing with moral dilemmas, experience has shown that some considerations can at least help manage them. The five steps that follow are taken from the writings of Tom L. Beauchamp and LeRoy Walters of the Kennedy Institute of Ethics at Georgetown University.[84] While these are by no means fool-proof, my hospital ethics committees and I have field-tested all of them and seen each one help. I still lack that magic wand but find these to be effective tools that help manage moral dilemmas.

Dealing with Moral Dilemmas

1. Obtain objective information: Although we usually assume moral dilemmas are created by opposing moral views and values, sometimes it is the basic facts of the situation which are cloudy. Getting more information about the diagnosis (what the illness is), co-morbidities (other illnesses which may be contributing factors), and prognosis (what the usual course of the disease is in patients with a similar degree of illness and substantially similar medical problems) can sometimes help clarify factual issues which then narrow the medical and moral options to be discussed. It is one thing to be told that your mother is gravely ill but that she might also recover. It is another thing to be told that her survival would be without medical precedent. Clarifying the facts in language which is as clear and unambiguous as possible often helps frame the situation more precisely. While this step may seem easy to accomplish, given the fact that most seriously ill patients are being cared for by several different medical specialists, getting their combined opinion, not just separate assessments of each organ system in isolation, can be a tough assignment. Nurses can sometimes help facilitate this as can hospital chaplains or ombudsmen. The patient and the family have the right to an opinion which ties all the relevant medical facts together.

2. Provide clear definitions of terms, both medical and moral, being used in the discussion. One of the reasons English is such a rich language is because words can have many shades of meaning. In addition to that, we sometimes use a word meaning one thing to us which turns out

to mean something quite different to another person. "Euthanasia" is one such term. Some people use it to mean "a mercy killing" in which one person deliberately kills another to end that person's suffering. That is also the sense in which we sometimes choose to euthanize our beloved pets that are ill. However, other people use the term euthanasia to mean something like "voluntarily-chosen natural death" when they refer to the withdrawal or withholding of life-supporting technology as a form of euthanasia. These two meanings of the term are quite different from each other, so it is easy to see how persons using these different definitions but unaware of the other meaning could be arguing with each other but actually talking about totally different events. Agreeing on one common definition for the critical terms in the discussion of a moral dilemma does not make the moral dilemma magically disappear, but it at least means that we are talking about the same problem while we are engaged in our debates. I have even seen a few occasions when clearing up confusing, idiosyncratic definitions led people to discover that they actually agreed with each other!

3. Seek a small piece of common moral ground. Because they are always accompanied by deep anguish and wrenching emotions, the debates about moral dilemmas frequently become very heated. Long-buried family conflicts rush to the surface again to be rehashed over a parent's prostrate body in the ICU. "I know why you don't care whether he lives or he dies. It's because you know that he always has loved me the best. That's why I'm the one fighting to keep him alive." There is no magic for dealing with these issues, either. There certainly were times when I might have considered selling my soul for a magic wand to resolve such confrontations had that option been available. Add to the already-volatile family mix the notoriously large egos of many physicians and you have a recipe for conflict. All is not hopeless, however. Sometimes all of the parties in the conflict can identify a small piece of common moral ground where they can focus on their joint interest rather than their differences. I have seen bitter conflicts subside to wary civility (remember, I said there was no magic bullet) when the warring parties were able to acknowledge that shared common interest. Often that small piece of common moral ground is that

all parties genuinely want to find and to do "the best" for the patient. They will continue to disagree about what the medical and moral expression of that "best" looks like in practice; outright conversion from one moral stand to another is rare. But if they can focus on their common commitment to identifying and doing "the best" for the patient, they can sometimes begin to see each other as fellow seekers after the good rather than adversaries to be vanquished. It then becomes much easier to listen to each other's viewpoints and sometimes a plan can be forged.

4. Using examples and counter-examples sometimes help turn a theoretical discussion into a more practical one and that is often very helpful for families. Terms like "futile," "hopeless," "hopeful," and "there is nothing more we can do" have a variety of meanings and implications. The use of examples of similarly-situated patients and the counter-examples of other patients can help clarify the medical staff's meaning for this specific patient. Examples can also help turn research information, which doctors use and interpret daily but most others do not, into useful information. This is especially true when the news media are trumpeting the "medical miracle of the day." When families offer an example or counter-example, the staff has the opportunity to learn more about their understanding of the situation and can then address confusion and misunderstandings.

5. Analyzing arguments is the final step suggested in this array of techniques to help deal with moral dilemmas. Philosophers are trained in analyzing arguments but all of us do this to some extent every day when we analyze the reasons politicians are giving for their latest policy proposal or when the school board explains why they are adopting a new curriculum. We all evaluate the reasons they claim support their conclusions and judge them to be adequate or not yet convincing. When we examine the arguments various persons involved in a moral dilemma put forth for inadequacies, gaps, fallacies, inconsistencies and unexpected consequences, we may find that they have argued their position logically and well. We may still disagree with it, but now we have to examine our own position to see why we disagree which helps us understand our own position more clearly.

If we can point out significant omissions, inconsistencies, or other failures in their position, they, too, will be challenged to rethink their stand and may see a need to modify it and perhaps move closer to our position.

TV doctors and nurses are rarely in doubt about anything. Confidently, seemingly without thought, they shout orders to their attentive staff and walk away from patient resuscitations with the reassuring comment, "He'll be fine." In real life the situation is most often much more complicated and less certain: genuine hospital resuscitations are far less successful, especially among the elderly, and no one would dare predict a complete recovery at such an early point. I have participated in multiple resuscitations of the same patient over the course of a few hours many, many times. When patients are first admitted, often through the ER, the clinical picture is usually unclear. We may honestly expect to use technology as a bridge when we first apply it. It is only as the patient's condition changes and we come to understand it more fully that doctors can then make the assessment that turns a stopgap treatment into a permanent one.

Fortunately the American bioethical community and many religions have concluded over the past 30 years or so that there is no moral difference between not starting a technology and removing it once it becomes apparent that it must be used permanently and the patient states that it is unwanted. It may feel different psychologically to withdraw a treatment than to withhold it in the first place, but there is a robust consensus that there is no important moral difference. I think this is good news for people, because it means that in the face of uncertainty about diagnosis (what is the medical problem?) and prognosis (what is the likely outcome of the disease in this case?), we can apply the technology and evaluate the patient's response to it. If it becomes apparent that the situation is one where the technology must be kept in place permanently and we have evidence that the patient does not want that done, then it can be removed. This scenario is often called "a trial of therapy" and it allows the patient the benefit of trying the therapy to evaluate its usefulness while not committing to continue if it cannot accomplish the hoped-for benefit.

There is another sense in which the use of medical technology involves a gamble. Callahan refers to this as "technological brinkmanship."

He writes, "It is well recognized by now that, if medical technology is pushed too far, a person can be harmed, that there is a line which should not be crossed. I define brinkmanship as the gambling effort to go as close to that line as possible before cessation or abatement of treatment."[85] But, he points out, "this seemingly obvious strategy assumes an ability to manage technology and its consequences with a delicacy and precision that medicine simply does not possess and may never possess."[86] Not only does the focus on technology mean a lesser focus on the person to whom the technology is applied, but also a greater difficulty in deciding when a patient is now in the dying process and cannot be restored to health. This means we don't know clearly when to stop gambling. The very nature of a gamble means that many times we are going to "lose," to make the wrong choice about the proper time to withdraw medical technology so as not to uselessly prolong dying.

Callahan says we have also conceptually confused ourselves by mixing up together the biological power of nature and disease to kill and the human power of technology to support various life functions even when they cannot restore health. Modern medicine, he argues, has come "to confuse its power to alter, control, or eliminate disease with its power to banish mortality."[87] The corollary of this is that when a patient does die, it is some person's fault, not the result of natural processes that at some point will kill every living being. No longer do we convincingly see ourselves as biological creatures fated to die someday. Rather, someone— the doctor who does not apply life-extending technology, the family who does not agree with the use of technology, or the patient who refuses technology through an advance directive—is responsible for that death. When we don't apply technology, then the patient is killed by the person who refuses, not the underlying disease. This, some say, dishonors the sanctity of human life.

There is a common-sense distinction between death as a result of disease or "natural causes" and death as a result of human mistakes, errors, or negligence. Whether God's initial plan for Eden was a paradise where human lives would be eternal is a matter for theological speculation, but all of us now alive live "east of Eden" in a world where death comes to all living creatures, including us. Callahan says we are confused "between physical causality (the impersonal, independent force of biological processes) and moral culpability (the responsibility of human beings for their actions, or omissions, in response to those processes)."[88]

From my viewpoint as a physician, there is a real difference between these two causes of death. As an anesthesiologist, I regularly inserted breathing tubes and placed patients on ventilators during surgery so that I could also administer paralyzing agents to relax their muscles and facilitate the surgeon's job. It is almost impossible to insert a breathing tube in an awake and healthy person; the reflexes we use to keep foreign bodies out of our breathing passages are some of the most difficult to frustrate in the entire human body. Just think back to the last time you choked while swallowing food! Once the muscle relaxant drugs wear off, patients fight to cough out the breathing tubes. Taking them out at that time does not cause death because the body is ready to breathe for itself again. Removing the breathing tube from a person who is permanently on a ventilator is different, however. They are on the ventilator in the first place precisely because they cannot breathe adequately on their own. Think back to the lady I described who was slowly becoming paralyzed by her ALS. When she arrived in the ER in respiratory failure a few months after her successful cataract surgery, was she dying from the ALS or because no one in the ER placed the breathing tube she said she did not want?

Previous generations never had to deal with questions like these, but we do. Joanne Lynn, M.D., a geriatrician and researcher who focuses on end-of-life issues, quotes one of her patients as saying, "No one in the Bible died like this."[89] The answers to these genuinely new questions are not to be found in the wisdom literature or the collective experience of our ancestors. We can and should look to these for information about our forebears' values and perhaps how they approached the novel problems of their day, but we cannot simply consult the Bible, the Talmud, the Koran, because nowhere do they mention ventilators.

A further confusion, Callahan asserts, has arisen because the traditional Roman Catholic teaching distinguishing between ordinary and extraordinary treatment has changed. For some time theologians believed that the main point of the original discussion was to distinguish between simple/ordinary and complex/extraordinary medical procedures. Instead, Callahan says, judgment was meant to take place on the moral level. It would be morally ordinary, for example, to give an antibiotic to a young person with an infection. On the other hand, it might be morally extraordinary to give the same antibiotic to a person dying of cancer who develops the same infection.[90]

The results of this shift from a moral evaluation to a purely technical one are not at all what upholders of traditional morality aim for. Judging technology only makes us hostages to technology. Callahan continues, "The value of life is in practice defined, not by religious or moral principles as traditionalists wish, but by technical capacities."[91] This is slavery, not moral freedom. If the traditional scriptural interpreters are to be believed, whatever technology is available must be used regardless of whether it restores health or increases suffering, all in the name of the sanctity of life.

Some Christians also feel that taking any direct action, e.g. withholding or withdrawing life-sustaining technology, is an attempt to "play God" and therefore morally inappropriate. The great Scottish philosopher David Hume decisively refuted this idea well over 200 years ago when he wrote, "If it is for God alone to decide when we shall live or we shall die, then we 'play God' just as much when we cure people as when we kill them."[92] Interestingly enough I have never heard a conservative Christian advance the claim that medicine is "playing God" when doctors give an antibiotic or take out an inflamed appendix, each of which can be life-saving. They choose not to see those illnesses as God "calling the patient home," or understand their decision to accept medical treatment as thwarting the will of God. Their objection to usurping the Almighty's prerogatives to decide when life should end is limited solely to medical decisions not to prolong life.

Moral decision-making is no less clear at the other end of the ideological spectrum. Callahan points out,

> *Those seeking a liberalization of older rules and mores seize upon the erasure of the distinction between nature and human agency as the occasion for a final and total control of human life through euthanasia and assisted suicide [but] they, no less than their opponents, have been tyrannized, this time by the idea that, if they can act, they must act. Disease must be banished to avert suffering; and if suffering cannot be banished that way, then it ought to be eliminated by euthanasia.*

To refuse to act decisively in the face of suffering, with direct killing if necessary, is to be responsible for it.[93]

This, too, is a conclusion based on two different sorts of confusion. As a physician, I believe that there is a significant difference between actively killing a patient, whether by directly-administered euthanasia or the provision of a prescription of a lethal dose of medicine (physician-assisted suicide) and allowing him or her to die peacefully when medical science can no longer restore that particular patient to health.

To be honest, I must report that capable philosophers and bioethicists do disagree on this point. One camp, articulately represented by James Rachels, states that there is no moral distinction between actively killing patients and allowing them to die. In fact, once it is clear that the death of the patient is the best possible outcome or "good" for that patient, swiftly killing them with direct euthanasia is more humane because it is associated with less suffering and faster than waiting for nature to cause their death.[94] Rachels criticizes an AMA statement that the cessation of treatment is not the intentional termination of life, saying, "Of course it is exactly that, and if it were not, there would be no point to it."[95]

Other capable philosophers such as Callahan do not accept this conflation of the power of nature and disease to kill and the capability of humans to kill as the same thing. There must be an underlying fatal disease for "allowing to die" to be possible. Otherwise, with or without treatment, the patient will recover (which is not to deny the benefit to the patient of timely and correct treatment, only to say it is hyperbole to call it "life-saving" when the patient would have recovered eventually without it). Rachels, says Callahan, confuses the different intentions when a person deliberately kills another and when a doctor steps back and allows a disease to kill a patient. We reserve the term "murder" for the deliberate killing of an innocent person and the specific intention of the murderer to make the other person dead. Doctors who remove life-support or do not start unwanted life-prolonging technology do not intend for the patient to become dead. Instead, they are making the different "judgment that it no longer makes sense, medically or morally or both, to continue life-extending treatments."[96] In fact, Callahan says that the judgment of medical futility of a treatment is not, and never has been, primarily a judgment about a patient's life at all, the decision that a particular patient "would be better off dead." Rather, it is a judgment about the limits of medical prowess and knowledge and the inability of medicine to offer any further benefit to that specific patient. "We can hardly be said to 'intend' death when we admit that we can no longer stop it," he says.[97]

Doctors have traditionally seen our role as healers, not killers, and many within the profession are deeply disturbed by the assertion of some physicians that it would be appropriate to adopt the dual roles of healers (when we can) and killers (when we cannot). The very use of the word "kill" makes us uneasy, and so proponents have often used softer, indirect terms to describe proposed medical killing. The Hemlock Society's handbook for committing suicide is called *Final Exit* and the process of committing suicide "self-deliverance." Dr. Jack Kevorkian referred to his practice of assisting in suicides and euthanasia as "medicide."

The other sort of confusion has to do with our responsibility for the actions and projects of other people. Callahan earlier criticized the liberal position for accepting the idea that to refuse to act in the face of another's suffering makes us responsible for that suffering. Thus, if we fail to euthanize another who asks us to end their suffering or will not assist in helping a person to a successful suicide, we become morally responsible for their suffering.

Doctors certainly are responsible when patients under their care do not receive adequate control of pain and other physical symptoms. But am I, as a physician, responsible for my patient's spiritual suffering? Philosophers thinking about this situation have often posited some version of the following story: I come upon a group of soldiers who are about to execute a group of people. The leader of the soldiers offers me the "honor" of executing one of the group, after which, he says, the rest will be allowed to go free. If I do not kill one, then the soldiers will kill the whole group (and maybe me, too). What is my moral duty? Some have argued that killing one from the group results in "the greatest good for the greatest number." But most people responding to this scenario cannot imagine actually doing that. We have no quarrel with anyone in the group. How could we pick any one of them to kill? And why should the soldiers' intention to kill suddenly turn into my moral responsibility to kill, even to preserve other lives? I am responsible for what *I* do, not what the soldiers do.

A similar confusion seems to underlie the idea that I become morally responsible for suffering if I am unwilling to do everything necessary to stop it, even killing a suffering person in the name of mercy. This is not to say that we should not be active advocates for friends and family who are ill: all such people need advocates because they simply do not have the strength to advocate for themselves. It does say, however, that arguments making us morally responsible for the sufferings of others when we are not the cause of those sufferings should be evaluated very carefully. There may be some moral sleight-of-hand going on.

It is one thing to aggressively treat disease when those actions may restore a patient to health. It may not be possible, and often is not in the case of the elderly, to return a given patient to the exact level of health they enjoyed before the illness, but when a level of function acceptable to the patient can be achieved, then treatment should be pursued. I am persuaded that, however one understands the sacred nature or the intrinsic value of human life, if we accept that idea, we owe every human that much. It is an enormous social injustice that in the richest country in the world and in a political climate advocating for a "culture of life," Americans do not do so. It seems to me to be a different question, however, when it becomes apparent that a patient's illness is either going to be fatal or so severe that only a very partial recovery will be possible. Then the sorts of judgments in a person's advance directive might well come into play. Does obeying the directive mean that we are denying the sacredness of human life? Is there a way to combine the biological inevitability of death and the sacred nature of human beings to craft a theology of "the sanctity of death"?

Many Americans believe that human life is sacred from the moment of conception, and thus are morally opposed to all, or almost all, abortions. Many of these same people also fervently believe in capital punishment. Their explanation of this apparent disjunction is that a criminal who has been fairly convicted of a capital crime has forfeited by his or her own action their right *not* to be killed by society. It is likely that the condemned man or woman ignored the sacred or intrinsically valuable nature of life by taking it from someone else, but how does that change the sacredness of the killer's own life? We also permit killing in self-defense and in "just" wars, although presumably the lives taken in either case are also marked by sacredness. Thus most Americans already make some concessions to the notion of the absolute sacredness of human life. We already believe in making distinctions in this area.

Pastoral counselor A. Joseph Baroody has attempted to do just that by rethinking what it means to be created in the image of God and what it means to die.[98] His "sanctity of death" ethic challenges the absolute nature of the sanctity of life doctrine. He makes additional distinctions, offering four principles as the theological basis for this belief:

(1) Being created in the image of God is not simply limited to the human race; at the very least some social mammals also bear God's image.

(2) Humans, while possibly the most advanced form of God's creation, are not its centerpiece. We exist to serve as much as be served.

(3) Human death represents both moral disorder and God's natural order of creation.

(4) As a part of moral disorder, human death reflects God's wrath and judgment. As a part of God's natural order, human death has a certain intrinsic sacredness that reflects God's grace and love. Therefore intentionally causing or allowing the death of a patient who has no quality of life can be a humane response and an expression of God's grace to human suffering.[99]

His proposal is that "what makes both life and death matter is that both are sacred."[100] We can see death not as a violation of life's sacredness, but as sacred in itself, and it therefore can teach us to value the meaning of life. "Death levels the playing field. It tells us what we do not want to hear: that we are just like the rest of creation."[101]

Baroody quotes theologian Helmut Thielicke who wrote that death is both personal and biological, and that the biological side of death is the "medium" through which personal death occurs. "If we are talking about the duty of doctors to sustain life, we have to mean human life and not just biological life. . .At least a trace of self-awareness is part of human life. Only on this basis can we suffer ethically, that is, make something out of our suffering. This is the only reason why biological life should not be prolonged indefinitely when self-awareness and the possibility of suffering ethically have been irretrievably lost and only a vegetable type of life remains."[102] Baroody concludes by saying that "death teaches us that our significance lies not in our ranking among the planets, nor in our status among the species, nor in our ability to keep someone 'alive' indefinitely, but in God who created it all."[103]

John B. Cobb, Jr. is a Christian theologian who feels that we are very inconsistent in our use of the term "playing God." He says most people favor playing God by accepting vaccines, taking medication, and accepting surgery. Many also take their belief to the extent of taking the lives of others through warfare, capital punishment, or self-defense. "To leave life and death to natural processes," he says, "has a certain consistency. To exercise human control has a certain consistency. But to exercise human control at all points, except one, and to forbid it there (removing life-sustaining technology), requires justification that cannot be found in a general prohibition against 'playing God.'"[104]

As a physician I have often seen death become a means of healing for an individual. When medical technology has reached its limits and restoration of health is impossibility, death becomes a means of grace for that person. In ordinary conversation we recognize this when we call an individual death "merciful" or "a blessing." One of my Hiram College students, Chris Mathews, wrote in an essay that sometimes death is "a sheep in wolf's clothing," which captures both the sense of laying down one's overwhelming physical burdens and our fear of death as always evil quite cleverly. That is not the same as saying that death does not sting or that we should welcome it prematurely. But even if a single fatal disease does not come our way, eventually our bodies simply wear out under the assault of time. It is our fate as biological creatures to have a limited lifespan.

For people who are not believers and for whom a "sanctity of death" argument is not helpful, Callahan offers another conceptual alternative: an "acceptable death." The hallmarks of an acceptable death are that it comes at a time when (1) further efforts to postpone it are likely to deform the process of dying or (2) when there is a good fit between the inevitability of death and the person's particular circumstances. Death, he says, can be "premature" in its timing when a person dies in youth or substantially earlier than biologically necessary. Death can be "merciful" or "a blessing" when "in the life being lived the possibility of enjoying the goods of life has been forever lost."[105] It is "tragic" when its circumstances are terrible or leave a mark on other people, as is often the case with the death of children and young people. All these statements use ordinary language "well-rooted in the past experience of death" as a guide.[106] An acceptable death is neither biologically nor morally wrong. An acceptable death occurs when medicine has "sought to enhance life but not at the cost of deforming death."[107]

So what does the sacred nature or the innate, intrinsic value of human life require of us? Tough decisions, hard questions, careful weighing of benefits and burdens, not only of the treatments or technology involved but also of the life achieved once they have done their work. There is no simple calculation that leads to one right answer for all people. Some people want everything medical technology has to offer applied to them until the final possible instant of biological existence, regardless of whether they have even a shred of consciousness. Others are willing to accept the burdens of medical technology as long as they appear to support healing but not as a permanent sustenance of "life" when healing cannot be medically achieved. Most people have no idea what they want because they have not done the very hard work of confronting these perplexing and difficult issues. But whether you choose to tackle this wrenching process of deciding for yourself or not, I can promise you this: someday you will die. Biological immortality is not an option. What is optional is having some control over how that death occurs.

CHAPTER 5

Pain—and Suffering?

"LIFE IS HARD AND THEN YOU DIE," MY PARENTS' FRIEND BETTY USED TO SAY. IT is a sentiment shared by many people of her generation who lived precariously through the Great Depression. While people living in Third World countries today might agree, most Americans do not. We seem to have decided that ours are privileged lives. We are fated to do well and be successful, and if we are not, it is clearly somebody else's fault and they should pay for it. Little pain and no suffering is our deserved lot in life. Thus, rather than expecting to suffer, we seem surprised when suffering strikes us. Why is this so?

One of the problems with suffering today is that so many people have no explanation for its purpose that is personally convincing to them. Betty's generation was more likely to claim a religious tradition that had a position on the meaning of suffering in human life and an explanation for its frequency. Many of us have no such context in which to experience suffering, so when it strikes us, it seems meaningless, random, pointless, useless, an evil to be avoided at all costs.

Any discussion of end-of-life issues must include the phenomena of pain and suffering, for during the process of dying there is likely to be some of each. While hospice and palliative care can relieve and control almost all physical pain, the approach of death often is associated with mental suffering, which requires a different kind of treatment. The words "pain" and "suffering" are almost always spoken of as if they were conjoined twins who could not be separated. And yet, just a little reflection shows that they are not necessarily linked at all. We can experience pain without suffering, suffering without pain or both together.

Pain is a physical sensation caused by trauma or disease of some bodily tissue. This launches a complex chemical reaction that attracts white blood cells to the area to fight off bacterial invaders, sets off the blood clotting mechanism, starts the process known as inflammation, and uses chemical messengers to tell the brain about what has happened by passing painful signals along nerves. Pain can also be caused by cancer growing into or pressing on nerve tissue within a small space and by permanent scarring along nerves after damage following some viruses, as sometimes happens with shingles. But by "pain" we are ordinarily referring to something that is happening to the physical body. A few people are born without the ability to perceive pain. While this may seem like a blessing, in fact it is not. Pain warns us of damage to our bodies, such as when we touch a hot stove and immediately withdraw our hand. In the absence of pain to cause the withdrawal, the damage continues to be inflicted until something else (perhaps the smell of burning flesh) catches our attention.

Suffering is a psychological state characterized by anxiety, fear, and a sense of dread or foreboding. How long will the pain last? Will it ever go away? How much worse will it get? Can it be treated? Will it be treated? How soon? Since all of these questions are about the pain being experienced, it is easy to see why pain and suffering so often go together experientially and linguistically. But they need not occur together. New mothers have regularly insisted that the pain of labor, which certainly seemed very real both to them and to me as an anesthesiologist seeking to moderate it with epidural analgesia, is forgotten the instant their newborn child is placed in their arms. It was real pain but not suffering. Daniel Callahan points out that the pain of the victorious long-distance runner leads to real pleasure, not suffering.[108] On the other hand, very real suffering can occur in the absence of physical pain. Imagine being told that your child, serving with the military, has been killed, or that you have a fatal, but not yet painful, disease. You may have no physical symptoms yet, but hearing the devastating news causes real suffering. A spiritual cause—a sense that life is ultimately without any significance or that one has wasted one's life now that it is too late to remedy the situation—can cause suffering, too, again with no physical pain involved.

Callahan says, "No moral impulse seems more deeply embedded than the need to relieve human suffering."[109] All of the great world religions call us to do so. It is the aim of much charitable giving and of national, state, and local social welfare programs. The twin aims of medicine are often expressed as the prolongation of life and the relief of suffering. But what is a doctor to do when prolonging life can only occur by prolonging suffering, too? When these aims conflict, which one is really primary? What are we as individuals, and what specifically are doctors, called to do about pain and suffering?

Pain turns out to be the easier of the two to deal with, so I'll start there. I believe my role as a physician obligates me to manage pain as a physical phenomenon and to do so to the satisfaction of the patient. Hers is the only voice which can judge the success of my efforts. Doctors have not always believed this, however. When I was in medical school we were taught that patients usually overestimate the pain they are in (!) and that many patients who complained of inadequately treated pain were in fact drug abusers out to con us into supporting their habits. I was taught that doctors and nurses are better judges of pain than the person experiencing the pain or that, at minimum, I should filter the patient's report of pain through the lens of my own perception of their pain level and act mostly on the latter. We were also cautioned that narcotics are highly addictive and powerful respiratory depressants, so we should use them in deliberately small quantities to avoid both the tragedy of helping to create an addict or inadvertently harming, possibly killing, a patient. Because of these caveats, I was taught to order pain medication by listing a range for the dose (thus allowing the nurse actually giving the medication the opportunity to independently judge how much to give), a range of time between doses (again giving the nurse some choice about how often to administer the medication) and then finally adding the initials "p r n" meaning "as needed" (which allowed the nurse to decide that no dose was "needed"). A typical order might have been "Demerol 50-75 mg IM q 4-6 h p r n" which translates to "50-75 milligrams of Demerol as an injection every 4 to 6 hours as needed."

When a patient decided it was time for a dose of pain medication, they rang for their nurse, waited until the call was answered, reported that they needed pain medication, waited while the nurse assessed their pain and checked the chart to see when the last dose has been given, waited while the nurse prepared and delivered the medication if the criteria were judged to have been met, and then waited some more for the dose to become effective. In retrospect I am appalled to think that we ever thought this methodology was appropriate.

During my stint as an anesthesiologist, we came to take pain seriously. It is now considered to be "the fifth vital sign" along with pulse, blood pressure, temperature, and respiratory rate, which nurses in hospitals and nursing homes check every few hours or more often in an ICU. We also accept that the level of pain is whatever the patient says it is and not what we guess it to be based on their appearance. We use a 10-point pain scale and patients coming for surgery are told about its use pre-op so they are prepared to use it post-op. More enlightened narcotics orders may still have the range of doses but they are now tied to reported pain levels. Better still, we have devices which allow patients to give themselves IV pain medication (within limits). Numerous studies have shown that when patients control their pain medication (often called Patient-Controlled Analgesia, PCA or "pain pumps"), they both use a total lower dose than with older methods of prescribing pain meds and they experience a great deal less pain because they can give themselves a small "booster" dose as soon as their pain begins to increase.

We also now recognize that, while it is easy to spot people with acute pain, for example someone brought to the ER with a freshly broken arm, those with chronic pain do not show the same signs of grimacing, sweating, looking pale, or tearing. People can have substantial chronic pain and yet outwardly appear quite comfortable. In the old days, when we privileged our outside evaluation of their pain, we would have said (and did) that they were overstating their discomfort, so we under-treated them. Now, thankfully, we know better.

In fact, a new subspecialty in anesthesiology since my days as a resident is Pain Management and many hospitals have a service that is prepared to treat pain from any cause 24/7. When drugs fail it is often possible to significantly relieve pain, even cancer pain, using injections of local anesthetics and other new technologies like spinal cord stimulators. The rise of hospice and palliative care has also added a great deal of new information about various kinds of pain and what types of treatment are best for each.

It is very humbling for me to go back and read first-hand and second-hand accounts of patients whose pain, even when they were dying, was poorly treated. It was never the case that medical personnel wanted to torture patients. It was the case that mythology had crept into medical practice and this, combined with arrogance that allowed us to trust ourselves more than patients' reports and lack of basic research into pain, led to terrible sins of commission and omission.

Journalist Stewart Alsop wrote shortly before his own death in 1975 about the experiences of his hospital roommate, another terminal cancer patient. I share his observations here not to frighten you but to make sure you understand what need not happen today

Jack had a melanoma in his belly, a malignant solid tumor that the doctors guessed was about the size of a softball. The cancer had started a few months before with a small tumor in his left shoulder, and there had been several operations since. The doctors planned to remove the softball-sized tumor, but they knew Jack would soon die. The cancer had metastasized—it had spread beyond control.

Jack was good-looking, about 28, and brave. He was in constant pain, and his doctor had prescribed an intravenous shot of a synthetic opiate, a pain-killer or analgesic, every four hours. His wife spent many of the daylight hours with him, and she would sit or lie on his bed and pat him all over, as one pats a child, only more methodically, and this seemed to help control the pain. But at night, when his pretty wife had left (wives cannot stay overnight at the NIH clinic) and darkness fell, the pain would attack without pity.

At the prescribed hour, a nurse would give Jack a shot of the synthetic analgesic, and this would control the pain for perhaps two hours or a bit more. Then he would begin to moan, or whimper, very low, as though he did not want to wake me. Then he would begin to howl like a dog.

When this happened, either he or I would ring for a nurse, and ask for a pain-killer. She would give him some codeine or the like by mouth, but it never did any real good—it affected him no more than half an aspirin might affect a man who had just broken his arm. Always the nurse would explain as encouragingly as she could that there was not long to go before the next intravenous shot—"Only about 50 minutes more now." And always poor Jack's whimpers and howls would become more loud and frequent until at last the blessed relief came.

> *The third night of this routine, the terrible thought came to me.*
> *"If Jack were a dog," I thought, "what would be done with him?" The*
> *answer was obvious: the pound and chloroform. No human being with*
> *a spark of pity could let a living thing suffer so, to no good end.*[110]

Several things need to be said about this passage. First, it dates from the early 1970s: it does not describe current practices and especially not hospice-style care for the dying. It is worth noting that it took place in one of the nation's premiere research institutions, the National Institutes of Health in Bethesda, Maryland. This was "state-of-the-art" care at the time. What this story clearly demonstrates is the failure of the type of pain management I was taught at that time. Jack's pain was never adequately controlled; it only varied from excruciating to terrible. Because it was never lowered to a point of tolerability, Jack was using almost all of his available energy just dealing with his pain. Although the story does not tell us, I am morally certain that the nurses, who certainly must have felt frustrated about their inability to make Jack more comfortable, had called his doctor many times to ask about increasing the amount or frequency of his doses. I am also sure they were told either that (1) no one wanted Jack to become an addict; therefore, he could not have any more pain medication, or (2) if the nurse gave any more medication, Jack could stop breathing from the larger dose and then he would die because of medical error, not melanoma. No increase in dose or frequency was "safe." Those are the myths I was taught and that we confidently told each other while feeling truly wretched about the pain and suffering that we were not controlling.

Today we know that addiction requires more than just drug exposure. It occurs when people who do not have severe pain take narcotics looking for a psychological effect, the drug-induced "high." Some people do acquire the prescription that leads to addiction because they are experiencing real pain at that time. But patients get into trouble when they continue to take pain pills for garden-variety headaches or other symptoms for which a strong narcotic is not appropriate. The narcotic makes the headache disappear and may even make the patient feel "well," so the next time they want to feel "better," they take another pill. This is the setting in which narcotics appropriately prescribed become the fuel for drug addiction. People like Jack who are given appropriate pain relief simply do not become "addicted" in the sense of craving drugs when the pain is gone.

We also know that daily exposure to narcotics causes a phenomenon doctors call "tachyphylaxis." This means that after a few days of regular use of a drug the body becomes more adept at metabolizing it, so it takes a larger dose to get the same degree of pain relief. Thus many dying patients gradually require larger and larger doses to obtain adequate pain control. To a new nurse caring for such a patient for the first time, a prescribed dose of medication may seem huge, but in examining the patient's chart, the pattern of a gradually increasing dose is very clear. This is not evidence of "drug-seeking behavior" or addiction, but the phenomenon of tachyphylaxis at work. It is also one reason why my mother's hospice nurse was so firm with me about not fixating on the dose of liquid morphine she might receive but giving enough to accomplish the goal.

There are two important things about Jack's wife in this story. In this pre-hospice glimpse of death in a hospital, note that "the rules" forbade her from staying overnight even though he was in the final stages of dying and their last earthly parting was looming. Even the fact that she had found a non-medical way of helping to ease his pain was not enough to gainsay "the rules." That would never happen in hospice, where care is all about comfort.

Secondly, Jack's wife found a way to help control his pain that worked! Once doctors started to study pain, we discovered the reason that her systematic patting helped him. Medical researchers Ronald Melzack and Patrick Wall propounded what came to be called the "gate control theory of pain." The pathways in the spinal cord that carry pain impulses up to the brain have the ability to pass a limited number of signals through what functions as a "gate" at each spinal cord level. Imagine a crowd of people leaving a large stadium that have to line up to get out through the exit gates. Many people can walk side by side through the corridors but at the actual gate, only a few at a time can go through. Both pain impulses and other non-painful, sensory impulses pass through this same gate. By flooding the gate with non-painful impulses generated by rubbing or patting (as mothers have instinctively known for millennia), fewer painful impulses can get through, so the perception of pain is lessened. Jack's wife was really lowering his pain but she was kept by the rules from doing so at night when pain typically seems worse since these are fewer distractions than during the day.

James Rachels quotes Alsop's story in his book *The End of Life*. The chapter in which it appears is called "The Morality of Euthanasia," and unless you have a heart of stone, by the time you got to the end of that chapter you, too, probably felt that euthanasia would have been merciful. But as I shall argue in Chapter 7, euthanasia is a very drastic measure to treat medical ignorance and inept practice (even when it is state-of-the-art practice for its time). Had researchers never decided to study what we all "knew" about pain, we would still be explaining Jack's lessened pain from his wife's ministrations as mere psychological distraction and not a real physical phenomenon. We would never have developed PCA pumps that allow a patient to keep the blood levels of analgesics within a therapeutic range at all times.

Finally, Jack's story is a reminder of how hospice has changed care for the dying. Today Jack would at least have the opportunity to die in the setting of his own choosing, mostly likely not at the NIH without his wife. He and she would have access to nurses who have turned pain control for the dying into an art form. His wife would have vials of liquid morphine (which hospice nurses have called "God's gift to dying patients") which can be given by dropper under the tongue and work almost as fast as if given intravenously. Jack's entire family would have the emotional, psychological, and spiritual support of hospice to accompany them on Jack's premature journey to death. By keeping Jack acceptably comfortable, if not totally pain-free, and by making the measure of the adequacy of pain treatment his alone, he would have had some energy to devote to final goodbyes, to mending relationships, to reminiscing with his wife about their life together, and to prepare spiritually for his death. As it was, 100% of his energy was consumed by dealing with his pain. That probably shortened his life by a few days, which, given the circumstances, may have been a very well-disguised blessing.

Alsop's roommate should never have died like this, but he did. I have talked to people like Jack's wife who have been permanently and deeply scarred by watching a loved one die horribly. They are profoundly suspicious that they will be forced to suffer as Jack did and they are among the most enthusiastic proponents of euthanasia or physician-assisted suicide I have personally met. They would literally rather kill themselves or have a doctor kill them than endure what Jack was forced to endure (which is understandable) and they are not at all reassured by descriptions of progress in treating pain (which is sad). *Do not let anyone you know die like this. It is unnecessary. It is immoral.* Even persons who cannot accept the passivity of hospice can, through palliative care programs or with the care of a knowledgeable physician, avoid this kind of brutal death.

Does this mean that hospice can eliminate all suffering associated with dying? No, it does not, and to explain that, we need to return to the nature of suffering again. What hospice and palliative care can do, and actually achieve, is really good control of pain as a physical phenomenon. Pain medications, like all drugs, have their side effects. Not only do they cause respiratory depression in high doses, but they also can cause nausea and constipation. Hospice nurses have also elevated dealing with these side effects to an art form. Because hospice programs prioritize comfort and caring, they take symptoms that sometimes strike doctors as trivial with utter seriousness. I remember now with embarrassment that as an intern when we did stop by a dying patient's room to ask how they were doing, if they offered a symptom like constipation we would often ruefully chuckle together in the hall while we ordered the laxative or stool softener. "He's dying," we would say to each other, "and all he cares about is a bowel movement." Hospice is much smarter than we were and responds to whatever symptoms are bothering a patient with a determination to control them.

But some of the suffering associated with dying is not physical in origin or related to physical problems such as poorly controlled pain. At least some of it is religious or spiritual or existential. "Why must I die and leave everything I love behind?" "What will happen to my family when I am gone?" "What is the ultimate meaning of life?" "Of my life?" "Did I make a difference?" "Will I truly be missed when I am no longer here or will I be forgotten?" These are at root spiritual questions and they can be addressed by people trained to be religious and spiritual advisors.

As Daniel Callahan has pointed out, euthanasia would stop this sort of spiritual suffering (as it would have Jack's physical suffering), but it is a strange remedy for a spiritual problem:

The great temptation of modern medicine, not always resisted, is to move beyond the promotion and preservation of health into the boundless realm of general human happiness and wellbeing. The root problem of both illness and mortality is both medical and philosophical or religious. "Why must I die?" can be asked as a technical, biological question or as a question about the meaning of life. When medicine tries to respond to the latter, which it is always under pressure to do, it moves beyond its proper role.

It is not medicine's place to lift from us the burden of that suffering which turns on the meaning we assign to the decay of the body and its eventual death. It is not medicine's place to determine when lives are not worth living or when the burden of life is too great to be borne. . . . Medicine should try to relieve human suffering, but only that suffering which is brought on by illness and dying as biological phenomena, not that suffering which comes from anguish or despair at the human condition. . .the doctor may have no better answers to those old questions than anyone else; and certainly no special insight from his training as a physician. It would be terrible for the physician to forget this, and to think that in a swift, lethal injection, medicine has found its own answer to the riddle of life. It would be a false answer, given by the wrong people. . .[111]

Pain medication does not treat spiritual suffering, but hospice does not ignore it, either. All hospice programs provide access to spiritual counselors and ministers, priests and rabbis from many denominations who will work with a patient and his or her family to help deal with these pressing, sometimes agonizing questions. My mother's hospice nurse asked us several times if there were any spiritual issues to address and if we had access to support from our church or needed a hospice chaplain to come. Because hospice is a holistic program, this crucial area is not ignored.

Accompanying a dying person may well entail enduring some suffering ourselves. It can be excruciatingly painful, as I'm sure it was for Jack's wife, to watch a loved one suffer, to know that we would gladly take that suffering on ourselves if we could and to know that it is not possible to do so. Family or friends must be prepared to be advocates for anyone with a serious illness, especially if they are in a hospital or nursing home. Being seriously ill leaves one exhausted and without the strength to advocate for oneself. Someone must be prepared to become the patient's advocate.

Untreated or poorly treated physical pain and other symptoms must not be tolerated. If the usual measures are not effective, there are extraordinary measures which can be used if necessary.

Dying patients sometimes experience a sudden increase in pain that does not respond to the treatment they are then receiving. If increasing the dosage and frequency of those medications does not work, hospice patients can be briefly admitted to an inpatient hospice unit or hospital to use more aggressive measures, such as nerve blocks, to control the pain. A measure of last resort is called terminal sedation and involves using sedative medications to make the patient unconscious until death occurs. By removing consciousness we believe we are ending the perception of both pain and suffering; general anesthesia regularly does that for persons undergoing major surgery. The trade-off for the patient and the family is that interaction can no longer occur; therefore, terminal sedation is used relatively infrequently. But it is important to know that extraordinary measures do exist and can be used when necessary. Hospice really intends to make good on its goal of having no patient die in physical pain.

But we cannot advocate away the personal spiritual suffering that some people endure while they are dying. We can be sure they have access to spiritual or religious counselors and we can assure them of our constant care for and about them, but no one can "give" us a meaning for our lives. The good news is that, as spiritually painful as the journey to death may be, I have seen it also be an opportunity for personal, substantial growth at the end of life, which I will address in the next chapter. What a thought—growing while dying!

CHAPTER 6

Growth at the End of Life

Most of us think of being dead as a highly undesirable state of affairs. Therefore, we also tend to think that the process of reaching that stage—dying—must be totally negative, too. We often say that we envy people who drop dead on the golf course or die in their sleep, and that we hope for that type of death ourselves. Yet, I know people who, while dying, experienced a time of personal growth and sometimes progress within their family that was incredibly important to those involved. In fact, this episode of growth rates as so valuable that people who have shared the journey with a loved one often say how grateful they are that death did *not* occur quickly and abruptly. Thus, while approaching death always hurts, sometimes there are aspects that people acknowledge as irreplaceably valuable.

While end-of-life growth is different for each person, there are some common themes. First, the dying person in some sense sums up his or her life and its achievements, often by talking or writing about it. Looking through old pictures, rereading diaries or letters, and retelling family stories reviews and reassesses the life that is drawing to a close and affirms its value and impact on others. The life-review process allows for telling family stories and history only the dying person may know and that will otherwise be lost forever. Our culture prizes virtues such as honesty, loyalty, and generosity. Reviewing our lives allows us to document for our family and friends the unique ways we have lived out those important values.

Second, the dying often want to communicate to family and friends how dear and precious those relationships are to them. Some families find a new ability to communicate the depths of their love for each other. Others find the impetus to heal fractured relationships as the reality of impending death makes the reasons for estrangement seem trivial. Most families report a vastly increased sense of solidarity and mutual support as they practice caring for each other as well as for their loved one. Many dying people and their families sum up this time of growth as an experience of transcendence.

Much of this growth opportunity consists of conversation. What do dying people want (and need) to talk about? Dr. Susan Block has suggested that patients' central concerns at the end of life, once pain is adequately addressed, fall into three major categories: their families, their own psychological integrity and coping skills, and making meaning out of the inevitability of death and its rapid approach.[112]

Concern for one's family is only natural. Elderly patients worry about how their surviving spouse will fare after they are gone, especially if they are childless or their children live far away. For elderly widows and widowers death often means moving to a different living situation away from lifelong friends, and the dying are concerned about the impact of this change on their partner. Younger patients with minor children fret about how their death will affect their loved ones financially. Do they have enough life insurance so that the family will not have to move? Will a stay-at-home mother have to find a job to get by? Will college plans for the children have to change? These concerns ratchet up when a family is caring for another member with special needs, such as a child with mental illness or physical limitations. Middle-aged persons frequently worry about the fairly long average life expectancy of their surviving partner and the social change from being half of a couple to being a single person. People of all ages experience regret for the life experiences—births, graduations, marriages, family successes—they will miss out on sharing. It is only natural for dying persons to be concerned about family welfare after their death, to such an extent that hospice nurses often counsel families to reassure their loved one that they will not feel abandoned and to offer explicit "permission" to move on.

Worries about psychological integrity and coping skills are equally natural. People usually face their impending death with some qualms about their ability to do so. After all, it only happens once in a lifetime.

We have no chance to practice. Avery Weisman has described two different mental strategies for facing life-threatening illness: coping and denying.[113] Persons who rely on the second strategy defend against the mental stress of dying by avoiding thinking about unpleasant new realities. Those who use coping skills harness problem-solving abilities to manage all the changes associated with dying. Each of these techniques can be both adaptive (reducing stress and allowing time for psychological adjustment to a harsh reality) and maladaptive (preventing further psychological adjustment). Many patients pass through a period of denial when they first receive a fatal diagnosis, but then find the personal resources to move beyond denial to coping. This period of denial seems to allow them some breathing room to begin to adjust to their illness while not yet having to face its full reality. Some patients or family members, however, remain in deep denial throughout the illness, which limits their ability for a time of final growth at the end of life. Unfortunately, such people often forfeit their ability to use hospice care because it acknowledges that death will be the outcome of this particular episode of illness.

Finding some meaning to one's life in the light of approaching death is a frequent concern. Patients who have lived within a particular religious tradition or followed a spiritual discipline for many years will often already have a vocabulary of ideas about what makes life meaningful, but they still usually want to assess how their own life has measured up to the standards of their tradition. While this can be done introspectively, conversation with friends and loved ones allows for a time of mutual sharing. Many families are not expert at communicating with each other, especially about painful, unpleasant realities. But investing effort in talking with a loved one about his or her impending death can provide a real opportunity for growth as a family. Facing a crisis together, actually exercising fidelity, loyalty, solidarity and honesty in tough times, teaches everyone the value of caring for each other and is an excellent behavior model for children and teens.

At one time or another, everyone wonders "Why must I die?" and "How will I be remembered after my death?" Religions have always been there to provide the answers. Some people who have never adopted a particular religious tradition or set of spiritual practices or who have rejected them find themselves in a genuine existential crisis as death approaches. Hospice programs have highly skilled chaplains from almost all faiths readily available to help the dying person address these crucial questions. They also have a variety of other trained professionals if a representative from "organized religion" is not welcome.

Denial of dying is a common occurrence. If the person denying is a family member rather than the patient, this attitude can be cruel: questions about the ultimate meaning of life can be agonizing to a dying person and denial of the inevitable forces the patient to leave them unanswered. It is very difficult to explain to these people why a mental health practitioner appears suddenly on the scene to deal with this existential predicament.

Wonderful ways exist to help a dying person find and articulate meaning in his or her life. The most basic are direct questions about how the person hopes to be remembered and whether any relationships need to be healed or would benefit from attention now. Just telling the dying person how much he or she is valued can help. Susan Block has also published a list of suggested questions that will help to assess the psychological and spiritual status of patients with life-threatening illnesses. Some of these questions are "How have you made sense of why this is happening to you?" and "How have you coped with hard times in the past?"[114] Others might be "What will help you feel that you have lived up to your own ideals in the way you've dealt with your illness/your death?" and "What could you do that would help you feel that this has been a meaningful time for you and the people you care about?"[115] While her article is written for healthcare professionals, many of her questions are also relevant for family and friends to raise sensitively, assuming that the dying person is not in denial. Family members will probably have a good sense of whether the patient has moved from the initial stage of denial so common upon first receiving a devastating diagnosis to the point where such questions may be appropriate. Do *not* use these questions to bludgeon a patient into "accepting" that he or she is dying. Do not attempt to discuss more than one or two in a visit unless the patient clearly leads the discussion forward. These conversations serve as a springboard for the further thought and discussions, which can lead to personal and family growth. Merely asking these questions can lead a dying person to ruminate about life and its meaning, even if he or she does not answer them aloud.

Many people find that the writing of so-called "ethical wills," mentioned in Chapter 2, really helps the life-evaluation process. The term ethical will may seem overly legalistic and perhaps too daunting. After all, who writes their own property will, living will or healthcare power-of-attorney? Dr. Barry Baines, a hospice physician and proponent of ethical wills, instead asked his father, who had been diagnosed with lung cancer, to write a letter to him "about things that have been important to you in your life."[116] Baines' father wrote about the value of hard work, caring for and educating children, being honest and helpful to those in need, and loyalty to one's family. "The memories of my father come flooding back whenever I read this letter," Baines later wrote. "Although it's only a couple of handwritten pages long, it's a precious gift whose value can't be quantified."[117]

Writing such a document, whether called an ethical will or just a letter to the family, gives the dying person a precious opportunity to review the achievements in his or her life. We all have them. We may never have been on the cover of *Time* magazine, but most of us have at some time been faithful family members and friends who sacrificed for others, or been loyal and constant when betrayal would have been easier. If, in fact, your life has disappointed others who had reason to count on you, a letter gives you the opportunity to apologize (even if you cannot bring yourself to do so in person). You can even apologize to the dead— perhaps parents you let down or friends you abandoned. All this work opens the door to reconciliation with others and may even allow you to forgive yourself for your failures or shortcomings. We all have those, too.

Our grandparents and great-grandparents lived in a world radically different from ours and experienced amazing changes in their lifetimes, but few of them left documentation of their lives in diaries and letters. Thus, we prize even short anecdotes and observations from times gone by. End-of-life letters preserve precious family stories and keep them from being lost forever. Many people who have written such a document report that doing so has a spiritual dimension that led to a sense of completeness to their life. In a similar fashion, some have found that making plans for their funeral service allows them the opportunity to think about the role of faith in their lives, to say why a favorite scriptural passage or other reading resonates with them powerfully, to list favorite hymns or other music and to pass on spiritual observations to the next generation. Doing so also gives the family valuable information about one's wishes for a funeral or memorial service or relieves them of this duty altogether.

Personal growth at the end of life is by no means automatic, however, and it can only occur if certain preconditions are met. The first, absolutely mandatory, is that *pain must be controlled to the patient's satisfaction.* This may not mean a state of being totally free from all pain, but it must be managed to the point where the patient declares it tolerable. Persons experiencing pain beyond their point of toleration use most of their physical and psychical energy coping with the pain and thus have no resources with which to grow. A few may require so much medication to control their pain adequately that they sleep most of the time, and that makes the opportunity for growth less possible.

The second precondition is soundness of mind. Patients suffering from moderate to advanced dementia have little or no opportunity to grow personally as death approaches because of the mental ravages of their disease. However, growth can be accomplished at the point of first diagnosis even though the person is not yet "dying." Since dementia progresses with a relentless, downhill course, the opportunity for growth must be seized quickly or the ability to grow at all will fade away.

Most importantly, patients need to know that talking with their families, friends and caregivers about the issues on their minds is okay. Families, friends and sometimes even doctors (although less commonly than in years gone by), feel that they must "protect" the patient from the terrible reality of their approaching death by either not talking about it or denying that dying is what is going on. This is the norm in some cultures, and it is difficult to overcome. In the United States, some men, raised on the stoic image of a multitude of John Wayne-like characters, feel that they need to protect their dying loved ones from a difficult and harsh reality by denying their dying. Be aware that this kind of "protection," while well-meaning, imposes a severe burden of isolation on the dying person. Family members can turn to each other for comfort out of the patient's earshot, but there is little comfort for a patient to be assured that if he or she would only eat or walk more, he would get well. When families are in denial, even the mildest suggestion from the patient that he might not get well meets with forceful assurances that renewed health is right around the corner. This forces the patient both to deal with his impending death alone and to maintain the fiction that nothing is seriously wrong. Mortally ill patients, including children, usually have a strong suspicion that they are dying and, in fact, are often relieved to have that confirmed. Leo Tolstoy's masterful novella *The Death of Ivan Illyich* deals with this exact problem. Ivan is dying: he knows it, his doctor knows it, his family knows it, but everyone pretends that he is not dying to "protect" him. Only his faithful peasant-boy servant Gerasim acknowledges the fact. Ivan desperately wants to talk about dying with his family, but this shield of silence does not allow it. To use a modern expression, in this story death is the elephant in the room that everyone ignores.

Signing into hospice care requires an acknowledgement that death will be the outcome of this episode of illness; it acts as an antidote to this understandable but usually misguided tendency to "protect." As a part of their ongoing evaluation, hospice nurses regularly check about not only physical symptoms and their management but also communication issues. They will carefully and sensitively raise questions like the ones Dr. Block suggests. Hospice nurses are available to talk with family members as well as patients and they encourage and support effective communication. But patients who are not part of a hospice or palliative care program have the same need and, I think, the urge to communicate with family and friends. Please do not close off honest, loving communication with them. Erecting a wall of silence may seem like the compassionate thing to do, but it prevents discussion about the most important issues in the person's life. Silence may also prevent some effective strategizing about how future coping might take place and thus denies the dying person a chance to continue to contribute ideas to other family members.

Undiagnosed and untreated psychiatric disorders can also frustrate the possibility of growth at the end of life. These "represent abnormal responses to the stress of terminal illness *and are distinct from the normal sadness, grief, and worry that characterize the dying process.*"[118] Of course dying people are sad about the loss of their lives and the most precious relationships in those lives. This type of understandable grief, sometimes called "situational depression" or "demoralization" by psychiatrists, usually accompanies unpleasant circumstances and episodes of loss. Dr. Paul McHugh describes it as "a natural feeling of discouragement provoked by bad circumstances. . .similar to the downhearted state of, say, a bankrupt man or a grief-stricken widow."[119] However, he says, severe or clinical depression occurs as a symptom of many diseases. This mental state, he writes, "with its beclouding of judgment, sense of misery, and suicidal inclinations, is a *symptom* identical in nature to the fevers, pains, or loss of energy that are signs of the disease itself."[120]

About 25% of cancer patients experience major depression during their illness.[121] Depression (as opposed to appropriate sadness) left untreated unremittingly diminishes the person's quality of life, increases the perception of pain and other troublesome symptoms, and diminishes the ability to experience pleasure, to connect emotionally with other people, and to find meaning in the time remaining. Untreated depression causes anguish to family and friends and is a risk factor for suicide. This type of depression can and must be treated to improve the quality of life for the dying person.[122] Demoralization, by contrast, waxes and wanes with circumstances, comes in waves, and is often worse during the night or when the person is alone. Mood and spirits lift, however, when pleasant circumstances occur—an anticipated visit from old friends or grandchildren, for example.[123]

Anxiety and fear lead to significant symptoms in about a quarter of dying patients.[124] These symptoms are often amenable to direct exploration with questions such as, "What are you afraid of?" or "What do you imagine dying will be like?" Hospice nurses, in particular, deal with these questions and provide accurate information about what to expect as the disease progresses. They monitor patients for significant psychiatric disorders and recommend treatment where appropriate, but families should never hesitate to voice their own concerns.

Delirium occurs as a terminal event in up to 85 percent of patients with far-advanced disease.[125] Although the patient may not be troubled by this symptom, families and friends may find it intensely distressing. If delirium cannot be managed with medications, an option of last resort is "terminal sedation:" giving the patient enough sedative drugs so that he or she becomes unconscious and maintaining this level of medication until death occurs. Terminal sedation is used only in extreme cases because, while it removes the symptoms that are so painful to the family, the level of unconsciousness needed to mask their symptoms also keeps patients from interacting with anyone. One of the goals of hospice, keeping patients able to communicate with their loved ones to the point of death, cannot occur if terminal sedation becomes necessary. One of the many strengths of the hospice program for the dying is that it is provided by an interdisciplinary team with medical, nursing, psychosocial, and spiritual expertise who deal with the dying as their niche. This means that the appropriate team member can be rallied to help the patient and their family in a rapid and seamless fashion. Hospice nurses work with the family as death approaches to help reduce their anxiety about what to expect. They also emphasize their availability both for phone and in-person support 24 hours a day.

Many family members and friends of dying people are afraid to talk openly to them about dying because they feel that admitting that death might be the outcome of this illness destroys hope. Matthew Stolick claims that, by perpetuating only a curative model of medical care (as demanded by the military metaphor of medical practice as was described in Chapter 1), doctors actually lie to their patients, albeit perhaps unconsciously. Focusing *only* on curing the patient, he says, renders the doctor unable to address the existential fact of the patient's impending death.[126] "The lie reduces the possibility of reconciliation, closure, and intimacy between the dying patient and his or her family and friends and prevents the patient from a high quality of dying."[127]

But can the term "hope" have any meaning to a dying patient? Can it mean anything beyond "hope for a cure"? Stolick defines hope in the healthcare setting as "a wish for a future state of affairs, an imagined future state that is *not a guarantee* but is theoretically possible."[128] Nurse Delores Kreiger has written of four phases of hope during a terminal illness: acceptance of the diagnosis, consideration of treatment options, a focus on prolongation of life using palliative care to improve quality of life, and finally a peaceful death.[129]

While it is understandable that patients, families and friends may wish that a person did not have cancer, that wish alone will not change the course of the disease. Stolick says that "hope" in Kreiger's phase one is just that: hope that a lump is not cancer, for example. But even when that hope cannot be realized, there are other valid uses of the word. In phases two and three, "hope for a cure" may no longer be realistic, but hope for prolongation of life using available treatments may be quite attainable. In stage four, as death draws nearer, there can be valid hope for a peaceful death as defined by that particular patient, best orchestrated by a hospice team and including family and friends.[130] For so long, the meaning of "hope" has been reduced to "hope for a cure," that many of us feel that it is impossible to speak of hope in the presence of the dying. But Kreiger and Stolick show us, I believe, valid uses of the word. Using their definition, hospice would say that no patient is ever "hopeless" even as he or she takes the last breath.

Of course, patients and sometimes their doctors can have false hopes: hopes for a state of affairs that cannot come to pass, at least without supernatural intervention. Here again, the military metaphor for medical practice does us a disservice because it can only focus on "winning the war" against disease. Since biological creatures cannot be immortal, some disease or other *must* inevitably kill us. There must always be the final "battle" that cannot be "won." Note that colluding with false hopes forces friends and family members to avoid any area of conversation that might shed doubt on the hoped-for miraculous cure apparently waiting just around the corner. It also does not encourage the patient to put his or her affairs in order. Often, in my experience, the patient is literally only days or hours from death when they and their doctors finally admit that their hoped-for cure will not come to pass; by then, there is no longer the time and energy to turn to preparation for the death which is so close.

Many of my students are shocked when I raise the idea that a dying individual might continue to grow in personally important ways or that families might find this passage from life to death to have positive aspects. It may seem hard to believe unless you have personally experienced such progress at the end of life. The journey with a loved one or friend to their death, while emotionally painful and raw, can also be a time of profound growth when we get to give and receive care, exemplify the virtues of loyalty, faithfulness, and solidarity, and demonstrate our love in tangible ways. And that is no small achievement.

CHAPTER 7

Euthanasia and Physician-Assisted Suicide

Humans have struggled with death and destruction for all of recorded history: wars, famine, staggering levels of infant and maternal mortality, industrial or farming accidents, lives lost to now easily treated minor infections, the inability of the elderly to keep up with nomadic tribes, murder and mayhem. The list is very long. No one seems to have worried that anyone might live longer than he or she wanted and that death would need to be *summoned*. But that is exactly what some people are proposing, saying that in order to end our lives at the "right time" and in the "right way" for each of us, we need to legalize euthanasia and/or physician-assisted suicide, deliberate forms of killing.

Bioethicists have learned how important it is to be clear about the definitions of key terms, so let's start with these two. *Euthanasia* (from the Greek for "good death") occurs when one person deliberately kills another person for merciful reasons and is therefore sometimes called "mercy killing." The killer is often a family member or friend who is so distressed by the patient's suffering that he or she feels impelled to use death to relieve it. Euthanasia is called "voluntary" when requested by the patient and "involuntary" when he or she does not. Juries in general are very reluctant to convict a person who kills when the circumstances clearly support a merciful motive and no apparent venal motives can be found.

Physician-assisted suicide occurs when a physician prescribes a lethal dose of a medication for the express purpose of a patient's using it to end his or her own life. Unlike euthanasia, the patient rather than the doctor administers the drug, hence the use of the term "suicide." The law is very specific: the doctor prepares the drug but cannot administer it and the patient who must swallow it without anyone's assistance. Physician-assisted suicide has long been a legal procedure in Holland and Belgium. Oregon was the first U.S. state to legalize it; voters in Washington approved it in 2008, followed by Montana in 2009.

There has been intense debate within the medical and philosophical communities whether either euthanasia or physician-assisted suicide is ever morally legitimate and if there is any important moral difference between these two actions. Some experts argue that in either case the doctor bears the moral responsibility for the patient's death, either by directly administering the drugs that kill or providing them to the patient knowing of their deadly purpose. In either case, the patient dies. Others say there is significant protection for patients in having them take the drug themselves; no one can force them to take the deadly dose. Both practices probably have been very quietly practiced by some physicians in a few circumstances; doctors who chose to violate the law would have done so in secrecy so we have no accurate idea of how often this has happened.

The assertion that we have a "right to die" equal to our right to life has been recently proposed to support the legalization of euthanasia and/or physician-assisted suicide in America. At first this novel claim may strike you as very strange, for we ordinarily think that depriving a person of life is the worst possible harm in almost all circumstances. A consensus has emerged in Europe since World War II, for example, that capital punishment for murder, the wrongful, deliberate killing of another person, is morally mistaken; some people in the United States are advocating for a similar abolition of capital punishment here.

Philosophers have long articulated reasons why humans have a "right to life." English political philosopher John Locke wrote extensively in the 17th century about "natural rights," the most fundamental set of human rights, which we have simply by virtue of being human and not because any person, government or religion has bestowed them on us. Locke's favored trio of natural rights was "life, liberty and property." Our Declaration of Independence boldly states that "we hold these truths to be self-evident. . .that [Americans] are endowed by their Creator with certain unalienable rights, that among these are Life, Liberty and the pursuit of Happiness." Note that "Life" comes first, for it is necessary to be alive to exercise the other rights. The term "unalienable" is not one we use often. It contrasts with rights that are "alienable," or severable, such as the ownership of a particular piece of property that can be voluntarily sold or taken away using eminent domain. An unalienable right is one that cannot be taken away or even voluntarily surrendered. Thus our Declaration asserts that we cannot voluntarily give away our right to our own life, even if we no longer want to live it.

You can see how clearly Locke and philosophers who supported his ideas affected the Founding Fathers. (It needs to be acknowledged that both groups limited these rights to white males who owned property, but they have since been successfully extended to men of color and finally women.) You can also see, having stated that a right to life is unalienable, how strange the claim is that there might be an equally important "right to die." That is not to say that no philosophical argument for a right to die can be made, but that, given the ages-long arguments for a right to life, it is going to take some work to convince us.

Why might people need to proclaim a right to die equal to their right to life? Some advocates assert that patients are too regularly held hostage by a medical system that cannot simply step back and allow them to die when health and quality of life can no longer be restored in any meaningful way. In previous chapters we have discussed how the metaphor of medicine as warfare acts to promote this behavior. Not to fight with guns blazing away until death, the "Great Enemy," literally snatches the patient from the doctor's grasp is to collude with the enemy, and that is treason. In addition, dying has been turned from an event into a process that can be protracted by modern medical technology. The same technology that can sustain a gravely injured young body while it heals itself can be used to prolong the dying of an aged person whose body no longer can. Unfortunately, no red flags magically pop up when a person crosses the line from very sick (but potentially salvageable) to irretrievably dying. The difficulty of identifying the point at which dying begins is so great that doctors may not know when to back off on the continued use of technology and to apply the wishes stated in an advance directive.

Daniel Callahan claims that medicine practices what he calls "technological brinkmanship." While it recognizes that people can be harmed by overusing medical technology, he says, medicine also pushes technology right up to the line where benefit turns into burden. He calls this a ". . .gambling effort to go as close to that line as possible before the cessation or abatement of treatment. Common sense seems to dictate such a course: aggressively work to prolong life until it becomes futile, or harmful, to continue doing so; then, just as boldly, halt life-extending treatment.[131] But doctors do not have and may never acquire the ability to manage medical technology as exactly and precisely as this strategy implies we can. "The result of this continuing failure is the violence of death by technological attenuation, a stretching to the limit and beyond the power of technology to extend the life of an organ system [like the heart] independent of the welfare of the persons to whom they belong."[132]

Dying was simpler years ago when medicine had much less to offer. People got sick and either got better fairly quickly or died, and that was that. Today we also have to deal with the problem of incomplete recovery from treatment. Medicine can sometimes save a life but leave the patient with severe limitations, as the case of Terri Schiavo so poignantly showed us all in 2005. This forces us to confront very difficult and perplexing questions. When is a life "not worth living"? Who can make that decision: the patient, the family, the insurance company? On what moral grounds and for what reasons would someone make such a choice? Some of the suggested candidates for those important moral reasons are individual autonomy, unassuaged and untreatable suffering or the dictates of a particular religious tradition.

Autonomy is a notion near and dear to the hearts of all Americans, even if the term is unfamiliar. Autonomy, or "self-governance," is the liberty to pursue one's own individual version of the good life. To be respected as autonomous by others means the freedom to be left alone to live according to our most cherished values, even when other people disapprove of our choices. That leads people for whom ecological concerns are paramount to live off the power grid, grow their own food organically and recycle compulsively while others live in vast houses, drive SUVs, commute long distances to work daily, and demand fresh strawberries in January. We Americans particularly prize this freedom to live life on our own terms: rugged individualism is as American as apple pie. So it seems quite natural for some Americans to claim the right to die at the time and place of their own choosing as an expression of that individualism despite the fact that the idea is a historical anomaly, to say the least. Should people have the right, or at least the freedom to decide that their quality of life is not acceptable to them and choose to end their lives? That question raises several more perplexing moral problems.

Let's assume for the moment that a consensus exists—and it does not—that in America people do have the right or the freedom to end their lives. This still leaves us with several thorny problems. Is this true only for people who are dying, and if so, how close to the end? After all, in one sense we are all dying every day. What about severely injured people who are not dying and may not for many years, but who find life confined to a wheelchair or attached to a ventilator to be one they do not wish to live? What about people who have no detectable illness but are existentially unhappy? Should they be forced to at least try medication for depression or can they simply choose to end their lives? What about the teenager who has just gone through a bad breakup and thinks life can never again be worth living?

Most proponents of legalizing euthanasia and physician-assisted suicide do not address these questions. Usually they propose something that sounds much more modest: that the procedures should be limited to patients who (1) are terminally ill, with 6 months or less to live in their doctor's best estimation, (2) have "unbearable pain and suffering," and (3) freely and repeatedly state that they want to end their lives. All of these turn out in practice to be far less clear and simple than they seem at first reading. Doctors are notoriously poor at predicting dates of death, except in cases of cancer. For the majority of people, doctors simply cannot identify that crucial point.

Another reason given for the necessity of direct euthanasia or physician-assisted suicide is to prevent "unnecessary pain and suffering." Specifying "unnecessary" seems to imply a contrast with some necessary degree of pain and suffering, but many Americans today feel that all suffering is "unnecessary." Instead, we believe with almost religious fervor in immediate gratification and that we are destined to be happy and successful. These ideas would seem quite strange to previous generations who labored to save money for purchases rather than using credit cards, bought "starter" houses rather "McMansions" as first homes, and often drove only used cars for their lifetimes. A desire to stop "unnecessary suffering" often compels loving pet owners to euthanize animals who are terminally ill. Proponents of legalizing euthanasia often point out that we treat our pets better than we treat each other in this regard. This seems like a compelling argument, but psychiatrist Paul McHugh offers a spirited response:

> At the heart of the confusion lies the contention that if the aim of medicine is to eliminate suffering and if only the killing of the patient will relieve the suffering, then killing is justified. On this logic rests Dr. Kevorkian's repeatedly successful defense before the juries of Michigan [until his final trial for murder rather than assisting a suicide]. Yet the aim of medicine cannot simply be to prevent suffering. Not only would that be an impossible task, given the nature of human life, but it would diminish the scope of human potential—almost all of which demands some travail. The elimination of suffering is a veterinary rather than a medical goal.[133]

But what about "unbearable" suffering? Emotionally this term moves us to act at once: after all, the suffering cannot be tolerated! Surely it demands immediate relief. We have already discussed the difference between pain and suffering extensively in Chapter 5. Here let me only reiterate that there is no way for me as a doctor to know that your suffering is "unbearable" beyond your self-report. We do not have "suffering meters" in our foreheads for me to read. We do know that patients vary in their capacity to tolerate pain, so there is no "average" to turn to as a standard. The teenager who has been dumped by his girlfriend truly feels that his suffering at that moment is unbearable. Those of us who have preceded him in this experience know first-hand that both the pain and the anguish fade with time. The teen, however, does not yet know this personally; from his limited perspective, choosing death may seem entirely appropriate. Doctors also know that untreated clinical depression increases the perception of pain and suffering. Depressed patients may well say their suffering is unbearable, but the appropriate first-line treatment surely is an antidepressant pill, not killing them.

Finally, how "free" is the request to die? Are people seeking death to avoid the financial consequences of illness or the sense of "being a burden" on their families? Are there bona fide altruistic reasons for the ill to commit suicide? Or is there a danger that the "right to die" might become manipulated into a "duty to die," a duty to get out of the way?[134] People with serious illnesses are vulnerable and depend on their caretakers. If those caretakers make it clear that providing for the patient's needs is a great burden, especially if, as is most often the case, they are family members, will patients feel the need to request that their lives be ended?

Even the seemingly non-controversial requirement that a patient repeatedly request euthanasia, designed to allow a change of mind if, for example, the first request is the result of a particularly difficult day, becomes tricky in practice. Patients whose disease involves mental deterioration will have to choose euthanasia before they lose the ability to request repeatedly. Anyone who has taken a pet to be euthanized knows the ambivalence of choosing the day for death to come. We should certainly expect patients to feel a similar ambivalence; yet if they acknowledge this normal clash of feelings their doctor might decide that they are unsure and choose not to kill them. So patients are forced to pretense in the final moments of their lives. A vignette from Holland captures this perfectly. Dr. Ben Zylicz of the Dutch League of Doctors told BBC News: "I have heard about a patient where the family came from Canada because of a planned euthanasia. The patient said, 'No, not today, I don't want it anymore' and everyone pressed him saying 'look, your family came from Canada, they cannot do it again.'"[135]

Yet another reason why some advocate for the freedom to end one's life at the time and in the circumstances of our own choosing is that dying naturally from your disease is likely to rob you of a "death with dignity." To prevent this you must choose to die before you lose your dignity. When pressed to describe how illness robs an individual of their human dignity, advocates cite factors such as needing help with toileting and feeding, becoming bed-bound and requiring the time and attention of caregivers. Since most of this care is currently provided by kinfolk as an addendum to their regular jobs and duties, being the provider can be stressful. However, I also found that it profoundly gratifying when I was caring for my mother while she was dying in a hospice program. If it is morally good for us to care for others (and the all major world religions claim that it is), then there must necessarily be recipients of that care or we cannot give it. I think that the phrase "death with dignity" is a combination of some confused thinking and a rather malicious playing on our American worship of youthfulness. In a masterful essay called "Aging and Caring" in the *JAMA* "A Piece of My Mind" column, Paul Ruskin presents a compelling case history to a class of graduate nurses studying psychosocial aspects of aging:

> *The patient is a white female who appears her reported age. She neither speaks nor comprehends the spoken word. Sometimes she babbles incoherently for hours on end. She is disoriented about person, place, and time. She does, however, seem to recognize her own name. I have worked with her for the past 6 months, but she still does not recognize me. She shows complete disregard for her physical appearance and makes no effort whatsoever to assist in her own care. She must be fed, bathed and clothed by others. Because she is edentulous, her food must be pureed, and because she is incontinent of both urine and stool, she must be changed and bathed often. Her shirt is generally soiled from almost incessant drooling. She does not walk. Her sleep pattern is erratic. Often she awakens in the middle of the night, and her screaming awakens others. Most of the time she is friendly and happy. However, several times a day she gets quite agitated without apparent cause. Then she screams loudly until someone comes to comfort her.*[136]

Death with dignity proponents would undoubtedly say that this poor patient had passed beyond dignity, yet it is actually an accurate portrayal of the author's six-month-old daughter! How suddenly our evaluation changes when we realize this is a baby and not a demented elderly woman. But if caring for the baby is morally good, why isn't caring for the demented and dying equally morally worthy?

The dictionary definition of human dignity refers to innate or inherent qualities attributed to all persons simply because they are biologically human beings. None of these innate qualities requires any sort of performance test, such as toileting on one's own. Dignity is something a person has by virtue of being born human. Ruskin's little daughter has it as fully as the President of the U.S. although her capabilities are quite different.

Philosophers invested a great deal of professional time and argument on a closely related issue in the 1970s and '80s. They hoped that, if they could just reach a consensus on the defining characteristics of human "personhood," they could decide whether or not abortion was moral. If a fetus could be shown to be a human "person" in a rigorous philosophical sense, then, they hoped, everyone would agree that killing one was morally equal to killing an adult person. If, however, a fetus could be convincingly demonstrated not to fulfill the requirements for human "personhood," then perhaps a majority of people could agree that killing a fetus was different enough from killing a "person" that abortion should not be equated with murder and remain a legal option. Various lists of essential traits for personhood were proposed and hotly debated, and in the end, philosophers decided that the exploration of personhood was a blind alley that would not solve the controversy.

The relevant piece of this debate for our discussion of euthanasia and physician-assisted suicide is this: how did these philosophers (and how should we) think about the profoundly demented patient at the other end of life? Is he or she still a human person? The patient certainly does not meet any, much less all, of the proposed criteria that defined personhood. Yet no one seriously suggests that we could simply routinely dispatch the demented because they are no longer "persons." Rather, the conclusion was that personhood, whatever we mean by the term (closely tied to human dignity), so inheres in humans that newborn babies have it and demented people still have it. Illness and incapacity cannot cause us to lose our dignity.

In an article titled "Death with Dignity," philosopher Christopher Coope asks the reader to consider carefully what is meant by the wish that someone dies with dignity. What would that mean in practice? He points out that not everything we do can be done with dignity. "Would we understand what is meant by 'birth with dignity'?" he asks. "Could one ask which was the more dignified: a cesarean or a normal delivery?"[137] In my role as an anesthesiologist I attended hundreds of deliveries, and each one of them was in some sense a miracle. But "dignified"—never! Coope goes on to argue that what is really meant by this phrase is the negative corollary that it

> *is thought somehow to be undignified to be ministered to as helpless Just as we all once needed our nappies changing (sic), a process without the*

128

least trace of insult, so those of us who are temporarily able-bodied may one day need this service again. Any service can be provided in a way that shows lack of respect. But neither being in need, nor being helped, should be thought of as demeaning in itself.[138]

My own experience of being a patient bears out Coope's observation. The first week after having major abdominal surgery I was totally unable to wipe myself after a bowel movement and required the help of aides. They provided this service professionally and matter-of-factly and I in no way felt demeaned because I temporarily needed their assistance or by their providing it. Needing help from others, whether temporarily or permanently, is not the end of civilization as we know it. But the phrase "death with dignity" certainly suggests that dignity is related to what tasks we can and cannot do without assistance and that it is preferable to be dead than to need care from others. "Complaints about the 'indignities' of terminal illness—loss of control over bathroom functions, complete lack of mobility—are naturally going to seem offensive to [the disabled] who have struggled to assert their dignity under similar conditions."[139]

Some excellent philosophers would disagree with me, including Ronald Dworkin, Thomas Nagel, Robert Nozick, John Rawls, Thomas Scanlon, and Judith Jarvis Thomson, who wrote in the *New York Review of Books*, "Most of us see death—whatever we think will follow it—as the final act of life's drama, and we want that last act to reflect our own convictions, those we have tried to life by, not the convictions of others forced upon us in our most vulnerable moment."[140] They then suggested that we humans share a common fear that we will be remembered by family and friends as we are in our final illness. To avoid that, we need the ability to elect to die while we are still in a condition that reflects our "best" self, they say. Coope counters, "If one had dribbled one would forevermore be a dribbler. One would have been remembered with honor, by contrast, if one had perished suddenly in one's undribbling prime. But who is there who has such peculiar friends? If one is unfortunate enough to be burdened with them, it is surely this habit of linking indignity with incapacity which has made them that way."[141] I think it is relatively unlikely that our family and friends primarily remember us forever as we are in the last few days before our deaths. Rather, they remember our achievements, our loving relationship with them and the positive impact of our life.

Finally, proponents for the legalization of euthanasia and/or physician-assisted suicide say that patients need to be in control. By this they do not mean patients exercising the robust legal and moral rights they already have in America, including the option of creating an advance directive, appointing a healthcare proxy to make medical choices for them, and the right to refuse all life-sustaining therapy and medication. No, it is the ultimate control of choosing the date and manner of dying that they lobby for. There is an interesting and telling sociological divide here. Those advocating for this ultimate control are overwhelmingly white, upper-class men and women who have been lucky enough to have exercised control over most aspects of their lives. When they discover that they cannot control the fact that they are dying, they demand the next best thing: control over the timing and circumstances of their (uncontrollable) death. Poor and middle-class people, who exercise far less power over the circumstances of their lives, are not lining up to lobby for the opportunity to kill themselves. Many of them are still struggling to achieve the promise of "life, liberty and the pursuit of happiness." They are accustomed to not having much power in life and so are less offended when they discover they are dying.

But is this ultimate type of control good for us to have, even those of us who are fortunate enough to have had experience exercising power? "Power corrupts, and absolute power corrupts absolutely," said Lord Acton in a cautionary aphorism. I cannot imagine greater power than the power to choose to end your own life unless it is the dictator's power to kill thousands or millions. But few of us aspire to be a Stalin or a Hitler. Marjorie Williams, a former Washington *Post* staff writer, penned an essay in 1999 after the death of her mother under hospice care. She and her two sisters had all helped to care for her mother. She said:

> *I began to wonder if human beings can really be trusted with the suggestion that there are ways to make the process [of dying] manageable, to combat the loss of autonomy and control that are the essence of death. You bear the unbearable, in the orbit of a loved one's death, because you have to. If we come to believe that we and our families can*

sometimes be spared that, how many of us will be willing to endure it at all, under any circumstances?. . .Of the 21 people who secured lethal prescriptions from their doctors [in Oregon] in 1998, 15 of whom went through with their suicides, only one cited the fear of intractable pain. More than anything, these patients cited concerns about "autonomy and personal control. . ." But I wonder now if it is that very structure—the sensible, humane, normalizing particulars by which suicide is enshrined in social policy—that constitutes the threat, because it offers such reassuring authority to anyone who might be tempted to manage death away.[142]

For many years in most states committing suicide was illegal, even though a "successful" suicide could not be prosecuted. Many states have laws that make it illegal to assist another person's suicide. Psychiatrists have labored long and hard to convince both civil and religious authorities that suicide is "not an uncomplicated, voluntary act [but rather] an act provoked, indeed compelled, by mental disorder—such as a disorienting depression or a set of misdirected, even delusionary, ideas. In that sense psychiatry taught that suicidal people were not "responsible" for this behavior—no matter what they said or wrote in final letters or testaments—any more than they would be for epileptic seizures."[143] As a result of this consensus, laws against suicide have been repealed and the ban against burying a suicide in consecrated ground has been lifted. These psychiatrists strongly, even vehemently, reject the idea of "rational suicide": that you can add up the balance sheet of your life and dispassionately judge whether the minuses outweigh the plusses. It may seem tempting to think that a dying person, whose life horizon is a foreshortened one, could rationally make the choice to die sooner rather than later. However, research does not support this notion. Even a study of cancer patients enduring pain found they were not inclined to want euthanasia.[144] Many psychiatrists (but not all) feel that any request for assisted death is diagnostic of untreated depression.

But the idea of rational suicide is not limited to the dying. In an article in the Washington *Post*, Barron Lerner described the suicide of Carolyn Heilbrun, a former Columbia University professor of literature and mystery author (as Amanda Cross) who for years had spoken about her plans for suicide. Heilbrun had described life after 70 as "dangerous, lest we live past both the right point and our chance to die." But she did not commit suicide until she was 77. Barron says, "Her sixties, to her surprise, had been a source of astonishing pleasure. She wanted to keep writing, enjoy her family and friends, spend time in a new home, and keep certain promises."[145] I cannot help but wonder what other surprises and "astonishing pleasures" might have been in store for her had she not chosen to end her life when she did.

The heart of the point here is that, once we accept individual preferences as a bona fide reason for legalizing suicide, it is really impossible to put limits on "acceptable" preferences. How can we limit autonomy? Even if the medical profession proposes a very restricted conclusion— that autonomous, legally competent individuals who are terminally ill with self-reported unbearable pain and suffering might rationally want to die now rather than when their disease carries them off—we still have a huge problem. How do we get from your wish to die in these sad circumstances to my legitimate moral right as a physician to either directly kill you with euthanasia or assist your suicide by prescribing deadly medication? Where is the moral grounding for my action? Doctors are not required to prescribe medications or perform surgery just because a patient requests them. Doctors are required to have acceptable professional and moral grounds for any action they take, whether it is prescribing the appropriate antibiotic for an infection or taking out a diseased gallbladder. Doctors commit a moral wrong when they prescribe an antibiotic for a viral infection (because antibiotics do not kill viruses) or take out a healthy organ because they want to buy a new car. So doctors cannot simply agree to patient demands. In the United States a person cannot voluntarily sell him- or herself into slavery, even if it's the only way to pay off his debts. In part this law was enacted because the legislature decided that it is not morally sound for one person to have the degree of control over another, including the right to kill them, that slavery allows. Why would we give doctors the option of killing us simply because we ask them for it? If nothing else, the participation of German doctors in the atrocities of the Holocaust show that medicine is not morally strong enough to resist the temptations of ultimate power.

There is a long history of opposition to physicians helping patients to die. The Hippocratic Oath, the most widely known surviving Greek medical text, is believed to date to about 400 BCE. It is attributed to Hippocrates or the group of physicians around him known as the Hippocratic School. It contains two significant admonitions we need to consider here: "I will do no harm or injustice [to my patients]" and "I will not give a lethal medicine to anyone if I am asked, nor will I advise such a plan. . ."[146] The fact that some ancient physicians adopted such an oath suggests that other physicians would give lethal doses to patients. It has been traditional (but never required) that new physicians recite the Hippocratic Oath upon graduation. Various modern and often quite different updates have been written. Some medical schools, including the one I attended, choose to use another statement such as the Prayer of Maimonides (1135–1204), a Jewish physician, rabbi, and philosopher.

The injunction not to give lethal mediation to a patient has been the formal ethical standard of medical practice as well as the traditional standard practice for hundreds of years. The AMA has repeatedly and clearly stated, "Euthanasia is fundamentally incompatible with the physician's role as a healer, would be difficult or impossible to control and would pose serious societal risks."[147] But significant public challenges to the tradition arose in the late 1980s and early 1990s. In 1988 the *Journal of the American Medical Association (JAMA)* published an anonymous one-page story called "It's Over, Debbie." Written in the first person, it appears to describe a gynecology resident euthanizing a young woman dying of ovarian cancer after she says to him, "Let's get this over with."[148] Some literary critics have suggested that it is not the straightforward description of an actual event but rather a carefully constructed fictional narrative. In either case, the story resulted in a firestorm of letters to the editor, some supporting but most condemning the doctor's action. *JAMA's* editor said he had published the piece to create public discussion on the topic, and he certainly was successful in doing that.

Dr. Jack Kevorkian, a Michigan pathologist, came to national attention in 1990 when he assisted 54 year-old Janet Adkins, who had been diagnosed with Alzheimer's disease, in committing suicide. He met Mrs. Adkins for the first and only time the night before he assisted her suicide by hooking her up to a "suicide machine" in the back of his van. It contained a lethal mixture of drugs which she started flowing by pushing a button. By the time he was jailed nine years later, Dr. Kevorkian claimed to have assisted 130 people in ending their lives. Some of these people had life-threatening diseases but each was autopsied as an "unexpected death" and many were found not to have any disease at all. He was finally convicted of second-degree murder after videotaping himself directly killing a man with ALS or Lou Gehrig's disease. Dr. Kevorkian was freed from prison in 2007, having promised not to participate in either physician-assisted suicide or euthanasia.

In March of 1991 a very different story was published in the *New England Journal of Medicine*. In "Death and Dignity: A Case of Individualized Decision Making," Dr. Timothy Quill related the story of one of his patients, "Diane," who was diagnosed with leukemia.[149] He had been her physician for eight years, was intimately acquainted with her past medical history, and had worked with Diane to deal with depression and alcoholism. Although Dr. Quill encouraged his patient to consider aggressive treatment, up to and including a bone marrow transplant, she felt the odds, a 25 percent rate of cure, were not good enough to justify a toxic course of chemotherapy and its attendant hospitalization. The physician knew a great deal about Diane's coping skills and personal values, especially how important it was "to maintain control of herself and her own dignity during the time remaining to her."[150] Diane made it clear to Dr. Quill that preoccupation with fear of a lingering death would interfere with her ability to maximize the quality of her remaining time. He therefore referred her to the Hemlock Society's book on "self-deliverance," *Final Exit*, available in most bookstores.

The Society recommends asking one's doctor for sleeping pills or tranquilizers and hoarding them until a lethal dose has accumulated. Dr. Quill was not surprised when Diane called to request a prescription for barbiturates for sleep. He asked her to visit him before providing the prescription to be sure she was thinking clearly and not in despair. When he decided she was not, he wrote the prescription "with an uneasy feeling about the boundaries I was exploring—spiritual, legal, professional, and personal. Yet I also felt strongly that I was setting her free to get the most out of the time she had left, and to maintain dignity and control on her own terms until her death"[151] Diane did eventually use those pills to end her life. Although the District Attorney in Monroe County, New York where Dr. Quill practiced, asked a grand jury to indict him, they declined to do so.

This article generated much discussion among doctors but it took a different tone than conversations about Dr. Kevorkian. Dr. Quill had had a long relationship with Diane and knew her both as a patient and as a person, unlike Dr. Kevorkian who only saw his patients once before assisting them to die. Still, what Dr. Quill did was illegal under New York law. The debate as to his guilt or innocence has continued among physicians and bioethicists to this day.

So why not permit euthanasia and/or physician-assisted suicide? Opponents have a host of arguments against these proposals. For some people the religious assertion that only God should decide when life ends is decisive. However, we live in a pluralistic society with many different sources of value; not all American agree that choosing deliberately to end life is morally wrong. Society, and especially doctors who are pledged to "do no harm," have special responsibilities to vulnerable populations who are susceptible to manipulation by others into seeing themselves as "useless burdens" on their families and society. The professional codes of both nurses and doctors forbid them to participate in performing capital punishment. Opponents of euthanasia or physician-assisted suicide feel quite strongly that doctors must comfort always, cure when they can, but never kill, even indirectly. They fear that, if doctors can both cure and kill, over time patients will come to distrust physicians as a group and that everyone's medical care will suffer. Some claim that if any health care personnel are involved in ending life as well as healing, patients will ultimately come to distrust all healthcare providers. They might support euthanasia if provided by a form of public executioner, but not by doctors, nurses, or EMTs.

Others have noted that the courts have largely left the doctor-patient relationship alone. Lawyer Susan Wolf notes that, secure in the historic pledge of doctors not to euthanize patients, "Judges generally have encouraged those involved in termination of treatment decisions to steer clear of the courts. . .Thus there has been an overall toleration of relatively informal, nonlegalistic processes and a trust in the commitment of physicians to do no harm."[152] She goes on to state that there is "a clear legal tradition of required and extensive review whenever a person is to be killed directly; capital punishment is the paradigm. Thus, were active euthanasia one of the options, it is hard to believe the courts would not require considerably more review, process and formality."[153] In other words, the courts cannot be reasonably expected to be casual or indifferent when one person proposes to kill another.

Some opponents feel that the relatively recent development of hospice care and palliative care make euthanasia and/or physician-assisted suicide unnecessary and socially dangerous. They fear that we already have too many socially accepted reasons for killing each other (wars, self-defense, capital punishment) and that we do not need to add another one. They are also apprehensive that removing the management problems of caring for the dying by killing them will decrease funding for research on hospice and palliative care. Access to palliative care is spotty, however. It is a very new medical specialty and very few physicians are trained in it. Those who are tend to cluster in big-city hospitals. Dr. Ira Byock, a hospice physician and current Director of the Palliative Care Program at Dartmouth-Hitchcock Medical Center calls physician-assisted suicide laws "an apology for a failed medical system."[154] To bring the profession up to speed, Byock suggests that all medical residents, whatever their specialty, undergo at least 100 hours of training and hands-on practice in palliative care and pain management.

Persons with disabilities feel especially threatened by legalized euthanasia because the Nazis' "Final Solution" started with disabled people whose lives were judged by the state as "not worth living" regardless of the individuals' evaluation of the worth of their own lives. Since this country does not (yet) recognize a right to health care, physician-assisted suicide opponents claim that the millions of Americans without access to programs such as hospice might feel economically forced to "choose" death over life. Similarly, medical bills are claimed to be the cause of 50 to 75 percent of U.S. bankruptcy filings, even among people with health insurance. The rising cost of health care, these groups argue, might force even people with insurance to opt for euthanasia or physician-assisted suicide to protect their family savings. Advocates for the demented and mentally ill worry about how persons in those groups might be manipulated into "requesting" euthanasia.

Medicine has traditionally been said to serve two goals: the preservation of life and the relief of suffering. The call for euthanasia and physician-assisted suicide directly pits these two goals against each other. According to hospice and palliative care experts, relief of suffering caused by the physical and mental symptoms of dying can be achieved without resorting to euthanasia or physician-assisted suicide in 95 to 99 percent of patients with access to hospice care. Should we ask medicine to be responsible for eliminating suffering, which is caused not by disease symptoms but by existential or spiritual terror? A lethal injection will stop that suffering, but should doctors provide it?

Daniel Callahan has weighed in on the role and limitations of medicine in eliminating human suffering:

The great temptation of modern medicine, not always resisted, is to move beyond the promotion and preservation of health into the boundless realm of general human happiness and well-being. The root problem of illness and mortality is both medical and philosophical or religious. "Why must I die?" can be asked as a technical, biological question or as a question about the meaning of life. When medicine tries to respond to the latter, which it is always under pressure to do, it moves beyond its proper role.

It is not medicine's place to lift from us the burden of that suffering which turns on the meaning we assign to the decay of the body and its eventual death. It is not medicine's place to determine when lives are not worth living or when the burden of life is too great to be borne. Doctors have no conceivable way of evaluating such claims on the part of patients, and they should have no right to act in response to them. Medicine should try to relieve human suffering, but only that suffering which is brought on by illness and dying as biological phenomena, not that suffering which comes from anguish or despair at the human condition. . . .

It would be terrible for physicians to forget this, and to think that in a swift, lethal injection medicine had found its own answer to the riddle of life. It would be a false answer, given by the wrong people. It would be no less a false answer for patients. They should neither ask medicine to put its own vocation at risk to serve their private interests, nor think

*that the answer to suffering is to be killed by another. The problem is
precisely that, too often in human history, killing has seemed the quick,
efficient way to put aside that which burdens us. It rarely helps, and too
often simply adds to one evil still another. That is what I believe euthanasia would accomplish. It is self-determination run amok.*[155]

What might happen in real life if euthanasia and/or physician-assisted
suicide were legalized? In 2002, Holland became the first Western
democracy to legalize euthanasia, having tolerated it for almost 30 years.
We would be foolish to ignore their experience. Holland, however, is very
different from the United States. The Netherlands has a long tradition of
tolerance dating to the 16th and 17th centuries when the nation fought
to secure its political and religious freedom and became a refuge for free
thinkers like Spinoza and Descartes who fled from religious oppression
elsewhere in Europe. The Dutch accept things that are anathema in the
U.S.: drug abuse, free needle exchanges for addicts, public displays of
prostitution, including naked prostitutes sitting in store windows in
Amsterdam's red-light district.[156] Despite the fact that both Roman
Catholicism and Calvinism are prominent in the history of the Netherlands, says Derek Phillips, professor of sociology at the University of
Amsterdam, "the Dutch are relatively uninterested in moral philosophy,
which has been the focus of attention in other Western countries, and
are unwilling to accept any moral absolutes and lacking in moral pas-
sion. . .The Dutch tend to equate morality with religion, seeing themselves as nonreligious. [A citizen] considers the single most important
social fact regarding morality in the Netherlands to be that indifference
often masquerading as tolerance."[157] America, by contrast, is considered
to be the most overtly religious democracy in the West. The Dutch differ
from Americans in that between 95 and 99.4 percent of the former have
health insurance, which also includes long-term care. This contrasts
sharply with the estimated 47 million U.S. residents who do not have
health insurance, much less long-term care coverage. Also, the population
of Holland, roughly 16 million people, is much smaller than the approximately 300 million Americans. For all these reasons, we cannot simply
extrapolate from the Dutch experience of euthanasia and physician-
assisted suicide to how legalization of these actions might play out here.

Euthanasia and physician-assisted suicide have been practiced in Holland without fear of prosecution for murder since the early 1980s after the Royal Dutch Medical Association and the Dutch courts reached an agreement. Guidelines were jointly developed and doctors could plead a defense of necessity if the guidelines were followed. Patients themselves had to make repeated requests for euthanasia that were judged to be "well-considered." The patient had to be terminally ill and experiencing "unbearable suffering with no prospect of improvement." Euthanasia was performed by a doctor only after the patient was evaluated by a second doctor who concurred with the diagnosis and prognosis. There must be no other reasonable solution (e.g. hospice) to the patient's problem other than euthanasia. Doctors had to keep complete written records of all cases and immediately report the death as a case of euthanasia to the local medical examiner. The examiner notified the prosecutor who decided whether to take the case to court, with the understanding that if the guidelines had been followed no charges would be filed. These guidelines seem reasonable at first reading and when they were first adopted, they were applied to people who were terminally ill, often with cancer. Guidelines like these, and similar ones in Oregon's physician-assisted suicide legislation, are often claimed to protect patients. Does the Dutch experience demonstrate that they work?

A BBC news report in November 2000 offered some frightening facts. It cited a 1995 *Lancet* study that had found that despite the legislation, almost two-thirds of Dutch euthanasia and/or physician-assisted suicide cases went unreported.[158] No one likes extra paperwork, so perhaps the doctors were following all the guidelines but skipped the requirement to keep complete case records and notify the local medical examiner of a euthanasia death. Natural deaths from disease simply require a death certificate signed by the doctor with no reporting requirements.

But the BBC reports uncovered others problems as well. They also discovered that 29 percent of euthanasia cases occurred without the patient's explicit request.[159] Indeed, the *Remmelink Report*, the first official government study of Dutch euthanasia, published in 1991, listed 2,300 cases of voluntary euthanasia and 1,040 that were involuntary (without the patient's knowledge or consent). Of the involuntary patients, 14 percent were fully competent (able to state their own opinions and wishes) yet were involuntarily killed by their doctors. Seventy-two percent had never given any indication that they would want their lives ended.[160]

Although euthanasia in Holland supposedly honors individual autonomy, doctors, not patients, are given the upper hand. Their reasons for having terminated patients involuntarily included "low quality of life" (in the doctor's opinion), "no prospect for improvement," and "the family couldn't take it anymore."[161] As a result, some Dutch people, especially the elderly, carry "life passports," documents stating their explicit wishes not to be euthanized if they become ill or are injured. To what extent these are honored is unknown.

Perhaps the most distressing lesion from Holland's example is the expansion, actually the explosion, of accepted indications for euthanasia tolerated by the Dutch courts and the public. If a person dying from cancer is euthanized, their life is shortened but perhaps not by much. If the patient reports unbearable suffering, we can all have a certain sympathy with their plight. We might even be tempted to think that we might make their same choice. And if euthanasia could be limited to those who were terminally ill, had unbearable suffering, asked repeatedly for euthanasia, and were examined by a second doctor to confirm their diagnosis, prognosis and report of suffering, we might agree that euthanasia was a compassionate social policy in extreme but limited circumstances. However, the practice in Holland has expanded steadily from the terminally ill to the sick but not yet dying to those with mental symptoms only to the merely unhappy with no physical or mental illness at all and to newborn infants.

In 1992 the Dutch Pediatric Association announced that it was issuing formal guidelines for killing "severely handicapped" newborns. "Both for the parents and children, an early death is better than life," said Dr. Zier Versluys, chair of the Working Group on Neonatal Ethics.[162] In 1993 the Dutch Justice Ministry proposed extending the court-approved euthanasia guidelines to formally include "active medical intervention to cut short life without an express request." Now some Dutch doctors provide "self-help" programs for adolescents to end their lives.[163] In 1993 the Dutch senior citizens' group the Protestant Christian Elderly Society surveyed 2,066 seniors on general healthcare issues. While not directly addressing euthanasia in any way, 10 percent of respondents voiced fears that their lives could be ended without their request, stating that they were "afraid that at a certain moment, on the basis of age, a treatment will be considered no longer economically viable, and an early end to their lives will be made."[164] The great irony of history here is that Holland was the only occupied country whose doctors refused to participate in the Nazis' euthanasia program. Today about half of the nation's doctors have performed euthanasia.[165]

A second government-sponsored study in 1995 showed an increase in the number of patients euthanized and a steady erosion of the "protection" offered by the formal guidelines for patient killing. In a famous case decided by the Dutch Supreme Court in June 1994, Dr. Boudewijn Chabot, a psychiatrist, was charged with improperly euthanizing "Netty," a middle-aged woman, after her abusive marriage failed, one of her sons committed suicide over a disastrous love affair, and her other son died from leukemia. She refused both his suggestion of antidepressants and participation in a grief support group, and without her being examined by a second physician, she was put to death. Dr. Chabot gave the defense of medical necessity, that death was the only remedy for her suffering. He sought opinions from seven colleagues but none of them independently examined the woman. He was found guilty, but the court declined to impose any penalty.[166] When personally interviewed by American psychiatrist Herbert Hendin, Chabot "was insistent that Netty suffered from no psychiatric disability of any kind, that she was not a psychiatric patient but a woman having a normal grief reaction, seeing a doctor because she wanted assistance with her suicide."[167] Hendin's evaluation is startlingly different. He wrote,

> *Netty needed someone who could tell her in a firm but kind way that she had never really lived for herself and that it was not to late to try. She could always kill herself, but she ought to give life a chance first. . . . No one should underestimate the grief of a mother who has lost a beloved child, but neither should one ignore the many ways life offers to deal with the feelings of loss, guilt, and pain of a child's death. The Dutch like to present patients with concrete alternatives. For Netty, it might have been possible to use her skills as a social worker and involve her in a facility or project devoted to youth suicide prevention.[168]*

Instead, Holland offered Netty the option of medically-assisted death.

In *Seduced by Death: Doctors, Patients and the Dutch Cure*, Hendin, who is also Executive Director of the American Suicide Foundation, shares other stories he heard directly from Dutch doctors on several visits to Holland to learn about the practice of euthanasia. Many of these doctors were practitioners of euthanasia and proud of their work. One shared a story of a colleague who, when dying of cancer at age 76, made a pact with his 74-year-old wife, who was not ill, to join him in suicide. Although she was physically well and did not claim to be irredeemably depressed, her suicide was assisted.[169] Another doctor told Hendin that a colleague

> *"had terminated the life of a nun a few days before she otherwise would have died because she was in excruciating pain, but her religious convictions did not permit her to ask for death. [Eugene] Sutorius [the Dutch attorney who defended Dr. Chabot] did not argue, however, when I asked why she should not have been permitted to die in the way she wanted. I said I had known terminally ill patients who were not religious, but for whom the need to struggle to the end was terribly important. Their right not to go quietly would seem to merit respect as much as the rights of those who wish a painless death. He agreed."[170]*

In yet another case, Hendin wrote, "a wife who no longer wished to care for her sick husband. . .gave him a choice between euthanasia and admission to a home for the chronically ill. The man, afraid of being left to the mercy of strangers in an unfamiliar place, chose to be killed. The doctor, although aware of the coercion, ended the man's life."[171] These and many other documented cases show that, once personal choice is accepted as a compelling moral reason for doctors to kill patients, limits on "acceptable" personal choices cannot in practice be enforced.

Are Dr. Hendin and other American critics of Dutch policy simply "cherry-picking" the cases that are most egregious? Apparently not, according to attorney and author Wesley Smith. Dr. Philip Nitschke, known as the Dr. Kevorkian of Australia, "believes in death-on-demand. A woman named Nancy Crick made headlines when she announced on Australian television and internationally through her website that she would commit assisted suicide because she had terminal cancer. But when her autopsy showed she was cancer-free, Nitschke admitted that he and Crick had known all along that she wasn't dying but pronounced that medical fact as 'irrelevant' because she wanted to die."[172] In an interview in 2001 the doctor stated that "suicide facilitation should be available to 'anyone who wants it, including the depressed, the elderly bereaved [and] the troubled teen' He even claimed that a 'peaceful pill' that could be used to commit a pain-free suicide should be available in the supermarket so that those old enough to understand death could obtain death peacefully at the time of their choosing."[173] Smith also feels it highly unlikely that legally facilitated death can be limited to the actively dying if it were practiced in the United States. "Once one accepts the noxious notion that killing is an acceptable answer to the problem of human suffering, how can it possibly be limited to the terminally ill?" he asks. "After all, disabled people, the elderly, and those with devastating existential grief caused by, say the sudden death of family members, may suffer more profoundly—and for a longer period of time—than the terminally ill."[174] This is precisely the conclusion that euthanasia in the Dutch experience teaches. Once the genie is out of the bottle, it cannot be contained.

In 1997 the U.S. Supreme Court reviewed laws passed in New York and Washington State that prohibited doctors from prescribing deadly doses of drugs to help patients end their lives. The Court ruled that there was no constitutional right to physician-assisted suicide, although individual states like Oregon could write such a law. In 2002 Belgium legalized euthanasia, becoming the second country to do so. Patients there must be conscious when the request is made and under "constant and unbearable physical or psychological pain" resulting from an accident or incurable illness. Minors cannot seek assistance to die. Every euthanasia case must be filed at a special commission to decide if the doctors have complied with the regulations. Opponents have threatened to take their case to the European Court of Human Rights. In 2008 Luxembourg also legalized euthanasia.

Reviews of hospice and palliative care in Holland are mixed. Some reports say that almost every hospital has a pain and palliative care unit attached to it. Another claims that there were only two hospices in the entire country in the mid-1990s and that the services they provided were very limited.[175] Critics in Holland have charged that some doctors make "euthanasia rounds" in nursing homes (whose cost is covered by Dutch health insurance) suggesting to elderly persons, and especially those without families, that they make the "brave" and "wise" choice for euthanasia. Critics of legalizing euthanasia in the U.S. point out our inability to control healthcare costs and the millions who have no health insurance. They fear that enormous pressure could be brought to bear on patients to choose death for purely economic reasons. There is no cheaper patient to insure than a dead one.

In 1994 Dutch television aired a documentary that followed Dr. Wilfred van Oijen, a Dutch GP, caring for and ultimately euthanizing his patient Cees van Wendel, who had ALS. Excerpts of the film were shown on ABC's *Prime Time Live*. At one point, Dr. van Oijen ruminates to himself as he is driving that he could have ordered a different wheelchair and computer for Cees. But, he says to himself, none of those would have stopped the man from succumbing to his disease, so what would be the point? But is that the attitude we want to enshrine in America? Paul McHugh warns us about the dangers of "hopeless doctors [who], ready to see patients as untreatable, produce hopeless patients. The combination of the two produces a zeal for terminating effort. 'What's the point?' becomes the cry of both patient and doctor."[176]

What is the alternative? McHugh shares the story of another terminal ALS patient, his colleague Nelson Butters, a neuropsychologist. Butters, he says:

> saw [the ALS] through to its natural end. In doing so—without making it his mission—he rebuked those who cannot (or will not) differentiate between incurable diseases, of which there are many, from untreatable patients, of which there are few. Although he said he'd rather die than be helpless, he also was willing to try the assistance his doctors offered him as his condition worsened. He had bad times. . .but after each procedure, and despite its implicit indication that his condition was progressing, he recovered his cheer as he found himself more comfortable and able to continue his work with students and colleagues and his life with his family.

Nelson, his family, and his doctors had achieved much together. They fought to enable him to sustain purposeful life as long as possible. They weathered distressing, powerfully painful portions of his clinical course. The doctors never suggested a poison to shorten his life. When there was still something to do, they encouraged him to try to do it and helped allay his reluctance at the prospect. And in the end they surrendered to the illness (by stopping his ventilator at his request) without betraying their mission or letting contemporary technology drag them along.

It was grim. Everyone who knew him was saddened to think that Nelson had to suffer so. But everyone also was struck by how he overcame the disease by staying purposeful, lively and wittily intelligent right through to the end, teaching much to all of us. I tell this story because many believe that permitting a progressive infirmity to continue right out to its natural end is cruel and pointless. It certainly is tough. Any gains need to be identified. In fact, the gains for Nelson Butters were several.

Most obvious among them was the continuation of Nelson's work as a scientist, an editor, and a teacher for many months, despite his illness. . .Another gain was an extended duration of Nelson's company to his family and friends. One of his daughters decided to help nurse him through his trials, and after his death, reflecting on all she had seen and done, she decided to take up a career in nursing incapacitated people.

Finally, there was the appreciation—to the point of amazement— on the part of his doctors of the value he fashioned from their efforts to help him. . . . I sensed the awe felt by the doctors themselves for what had been accomplished in the end. Almost despite themselves and their own feelings about this awful disease, they had been partners with Nelson in a great achievement. They had carried out excellently the task set before doctors—help the patient encounter and resist the chaos of disease for as long as possible—and thus preserve the purposeful character of life to its end.[177]

The debate on legalizing euthanasia or physician-assisted suicide in the United States will undoubtedly ramp up again. When it does, we will be debating issues of grave moral importance. There are many viewpoints on the morality, practicality, and prudence of adding direct or indirect physician killing to the kinds of killing we already accept as a society. To boil the issues down to the simplest terms, let me suggest that this will be fundamentally a debate about what kind of society we want to be. Do we want to help each other bear the burdens of life, which inevitably lead at some point to illness and death, or do we want to opt for the cheapest, most efficient solution of dispatching those who need our care in the name of mercy? Let me give Paul McHugh the last word:

> *To be one the side of life provides a source of sanity. Be on the side of life and your course is clear, your efforts concentrated, the rules coherent. Bad patches can then be overcome, and even bad luck such as befell my friend Nelson Butters can be turned into something good. Be on the side of death and things fall apart, chaos reigns, and the fearful passions evoked by conflicting aims make malice, misdirection, sentiment and compassion all look the same.*[178]

CHAPTER 8

"Is This the Illness That Should Be Allowed to Be Fatal?"

As Daniel Callahan has pointed out, death is a topic strangely outside theoretical medicine even if, like a rude salesman, it often has its foot in the doors of the practices of clinicians. It seems as if the project of modern medicine, having declared war on each and every disease that might kill us, is to make us immortal. But from a biological standpoint, that will never be achievable, and we should be glad. If the first creatures to populate our planet had been immortal, there would not have been enough room for our generation to be born! Our very chance at life depended on the deaths of the creatures, both animal and human, which lived before us. But if modern medicine truly does aim to eliminate all diseases one by one until there is nothing left for us to die from, it is on a collision course with reality.

Instead, Callahan says that medicine *needs to see death as the necessary and inevitable endpoint of medical care at some time.*[179] Does this mean that we should not seek to treat a serious childhood illness because someday that child will die? Certainly not. To carry that idea to an illogical extreme, we could euthanize babies as they are born to prevent all the future illnesses and suffering they will endure in their lifetimes. I don't know of anyone who advocates that. But if immortality is not an option, some illness or other is *necessarily* going to be the fatal one for each of us. How should medicine incorporate that reality into practice? How should the general public think about it?

Because we live in a youth-worshipping and death-denying society, it is difficult for us to face the inevitability of our own deaths and the deaths of those we love. Unfortunately, failing to face this reality does not turn away death; it merely leaves us unprepared when a critical illness does strike. Many families find themselves truly unprepared for a relation's death—especially when the crisis arrives in the form of an accident at a young age—because they have not yet talked about end-of-life issues. They have no idea what the accident victim wanted or did not want in term of care and they feel guilt and real uncertainty about the choices they are being forced to make. Some are so paralyzed that they literally cannot make *any* choices. Decision-making then falls by default to the medical team who make them based on their own values and experiences.

Courts and bioethicists refer a choice in which one person acts on behalf of another as "surrogate decision-making." It is always more difficult than when the patient's wishes are known. The better the surrogate knows the patient, the better he or she will make choices based on the patient's own values and standards. Although doctors are sometimes forced into the role of surrogate decision-makers, we are very uncomfortable in this role because we usually don't know the patient well enough to predict his or her wishes accurately. Durable powers-of-attorney for health care or other documents can legally appoint a health care proxy to make these choices for the patient, but these are only effective if the patient and the proxy have had extensive conversations about the subject's wishes, values, and goals.

Another type of decision-making is called "best interest standard" and happens when no specific information is known about a particular patient's wishes and no proxy has been appointed. In that case, the medical team takes a guess at what the "best interests" of an "average" person would be for guidance. Because we are all the products of many forces that shape us during our lives, whoever is called upon to make a "best interests" decision will inevitably do so from the biases of his or her own viewpoint, which may or may not be anywhere close to the patient's own.

Callahan says that bringing death within the bounds of medical practice will require a fundamental rethinking, both for doctors and the general public. He claims that we have expanded the military metaphor of "the war on disease" into a general war on nature. We no longer see nature as a force independent of human beings that causes things to happen. Rather, we have come to think of "nature" as the sum total of mankind's manipulation of our environment.[180] It is important to think carefully about this point, for how we think about "nature" affects other concepts that we hold and act upon.

An important way in which our concept of nature cuts close to the bone for physicians is in how we understand what happens when we withdraw or withhold life-sustaining treatment from a patient who is dying. Callahan argues that it is the underlying disease process, not the doctor's action, which kills the patient at this point.[181] For example, if an otherwise healthy person undergoes surgery and I withdraw the breathing tube inserted for my anesthetic at the proper time, the patient breathes on his or her own. However, if I withdraw the breathing tube from a patient with end-stage ALS (Lou Gehrig's disease) where the respiratory muscles have been paralyzed, the patient will die. Callahan would say that death resulted from the underlying disease and not from my action. This analysis, he states, preserves the distinction between nature's independent powers and human powers. Nature has injured the body too severely for life to continue despite medical care. Doctors are obliged to use their skills carefully and diligently, but not everyone survives either serious illnesses or major trauma. When these patients die, Callahan says, nature is morally responsible for their deaths, not human failure to rescue— unless, of course, there has been negligence in caring for the patient.

Other capable philosophers disagree with this analysis. They claim the only reason to withhold or withdraw life support is because the judgment has been made that the patient would be better off dead. Life support is being removed or not started specifically to allow the patient to die. If the treatment in question was not life-supporting, it would not be withdrawn or withheld. The moral question for them is not whether the doctor or impersonal "nature" kills, but rather whether the decision to use life support or remove it is made properly and for appropriate moral reasons. It is not morally different, they say, to directly kill a patient by active euthanasia or to stop life support. The moral crux is not the means by which the patient becomes dead but whether the choice for death has been made appropriately, ideally by the patient's direct request or by an advance directive. If this analysis is accepted, then the distinction between direct killing and "allowing to die" in the medical setting collapses. Philosophers who are persuaded by this line of analysis claim that, since suffering is often associated with the dying process, mercy forces the deliberate killing of patients—direct physician euthanasia—to limit that suffering.[182] These certainly are two starkly different viewpoints.

If "nature" is not an independent force that causes tsunamis and earthquakes and diseases but rather the sum total of human impact on the environment, then, at least in theory, the idea of "wars on disease," like the war on cancer, makes perfectly good sense. The military metaphor here suggests a firm purpose and determination to overcome the enemy. Every known disease will someday be conquered one by one and mankind will then become immortal. If this project is ultimately successful, we stand on the threshold of immortality.

But if nature, as Callahan argues, is an independent force, which we can study and modify only to some extent but which retains the ability to act totally apart from human desires, then the project to eradicate all diseases is fruitless. Nature dooms us as biological creatures to die of something someday. We may in the future eradicate cancer and heart disease, as we have smallpox and polio (at least in the Western world), but other processes associated with biological decay will fell us. So we make a very basic choice in which of these understandings we choose to accept. One choice suggests that mankind is in the process of, and someday will succeed in, bringing nature to heel, making it a well-behaved house pet that invariably comes when called. The alternative understanding sees the power of nature as something we can at best learn to predict and perhaps modify but ultimately not control.

To follow the implications of our choice again into the medical field, cryopreservation, the freezing of a person's body immediately after death in the hope of thawing it at a future time when the disease process that killed them has been conquered and they can be cured, makes perfectly good sense in light of this understanding of nature. If, on the other hand, we accept that some illness or other *must* inevitably be fatal, then we can ask when a serious illness strikes, "Is this the illness which will prove to be fatal? Is this the illness which *should be allowed* to be fatal?"[183]

In the first part of life, the answer to this question will most commonly be a resounding "No!" Most young people will want to be treated for a serious illness with the hope of recovering and living for many more years. This will not be true in every case, however. Cystic fibrosis is the most common fatal genetic disease in the United States. The life expectancy of its victims has dramatically increased, but it is still only about 30 years. A 30-year-old with lifelong CF who decides to allow an acute episode to be his or her final illness might be making an appropriate choice. In mid-life most people will want to treat diseases aggressively since they statistically have many years of life expectancy left ahead of them. Most adults work to support themselves and families and look forward to the new opportunities that retirement from that work in later years offer.

As we reach old age, however we define it, our options change, whether we like it or not. More of our life is behind us than it ahead of us even though we don't know how much more lies ahead. Many people find that their remaining life goals are even more important than they were before because they are sharpened by the realization that time is passing. For some, it is time to finally try to write that book or essay or poem. For others, it will be spending time with family and friends, something not possible in their youth and middle age due to the pressures and demands of work. Still others will finally get to play golf every single day.

So when a serious, possibly life-threatening, illness strikes, each person will have to think about the exact nature of that illness, their underlying general state of health, their age and what they have yet to accomplish in the remainder of their life. They need accurate information about the general outcome of persons with their illness while recognizing that generalizations never predict how a specific patient will do. Then they must factor in their deepest personal values before making a decision on how best, for them, to respond to this episode of illness. Because we are each individuals with a unique life story, medical profile, and unfinished life projects, it is very hard to generalize about what people in this situation "should do." The best help I can give is to suggest the most important elements to be considered.

One critical element is a person's individual religious or spiritual understanding of the place of death in human life. If your view of human life is "vitalistic," that is, that life per se is a pearl beyond price and must be preserved at all costs regardless of the burdens that might be imposed by life-sustaining medical treatment, then death is obviously to be postponed to the last instant possible and whatever medical treatment and technology might help achieve that is to be pursued. If your view is that life is valuable only insofar as it allows you to perform certain physical activities, like playing 18 holes of golf daily, and your illness will make that permanently impossible, then you might make entirely different choices.

Most people are somewhere between these polar opposites in their assessment. But first and foremost, how an individual thinks about the value of life and, therefore, the evil of death is a crucial element to be considered. Since these are deep religious, spiritual, and philosophical issues, it is not appropriate to consider them for the first time in the throes of a serious illness. While we may not have articulated them in just these or similar terms, most people do have some understanding of their thoughts about these issues, perhaps as a result of a life lived within a particular community of faith or years of devotion to particular spiritual practices. Once you understand something about your orientation toward the value of life you have an important piece of self-understanding in hand.

Secondly, you need access to accurate information about your diagnosis (what the disease process is) and prognosis (what typically happens to patients with this disease). Remember, this can only be given in terms of large populations of patients and doctors can only make educated guesses about individual patients. Even so, you need as much objective information as possible so you can begin to think about choices. If you have had a stroke, it may make a difference to you whether, in your doctor's experience with other patients, 1 or 10 or 50 or 95 percent of patients who seem to be similar to you (never identical, however) ever walk again and are able to return to playing golf or the piano or typing on a computer. If you are diagnosed with cancer, what are the treatment options for your particular kind and stage? Is surgery possible? Can chemotherapy or radiation therapy help? If you choose them, do they cure or merely palliate the underlying disease? What are the various benefits and burdens of each form of therapy? What are the benefits and burdens of no therapy at all? Is the one-year survival rate of the "average patient" 95 percent or 5 percent? If it is a very low percentage regardless of whatever therapy is attempted, you may want to prioritize your unfinished life projects very carefully so as to use whatever time you have left in the ways most meaningful to you. Alternatively, you may want to commit all of your physical and spiritual energy to fighting off your disease. Or you can do both. It is very important to remember that this is not really an either/or choice. Too often, patients are presented the choice of "fight" or "don't fight" as mutually exclusive options, and they are not. An equally valid and more holistic choice is "to hope for the best while planning for the worst."

As a part of this step, you need objective information about the various treatment options and the benefits and burdens of each. Unfortunately, every medical treatment comes with some burdens. Every drug has side effects; the antibiotic you need to treat your pneumonia may well also give you diarrhea, for example. Most of us know something about the burdens of chemotherapy and radiation therapy, but these must always be compared to the benefits those treatments hold out. You also need information on what the likely scenarios are if you choose not to accept any treatment. How do people die from this disease if not treated? What potential pain issues do you face? If cure seems unlikely even with treatment, how much time on average does treatment "buy" for a patient? What life projects could you accomplish with the gift of that much time?

It is important for people to understand that the presumption in modern medicine is to treat. Daniel Callahan writes that when he interviewed physicians trained after the Second World War, they "told me that they had a moral duty to save life at all costs. The quality of life, the actual prognosis, or the pain induced by zealous treatment were all but irrelevant. The technological imperative to use every possible means to save life was combined with the sanctity-of-life principle in what seemed the perfect marriage of medicine and morality."[184] Thus, within a few years of CPR being developed, it was standard policy that, if a patient died in a hospital, resuscitation was always attempted. Of course, when the patient had just died from widespread cancer or some other incurable illness, we all knew that (1) resuscitation would not be successful and (2) that outcome was good because to resuscitate a person dying of cancer today so she could die again tomorrow was a terrible mistake. But the presumption to "save a life" was so strong that we dared not talk about *not* attempting resuscitating openly among ourselves. Instead, doctors and nurses informally adopted ethically questionable practices like "show codes" where they appeared to attempt resuscitation but deliberately made ineffective choices so as not to risk a successful resuscitation. Another variant of this was a "slow code" in which the team responded slowly to the scene of a cardiac arrest if we thought resuscitation would be cruel and inhumane. These practices were ethically wrong in that they publicly purported to do one thing while actually aiming at the opposite.

When enough doctors and nurses were troubled by this conflict, the idea of writing Do Not Resuscitate orders in patient's charts arose. I was serving as chair of a hospital ethics committee when the medical staff first wrestled with a DNR policy and I remember vividly the impassioned debate about "not doing everything" to save a life versus not inflicting "painful and futile and medically inappropriate treatment on patients with incurable diseases."

Doctors also enjoy doing whatever is the work of their chosen specialty. Surgeons like to operate. Anesthesiologists like to anesthetize patients. Invasive cardiologists like to perform cardiac catheterizations and do angioplasties. This does not mean that ethical surgeons operate on healthy people simply because they enjoy operating. But since doctors derive satisfaction from doing their chosen work, left to our own devices we will *tend* to do what we have been trained to do. Therefore doctors who treat cancer, for example, will usually suggest that their patients accept treatment.

As you begin to integrate all of this information (something that does not happen instantly; it is a process and takes time), you are working towards acknowledging the fact that, like it or not, this present illness *might* be the one that will be fatal. If that is how it works out, how do you want to spend whatever time you have? Is your priority to wring as much time as possible from your illness? Then starting treatment as soon as possible is the game plan. If your highest priority is spending time with family and friends, even if that means not attempting possible therapies that would require extended time in the hospital or leave you unable to pursue valued activities, then a palliative care/hospice setting is the better choice for you. Many combinations of choices are possible. The exact combinations of facts as to the critical illness and underlying state of health cannot be predicted precisely in advance. The frail elderly (the largest number of Americans who die each year, about 40 percent) fall into a category in which the fatal illness is a "physiological challenge that would have been a minor annoyance earlier in life—influenza, urinary infection, pneumonia, or a broken bone."[185] For all these reasons, you can see that much of your thinking needs to have taken place in advance of the critical illness when time for decision-making is necessarily short and the choices are both complex and life-changing.

Of course, it is wise to remember that hypothetical choices made about a situation we are not currently facing often change when the situation becomes real, and that is to be expected. A fellow anesthesiology resident asked me on more than one occasion to promise to euthanize him should he ever become paralyzed and be permanently confined to a wheelchair. I told him that I could not do so as it violated both my medical and personal moral codes. I am certain that many, many people feel that way about being "handicapped," to use the old term. Yet disability theorists and advocates point out, "Wheel-chairs do not confine; they liberate. Voice synthesizers aid communication for people who can no longer speak. Diapers or catheters are akin to eyeglasses. Using the services and skills of a personal assistant who helps them get into and out of bed, eat their meals, or travel to their next appointment is no more shameful or embarrassing than it is for a non-disabled person to work closely with an administrative assistant or to value the expertise of a mechanic, plumber, or the magician who restores data after a computer crash."[186] Actor Christopher Reeve is an example of a person who faced life-changing alterations in his physical capabilities as a result of an accident but who found new ways to continue to use his talents in spite of quadriplegia. I doubt he would have chosen quadriplegia as a hypothetical good for his life, but when the accident occurred, he chose to pursue aggressive rehabilitation strategies and funded research aimed at helping other victims of accidental paralysis.

Callahan believes that we need to ask a different and more probing question with each serious illness: since some illness or other must be fatal, *what are the chances that allowing this illness to be the final one will in fact enhance the final days this patient values most?* If we choose to treat this episode of illness and are successful, what is the likelihood that the *next* illness will allow an equal or better final span?[187] Is this the illness that should be *allowed* to be fatal?

Let me share with you a story to illustrate this point. You have already met my dear friend Coreen who, during the years she helped me care for my mother, became another daughter to my mother and like a sister to me. At that time her own mother, Kay, was diagnosed with an unusual presentation of colon cancer. Kay had not ignored her symptoms, as some people do. She promptly went to her doctor when she first became suspicious that something was wrong. Kay chose to undergo surgery and subsequent chemotherapy for her disease, and initially she got the good result she was hoping for. Unfortunately, however, the cancer later reappeared in her liver. She tried a second round of chemotherapy and this time the side effects were worse and the response of the cancer more limited. When her oncologist suggested a third round with different drugs whose side effects were more challenging, she and Coreen, her only child, talked about her choices. Kay ultimately decided not to undergo further chemotherapy. Her doctor told her he thought she was making the wrong choice and asked her to return in a few days and talk through it with him again and she did so, but she did not change her mind. So far, so good: her doctor had shared his professional opinion with her, listened to her when she disagreed, and asked her to come back again so they could continue a conversation and the doctor could be sure that Kay really understood the implications of her choice not to pursue more therapy. But what Kay and Coreen never thought to ask and the oncologist did not tell them was how Kay would actually die from the natural progression of the cancer in her liver. Nor did he refer them at that point to hospice care, although he did discuss hospice as an option "someday."

Six or eight weeks after Kay decided not to seek further care, Coreen was at my house helping me with an 80th birthday open house for my mother when the phone rang. It was a frantic Kay. She had begun hemorrhaging copious amounts of bright red blood from her rectum and wanted her daughter right away. Kay lived about 30 minutes away. Although Coreen got there as soon as she could, by then Kay was so weak from blood loss that she could hardly stand. Unfortunately the oncologist she had been referred to did not practice at the nearest hospital, so Coreen and her mother, by now barely conscious, had to travel across town to get to the one where he did practice. Circumstances in the real world are often "untidy," and they certainly were for Kay and Coreen

156

this day. It happened to be the Saturday before Easter and when Kay and Coreen finally reached the ER at his hospital, they found that the oncologist was out of town for the weekend. Another oncologist covering for him had no information about Kay or the precise stage of her disease, so he could only offer the general advice that she probably was bleeding because the cancer had replaced so much of her liver that it could no longer make the proteins that allow our blood to clot. She could either have transfusions to replace those proteins or continue to bleed until she died, which would happen within an hour or so.

By now Kay was unconscious from low blood pressure. The ER doctors turned to Coreen for a choice. Since she was the durable power-of-attorney for health care for her mother, she was legally empowered to make this choice but mentally and emotionally unprepared. No one had suggested that a dramatic incident like this might be the outcome of cancer "invading" liver tissue. No one had suggested that death from hemorrhage might be a quick and painless way to die from cancer. No one had suggested that Kay and Coreen might want to talk through what the best response to this scenario would be from Kay's perspective. Now Kay could not contribute to a conversation. Coreen did what almost all of us would do when faced with an unexpected crisis: she voted to rescue her mother by authorizing transfusions. They were given and restored not only Kay's blood pressure but her ability to clot. Within a day and a half she was discharged home.

When her oncologist returned, he suggested that this was the right time to call hospice and that is what they did. Kay lived about six weeks more after this event. Eventually she developed pain (she had been essentially pain-free until then) which was treated by hospice with good, but not perfect, success. She died peacefully in her own home with Coreen caring for her with hospice support. Fortunately for both mother and daughter, passing on the option of a rapid, painless death from blood loss did not lead to a prolonged and painful death from some other mechanism.

Had Kay and Coreen had more information about likely deaths from liver failure including the idea of a sudden, painless episode of life-threatening bleeding, they could have considered whether this illness should be allowed to be fatal. Kay might then have stayed at home with Coreen at her side (but without the support of hospice because she was not yet a patient at that time) or she might have not received transfusions in the ER but been allowed to die there quietly and painlessly. But because no one had ever discussed this scenario and suggested the question, the two had never discussed possible answers, and so Coreen did what seemed right at the time.

The choice to postpone dying on that Saturday gave Kay six more weeks of life. During that time she and Coreen received the support hospice offers, and Kay had the opportunity for last goodbyes that would have been foreclosed by an abrupt death. She also suffered some pain and other troublesome symptoms. Thanks to hospice care, she did not die with uncontrolled pain or away from her home. Not all stories work out so well, however. Had Kay's pain been more difficult to manage, for example, or had other symptoms become very troublesome, she might have lived to regret Coreen's choice in the ER. Thankfully, in this case that did not happen.

Alternatively, we can postulate another scenario. Imagine the exact same set of characters and facts but add a new (and imaginary) fact: Kay's beloved grandson was going to be married in two weeks and she wanted more than anything to attend. She knew it was highly unlikely that she would live long enough to see a great-grandchild, but she certainly wanted to be there for that ceremony. Now the choice to transfuse Kay in the ER became quite different. The transfusions were not particularly painful or burdensome and they did control the bleeding. In this second, hypothetical, story Kay rallied and was extremely grateful to be able to attend the wedding.

To ask, "Should this be the illness that is allowed to be fatal?" *does not imply* that we should always choose to allow the patient to die now. It is simply asking a question whose answer must depend on the exact constellation of facts surrounding that particular patient at that instant in time. It is not a coded signal never to treat. The choice to treat is always a gamble about what the future might hold, both in terms of benefits and burdens and what the ultimately fatal illness will be like. But, depending on a patient's and family's values, it might well be a question worth asking because this particular illness at this particular time might represent a good confluence between the inevitability of death from some disease and the patient's current life situation.

So what would medicine look like if we took Callahan's challenge to incorporate death as the necessary and inevitable endpoint of medical care? First, the tension between theoretical and clinical medicine would disappear. Clinical medicine has always had to deal with the fact that people die. Now theoretical medicine would also acknowledge that people eventually die of something despite the "war" on individual diseases. Second, hospice/palliative care would become usual, conventional medical care for the seriously ill and the dying, not special programs. With every significant, potentially life-threatening illness doctors would help patients and families to decide if this was likely a fatal illness—and whether it should be allowed to be. Their answers would then guide the medical choices that were made.

CHAPTER 9

"The Rules" According to Dr. Buckley

Congratulations! You have persevered through some difficult material and, despite the discomfort raised by the subject, stuck with it. In this final chapter, I want to leave you with a succinct review of the most important points I have tried to make in the text. I developed these "rules" for a class at Hiram College. While their title, inspired by the sitcom *Seven Rules for Dating My Daughter*, is a bit frivolous, their content is anything but. So here goes.

Rule #1: Death is not optional.   Pretending you are immortal may seem easier at present, but it does not change your ultimate fate. If you want some control over how your life ends, you must face the fact that you will die someday and begin to prepare for that day right now. If you don't, the experience of the overwhelming majority of people shows that you will be so panicked when a potentially fatal illness is diagnosed that you will not be able to think calmly and effectively. People who put off the discomforting work of thinking about the end of their lives most often end up swept away in the currents of medical practice and die in a hospital or nursing home. But you *can* have control over many aspects of the end of your life.

Rule #2: It takes planning to achieve death on your own terms.   Some of us will die in accidents and not have the opportunity to shape our dying. But most of us have the chance, if we only make use of the time. Think about how you would like your death to be and then plan so that your wishes can be honored. Do not put off doing so: remember that Karen Ann Quinlan, Nancy Cruzan, and Terri Schiavo were all in their twenties when they suffered their catastrophic events. Youth does not guarantee immortality. You can expect your desires to change as you age, and plans can always be changed to accommodate your updated wishes. These changes are much easier to accomplish than the initial planning process, which is the daunting one. So plan earlier rather than later, when it may be too late to plan at all.

Rule #3: Document your desires for the end of your life in advance directives.   Solidifying your vision of an "ideal" end to your life story may be a solitary endeavor or it may require discussions with family and friends. Your attempts to broach the subject may be rebuffed as "premature" or "morbid," but please persist; your local hospice has booklets with helpful conversation-starters. (The Appendix reproduces one such document from the Hospice of the Western Reserve.) When you have made your choices, you need to execute the form or forms of advance directives that are legal and necessary in your state. Check the website of your state bar association for the documents you will need. In many states you will require a health care proxy, a person to hold your healthcare power of attorney. It is prudent to name at least two people so that if the primary person can or will not serve, the second can begin to make decisions on your behalf. Select these people with care, for you are asking them to assume a great responsibility. Then discuss your wishes, values, and hopes for your death with them so they have a strong insight into your choices.

Rule #4: Do not allow yourself or a relative or friend to die with uncontrolled pain.   Hospice has turned end-of-life pain management into an art form, one excellent reason for involving it in the vast majority of deaths. In the very rare case when expert pain management fails, remember that terminal sedation is an option of last resort and abolishes all pain. Palliative care can assist with troublesome symptoms earlier in an illness and increasingly this will become more widely available. Remember that seriously ill patients probably won't have the energy to battle an unresponsive "system," so be prepared to be an advocate for your loved one or friend if necessary. Do not permit suffering from poorly treated pain to continue! It is unnecessary.

Rule #5: Dehydration at the end of life is neither painful nor associated with suffering.   According to hospice nurses, the group with the greatest current reservoir of experience dealing with dying people, dehydration seems to cause the release of natural endorphins, chemicals in our brains that make us feel good. It makes sense that evolution might have developed such a mechanism, as dehydration is a primary terminal event in nearly all animal deaths, including, until recently, human beings. Do not accept the use of the term "starving to death" for refusal of food and water at the end of the dying process. Starving is indeed a painful experience for otherwise healthy people, but as death becomes imminent, the lack of desire for food and water is a normal part of the body's shutting down. As long as their mouths and lips are kept moistened, dying people do not "suffer" from lack of what can no longer sustain their bodies.

Rule #6: Medical practice as "warfare" is not a helpful metaphor and needs to be jettisoned.   At least at the end of life. The idea of waging war on disease covertly suggests that when all diseases have been defeated, humans will become immortal. But that is simply not true, and perhaps not even desirable. Most people today will contract one or more chronic diseases that they will manage but never "defeat." In wartime we do not manage anything with our enemy. Some people experience an illness as a time of rebirth, another phenomenon the warfare metaphor omits. Seeing death, even in extreme old age, as a battle lost, leads the medical system to postpone discussions about end-of-life issues until too late in the process and to over-treat the dying. No longer seeing death as the "great Enemy" in every illness would allow hospice to become a standard part of medical practice, rather than a special program utilized by only a few persons.

Rule #7: Withholding and withdrawing medical treatments are morally equal actions.   The bioethical and religious communities have spent decades debating this conclusion and have reached a very robust consensus. This is actually good news for patients, because it means that when a health situation is not clear, doctors can try treatments for a time to see if they will be beneficial. If they prove not to help, they can be stopped without moral qualms.

Rule #8: Competent adults have the legal right to refuse life-sustaining or life-saving treatments. This has been recognized by the U.S. Supreme Court as a "liberty interest" or "negative right," a right to be left alone. Such refusals are not morally like committing suicide even if they result in death. Some people are concerned that choosing not to accept life-sustaining treatments will invalidate their life insurance policies, most of which deny benefits when the policy holder commits suicide. But the Supreme Court's decision has made it clear that patients and their health care proxies can choose to forego or stop such treatments when they are unwanted. This includes the right to refuse food and fluids.

Rule #9: There is a crucial difference between pain and suffering. The medical profession can and must treat pain, a physical phenomenon, but we have no special training or expertise to treat suffering, which is often spiritual or existential in nature. Suffering people need to be referred to those who have the expertise to help them, often religious advisers. Society should not expect medicine to "treat" suffering with a lethal injection. Poorly treated pain as a physical phenomenon indeed leads to suffering. Do not allow that to occur. It is not necessary. If your doctor cannot manage your pain adequately, get another physician who can. See Rule #4.

Rule #10: We are profoundly shaped by the deaths we witness, especially in our own families. When deaths are poorly managed, when dying people suffer from isolation from their loved ones and friends, when pain is not adequately controlled, the anguish of losing a loved one is magnified by needless suffering. But medicine already knows how to mitigate pain using palliative care and hospice programs. Now you know about them, too. Persons who are willing to be proactive, to decide how and where they wish to spend their final days and then execute the appropriate advance directives to ensure that their choices are honored, can prevent needless emotional suffering. In fact, some dying people and their families experience real personal growth during the dying process.

Of course, death still stings. It ruptures the most profound human relationships, and it is never easy to endure the loss of one we love. But we can make death "tame," if still unwelcome. People can choose to die in their homes, surrounded by friends and family, rather than in hospitals hooked up to a variety of machines. We have many, many choices nowadays, if only we elect to make use of them. I hope this book has introduced you to information you did not know and motivated you to make use of your "choice muscles" to shape the end of your life in the manner you choose.

Afterword

As you learned in the Introduction, I had a cancer scare as I was starting to write this book. That particular episode proved not to be cancer. However, the next time I was not so lucky. In early 2009 I was diagnosed with cancer of the uterus. As I underwent months of surgery, radiation, and chemotherapy, I moved from considering my own death as a distant, hypothetical event to one possibly much closer than I liked. That experience sent me back to review the contents of this book from a new vantage point. Did I still believe what I had written?

Yes, I do. More confidently than ever I stand behind the information I have shared with you in these pages. My diagnosis led to some uncomfortable discussions with my family. I have advance directives in place but it seemed prudent to discuss the disposition of certain family "treasures" in my home should something catastrophic happen during surgery. This was very difficult for me and for the brother who is the executor of my will. When I started chemotherapy, I had to decide if I would agree to suspend the DNR order in my living will on the days when I was receiving treatment. Each one of these events made me realize how crucial it is to have done some preparatory thinking about difficult end-of-life issues. It is overwhelming to learn that you have a potentially fatal disease, and it takes quite a bit of time to adjust to that harsh new reality. But decisions about treatments like surgery often cannot wait while you adjust to the diagnosis and begin to think more clearly. If you have done none of the thinking I recommend in this book, you are even more overwhelmed and panicked.

So, do the uncomfortable work I have outlined. Face the fact that you will die someday and begin today to plan for how you envision that end occurring. Document your choices according to the laws of the state where you reside in advance directives. Give your family the gift of only needing to honor your choices, not making life and death choices on your behalf when they do not know what you wanted for yourself. It is the best final gift you can ever give them.

End Notes

Introduction

1. Daniel Callahan, "When Self-Determination Rums Amok," *The Hastings Center Report*, March-April, 1992, 55.

Chapter 1

2. Daniel Callahan, *The Troubled Dream of Life: In Search of a Peaceful Death* (New York: Simon & Schuster, 1993), 33.

3. Abigail Van Buren, "Dear Abby." *Cleveland Plain Dealer*, June 5, 2006, E2.

4. Thomas Lynch, "Good Grief," *AARP Magazine*, July-August, 2005, 29.

5. Ibid.

6. Ibid., 28-29.

7. Thomas Lynch, "Good Grief," *The Christian Century*, July 26, 2003, 22.

8. Callahan, op. cit., 26.

9. Ibid.

10. Callahan, op. cit., 12.

11. Ibid., 54.

12. Melinda Kapalin, personal communication.

13. Melinda Kapalin (2006) "Gifts of Grace from Terminally-Ill Children: The Benefits of Children Writing Their Own Life Stories," Unpublished Master's degree capstone paper, Hiram College, Hiram, OH, 10.

14. Karen Donley-Hayes, "At Face Value," *Journal of the American Medical Association*, June 21, 2006, Vol. 295, No. 23, 2701-2.

15. Regina Brett. "George, canoe not done yet." *Cleveland Plain Dealer*, July 7, 2006, B1.

16. Ibid.

17. James F. Childress, "Metaphor and Analogy," *Encyclopedia of Bioethics* (New York: Simon & Schuster Macmillan, 1995), 1766.

18. Anne Hunsaker Hawkins, *Reconstructing Illness: Studies in Pathography* (West Lafayette, IN: Purdue University Press, 1993) cited in Childress, op. cit. 1766.

19. Dolores Krieger. *Foundations for Holistic Health Nursing Practices: The Renaissance Nurse* (New York, Lippincott Williams & Wilkins: 1981) cited in Matt Stolick. "Fostering True Hopes of Terminally Ill Patients." *BIO Quarterly* Vol. 17, no. 2, 3.

20. Ibid., 4.

21. Katherine C. Grier, *Pets in America: A History* (Chapel Hill, NC: University of North Carolina Press, 2006), 226.

22. Callahan, op. cit., 190, emphasis added.

23. Ibid., 58.

24. Ibid., 51.

25. Ibid., 51.

Chapter 2

26. William H. Colby, *Unplugged: Reclaiming Our Right to Die in America* (New York: American Management Association, 2006), 237.

27. C. E. Schneider, *The Practice of Autonomy: Patients, Doctors, and Medical Decisions* (New York: Oxford University Press, 1998) cited in Fagerlin, Angela and Carl E. Schneider, "Enough: The Failure of the Living Will," *The Hastings Center Report* 34:2 (2004): 33.

28. Centers for Disease Control and Prevention, National Center for Health Statistics, "Deaths/Mortality," http://www.cdc.gov/nchs/fastats/deaths.htm.

29. SUPPORT Principal Investigators. "A Controlled Trial to Improve Care for Seriously Ill Hospitalized Patients: The Study to Understand Prognoses and Preferences for Outcome and Risks of Treatment (SUPPORT), *Journal of the American Medical Association* 274: 1591-98 (1995).

30. Joanne Lynn et al., "Prognoses of Seriously Ill Hospitalized Patients on the Days before Death," *New Horizons*, 5: 56-61 (1997), quoted in Colby, op. cit., 111.

31. Callahan, op. cit., 44.

32. Earl A. Grollman, "Ethical Wills: Values with the Valuables," *Frontline* (Summer, 2002) 1.

Chapter 3

33. Maggie Callanan and Patricia Kelley, *Final Gifts* (New York: Bantam Books, 1993), 83.

34. Bruce Jennings, Gregory E. Kaebnick, and Thomas H. Murray, eds. *Improving End of Life Care: A Hastings Center Special Report,* November-December, 2005, 45.

35. "Hospice: A Service That Satisfies—But Is Unavailable to Many Dying Americans," *State Initiatives in End-of-Life Care* 17 (November, 2002), 2.

36. Doyle, D., Hanks G.W., MacDonald, N. *Oxford Textbook of Palliative Medicine,* 2nd Ed. (Oxford: Oxford University Press, 1998) cited in Timothy E. Quill, *Caring for Patients at the End of Life: Facing An Uncertain Future Together* (Oxford, Oxford University Press, 2001), 4.

37. Jennings, op. cit., 44.

38. Greg A. Sachs, "Sometimes Dying Still Stings," *Journal of the American Medical Association* (2000;284), 2423.

Chapter 4

39. Elaine Pagels, *Adam, Eve and the Serpent* (New York, NY: Random House, 1988), 39, cited in Joe Baroody, "Life and Death Matters: Toward a Sanctity of Death," *The Journal of Pastoral Care* Fall, 1999, Vol. 53, No. 3, 298.

40. American Medical Association Policy 22.21. Available through the AMA Policy Finder at *http://ama-assn.org/ama/pub/about-ama/our-people/house-delegates/polifyfinder.page*

41. Ronald Dworkin, *Life's Dominion: An Argument About Abortion, Euthanasia and Individual Freedom* (New York: Vintage Books, 1994), 13.

42. Callahan, op. cit., 59.

43. Albert Jonsen, *The New Medicine and the Old Ethics* (Cambridge, MA: Harvard University Press, 1990), 52, quoted in Kohn, Martin. "On Futility." *Bio-Quarterly* Vol. 8, No. 2, 1999, 1.

44. Howard Brody. *The Healer's Power*. (New Haven: Yale University Press, 1992), 182, quoted in Kohn, op. cit., 2.

45. Ibid.

46. Regina Brett, "Should we fight to preserve life?" *The Cleveland Plain Dealer,* April 3, 2005, B1.

47. J. Morris, S. Morris. "ADI: Assessment measures for use with frail elders." In J. Teresi, M. Lawton, D. Holmes, M. Ory. eds. *Measurement in Elderly Chronic Care Populations.* (New York: Springer, 1997), 130-56. cited in Muriel Gillick. "Rethinking the Role of Tube Feeding in Patients with Advanced Dementia." *New England Journal of Medicine*, Vol. 342, No. 3, January 20, 2000: 207.

48. R. M. McCann, W.J. Hall, A. Groth-Juncker. "Comfort Care for Terminally Ill Patients: The Appropriate Use of Nutrition and Hydration," *Journal of the American Medical Association*, Vol. 272, 1994: 1263-6, quoted in Gillick, op. cit., 207.

49. Colby, op. cit., 158.

50. American Medical Association Policy Finder, "E-2.20 Withholding or Withdrawing," *http://ama-assn.org/ama/pub/about-ama/our-people/house-delegates/polifyfinder.page.* accessed July 12, 2006.

51. Colby, op. cit., 156.

52. Printz L.A., "Terminal dehydration: A compassionate treatment," *Archives of Internal Medicine* 152:697-700, 1992, cited in Joyce V. Zerwekh, "Dehydration: A Natural Analgesic When Death Is Imminent," *Critical Care Specialist* Vol. 1, No. 1, July-August, 1993, 3.

53. Colby, op. cit., 40.

54. Callahan, op. cit., 81.

55. M. Kaw, G. Segas, "Long-Term Follow-up of Consequences of Percutaneous Endoscopic Gastrostomy (PEG) Tubes in Nursing Home Patients." *Digestive Disease Science* 1994:39: 738-43, cited in Gillick, op. cit., 206.

56. Gillick, op. cit., 206.

57. Barry Siegel. "A Debate over Life after Death." *Los Angeles Times* 10 Feb 1997. http://articles.latimes.com/1997-02-10/mews.mn-27239_1-brain-death. Accessed 10 April 2011.

58. Albert R. Jonsen, "What does life support support?" *The Pharos* Winter, 1987, 4.

59. Ibid., 7.

60. Ibid.

61. Michael Kirsch, M.D., "Organ donation stirs life-or-death debate," *The Cleveland Plain Dealer*, June 28, 2003, E3, emphasis added.

62. A.J. Rosin, M. Sonnenblick. "Autonomy and Paternalism in Geriatric Medicine: The Jewish Ethical Approach to Issues of Feeding Terminally Ill Patients, and to Cardiopulmonary Resuscitation," *Journal of Medical Ethics* 1998;24: 44-8, quoted in Gillick, op. cit., 208.

63. Allen Verhey, *The Christian Century*, April 19, 2005, 9.

64. Ibid., 9-10.

65. Ibid., 10.

66. Ibid.

67. Ibid.

68. Ibid.

69. *The Christian Century*, April 19, 2005, 15.

70. Ibid.

71. Ibid., 14.

72. Ibid.

73. Ibid., 15.

74. Callahan, op. cit., 183.

75. Ibid., 183-4.

76. Ibid., 184.

77. Ibid., 59.

78. Pagels, op. cit., 127-150, cited in Baroody, op. cit., 298.

79. Callahan, op. cit., 70.

80. Ibid., 71.

81. Colby, op. cit., 42.

82. Ibid., 157.

83. Tom L. Beauchamp and LeRoy Walters, *Contemporary Issues in Biomedical Ethics*, 6th Edition (Belmont, CA: Wadsworth, 2003), 4.

84. Ibid., 4-7.

85. Callahan, op. cit., 41.

86. Ibid.

87. Ibid., 89.

88. Ibid., 66.

89. Bruce Jennings, Gregory E. Kaebnick, and Thomas H. Murray, eds. *Improving End of Life Care: A Hastings Center Special Report*, November-December, 2005, 14.

90. Callahan, op. cit., 70.

91. Ibid.

92. David Hume cited in James Rachels, *The End of Life: Euthanasia and Morality* (Oxford: Oxford University Press, 1986), 163.

93. Callahan, op. cit., 71.

94. James Rachels, "Active and Passive Euthanasia," *New England Journal of Medicine*, Vol. 292, no. 2 (January 9th, 1975), 79.

95. Ibid., 80.

96. Callahan, op. cit., 77.

97. Ibid., 78.

98. Baroody, op. cit., 299.

99. Ibid.

100. Ibid., 301.

101. Helmut Thielicke, *Living With Death* (Grand Rapids, MI: William B. Eerdmans Publishing Co., 1983), 79-80; quoted in Baroody, op. cit., 302.

102. Ibid., 307.

103. Ibid.

104. John B. Cobb, Jr. *Matters of Life and Death* (Louisville, KY: John Knox Press, 1991), 48.

105. Callahan, op. cit., 180.

106. Ibid.

107. Ibid., 185.

Chapter 5

108. Callahan, op. cit., 95.

109. Ibid., 94.

110. Rachels, James. *The End of Life: Euthanasia and Morality.* New York: Oxford UP, 1986, 152.

111. Daniel Callahan. "Self-Determination Run Amok," *The Hastings Center Report,* March-April, 1992, 55.

Chapter 6

112. Block, Susan D. "Psychological Considerations, growth and transcendence at the End of Life: The Art of the Possible." *Journal of the American Medical Association* 285:22 (13 June 2001): 2898.

113. Weisman, Avery. *Coping with Cancer.* Ney York, NY: McGraw Hill, 1979, quoted in Block, op. cit., 2899.

114. Ibid.

115. Ibid., 2902.

116. Baines, Barry K. "Ethical Wills: Preserving Your Legacy of Values." http://www.cancerlynx.com/ethical_wills.html. 1.

117. Ibid.

118. Block, op. cit., 2901.

119. McHugh, Paul R. "The Kevorkian Epidemic." *The American Scholar* 66 (winter 1997), 16-17.

120. Ibid., 17.

121. Block, op. cit., 2901.

122. Ibid.

123. McHugh, op. cit., 18.

124. Block, op. cit., 2901.

125. Ibid.

126. Stolick, Matt. "Overcoming the tendency to Lie to Dying Patients." *American Journal of Hospice and Palliative Care* 19:1 (January/February 2002), 29.

127. Ibid., 30-31.

128. Stolick, Matt. "Fostering True Hopes of Terminally Ill Patients." *BIO Quarterly* 17:2 (Summer 2006), 3.

129. Krieger, Delores. *Foundations for Holistic Nursing Practices: The Renaissance Nurse.* New York, NY: Lippincott, Williams and Wilkins (June 1981); quoted in Stolick, Ibid., 4.

130. Stolick, Ibid., 4-5.

Chapter 7

131. Callahan, op. cit., 41.

132. Ibid., 41.

133. McHugh, op. cit., 23.

134. Hardwick, John. "Is There a Duty to Die?" *The Hastings Center Report* 27.2 (March-April 1997).

135. "Holland: Bending the Rules?" BBC News 28 Nov 2000. http://news. bbc.co.uk/1/hi/health/background_briefings/euthanasia/331270.stm. Accessed 10 April 2011.

136. Ruskin, Paul E. "Aging and Caring." *Journal of the American Medical Association* 284 (2000): 2423.

137. Coope, Christopher. "Death with Dignity." *The Hastings Center Report* 22.2 (March-April 1992): 37.

138. Ibid., 38. Italics in original.

139. Keizer, Garret. "Life Everlasting: The Religious Right and the Right to Die." *Harper's Magazine* Feb 2005: 6.

140. Dworkin, Ronald, Thomas Nagel, Robert Nozick, John Rawls, Thomas Scanlon, and Judith Jarvis Thomson. ("Assisted Suicide: The Philosophers' Brief." New York Review of Books, 27 March 1997) quoted in Coope, op. cit., 38.

141. Ibid.

142. Williams, Marjorie. "Death Is Not a Matter of Policy or Control." *Cleveland Plain Dealer* 22 Nov 1999.

143. McHugh, op. cit., 22.

144. Ibid., 16.

145. Lerner, Barron H. "A Calculated Departure: For Someone in Good Health, Can Suicide Ever Be a Rational Choice?" *Washington Post* 2 March 2004: 6-7.

146. "The Hippocratic Oath." www.nim.nih.gov/hmed/greek/greek_oath.html, accessed January 13, 2013.

147. "Euthanasia." American Medical Association Policy 22.21. http://www.ama-assn.org/ama/pub/physicianresources/medical-ethics/code-medicalethics/opinion221.page, accessed January 13, 2013.

148. "It's Over, Debbie." *Journal of the American Medical Association* 259.2 (* Jan 1988): 272.

149. Quill, Timothy E. "Death and Dignity: A Case of Individualized Decision Making." *New England Journal of Medicine* 324.10 (7 March 1991):691-694.

150. Ibid., 692.

151. Ibid., 693.

152. Wolf, Susan M. "Holding the Line on Euthanasia." *The Hastings Center Report* Special Supplement, Jan-Feb 1989:13.

153. Ibid., 14.

154. Keizer, op. cit., 6.

155. Callahan, Daniel. "When Self-Determination Runs Amok." The Hastings Center Report 22.2 (March-April 1992): 55.

156. Hendin, Herbert. *Seduced by Death: Doctors, Patients and the Dutch Cure.* New York: W. W. Norton & Co., 1997, 135.

157. Ibid., 142.

158. "Holland: Bending the Rules." BBC News. http://news.bbc.co.uk/1/hi/health/background_briefings/euthanasia/331270.stm, 2.

159. "Euthanasia Controls Failing." http://news.bbc.co.uk/2/hi/health/280034.stm., 1.

160. "Euthanasia in the Netherlands." International Task Force. http://www.internationaltaskforce.org/fctholl.htm, 3.

161. Ibid., 17.

162. Ibid., 23.

163. Ibid., 26.

164. Ibid., 32.

165. "Holland: Bending the Rules." 2.

166. Hendin, op. cit., 47.

167. Ibid., 86.

168. Ibid., 71.

169. Ibid., 57.

170. Ibid., 79-80.

171. Ibid., 93.

172. Smith, Wesley J. "Noxious Nitschke." http://nationalreview.com/zcript/primntpage.p?ref=smithw/smith200411150826.asp 1.

173. Ibid., 1-2.

174. Ibid., 2.

175. "Euthanasia in the Netherlands." 22.

176. McHugh, op. cit., 19.

177. Ibid., 25-27.

178. Ibid., 27.

Chapter 8

179. Callahan. *The Troubled Dream of Life.*, op. cit., 188-191.

180. Ibid., 62-67.

181. Ibid., 76-82.

182. Ibid., 76.

183. Ibid., 190.

184. Jennings, Bruce, Gregory E. Kaebnick, and Thomas H. Murray, eds. "Improving End of Life Care: Why Has It Been So Difficult?" *Hastings Center Special Report,* 6.

185. Ibid., 16.

186. Ibid., 33.

187. Ibid., 190-191.

References

Alsop, Stuart. "The Right to Die with Dignity." *Good Housekeeping* Aug. 1974, quoted in Rachels, James. *The End of Life: Euthanasia and Morality.* Oxford: Oxford UP, 1986.

Anderson, Megory. *Sacred Dying: Creating Rituals for Embracing the End of Life* 2nd ed. New York, Marlowe & Company, 2003.

> Anderson says her book is about bringing spirituality, through ritual, into the physical act of dying. She explores simple, achievable ways to create sacred space around the dying, the use of rituals to let go of emotional burdens, rituals to comfort and release the dying body, and the use of music to create transcendence and healing. This book will help those who have questions and concerns about practical ways to address many of the spiritual issues that accompany the dying process.

"Background About Euthanasia in the Netherlands." Patients Rights Council. *http://www.patientsrightscouncil.org/site/holland-background.* Accessed 10 April 11.

Baroody, Joe. "Life and Death Matters: Toward a Sanctity of Death." *The Journal of Pastoral Care* 53.3 (Fall 1999): 298-307.

Beauchamp, Tom L., LeRoy Walters, Jeffrey P. Kahn, and Anna C. Mastroianno, eds. *Contemporary Issues in Bioethics*, 7th ed. (Belmont, Cal.: Thomson Wadsworth, 2008).

> A wonderful general introduction to bioethics from the Kennedy Institute of Ethics at Georgetown University. Each edition updates the essays in the volume and each section starts with very helpful introductory material. Chapter 6, "Death and Dying," might be useful to readers as a general introduction to the ethical issues which often accompany decisions at the end of life.

Block, Susan D. "Psychological Considerations, Growth, and Transcendence at the End of Life: The Art of the Possible." *Journal of the American Medical Association* 285.22 (13 June 2001): 2898-2904.

Brett, Regina. "George, canoe not done yet." *Cleveland Plain Dealer*, July 7, 2006, B1.

Brett, Regina. "Should we fight to preserve life?" *The Cleveland Plain Dealer,* April 3, 2005, B1.

Byock, Ira, M.D. *Dying Well: Peace and Possibilities at the End of Life.* New York: Riverhead Books, 1997.

> Byock, a former president of the American Academy of Hospice and Palliative Medicine, has been a prominent spokesperson for the hospice movement. In this book he shares stories of patients facing death on their own terms with the help of hospice care, emphasizing the possibilities for love and reconciliation in the face of tragedy, pain and conflict. Byock's goal is to make the end of life as meaningful and precious as the beginning.

Callahan, Daniel. *The Troubled Dream of Life: In Search of a Peaceful Death.* Washington, D.C.: Georgetown UP, 2000.

> Callahan is a co-founder of The Hastings Center, one of the two major bio-ethical think tanks in America. He served as its president from 1969 until 1996. He has written extensively on biomedical ethical issues, including this book focused on issues at the end of life.

Callahan, Daniel. "Pursuing a Peaceful Death." *The Hastings Center Report,* (July-August, 1993), 33-38.

Callahan, Daniel. "When Self-Determination Run Amok." *The Hastings Center Report*, 22 2 (March/April, 1992), 52-55.

Callanan, Maggie and Patricia Kelley. *Final Gifts: Understanding the Special Awareness, Needs and Communications of the Dying.* New York: Bantam Books, 1992.

> A small but important volume by two hospice nurses based on their years of experience with dying patients. It provides useful information not only for families accompanying a dying loved one but for those who are unfamiliar

with the dying process and thus may miss important communications from dying loved ones.

Cobb, John B., Jr. *Matters of Life and Death*. Louisville: Westminster/John Knox Press, 1991.

> A reflection on life and death from an eminent American Christian theologian and teacher. It may be helpful in dealing with the spiritual issues which arise when we contemplate our own deaths in the future. Cobb, a major explicator of process theology, addresses life and death from a progressive viewpoint which may be new to those whose background is more conservative or fundamentalist.

Colby, William H. *Long Goodbye: The Deaths of Nancy Cruzan*. Carlsbad, Cal.: Hay House, 2002.

> A detailed recounting of the story of Nancy Cruzan, a young woman who became vegetative following a car accident. 7 years later her family went to court to ask permission to remove the feeding tube that was keeping Nancy's body alive. The case went to the U.S. Supreme Court as the first right-to-die case. Colby was the attorney who became involved with the Cruzans early in their struggle so he writes from a first-hand perspective.

Colby, William H. *Unplugged: Reclaiming Our Right to Die in America*. New York: AMACOM, 2006.

> Written after *Long Goodbye*, this book turns to a more general look at why modern medicine has created such morally complex problems at the end of life. It is based on court records, personal interviews, and Colby's first-hand vantage point as a leading legal expert in end-of-life issues. Although the book is written in non-technical language, he does not shy away from the complexities often involved in making medical decisions at the end of life, especially when patients cannot speak for themselves.

"A Controlled Trial to Improve Care for Seriously Ill Hospitalized Patients: The Study to Understand Prognoses and Preferences for Outcome and Risks of Treatment (SUPPORT)." *Journal of the American Medical Association* 274 (1995): 1591-98.

Coope, Christopher. "Death with Dignity." *The Hastings Center Report* 27.5 (Sept.-Oct.1997): 37-39.

"Deaths/Mortality." Centers for Disease Control and Prevention, National Center for Health Statistics, *http://www.cdc.gov/nchs/fastats/deaths.htm*. Accessed 10 April 2011.

Donley-Hayes, Karen. "At Face Value." *Journal of the American Medical Association*, 295.23 (June 21, 2006): 2701-2.

Dunn, Hank. *Hard Choices for Loving People: CPR, Artificial Feeding, Comfort Care, and the Patient with a Life Threatening Illness*. Lansdowne, VA: A&A, 2001.

> Dunn is a graduate of the Southern Baptist Theological Seminary in Louisville, KY and since 1983 has been a full-time nursing home and hospice chaplain. In this small work he uses his years of experience with dying patients and their families to discuss in practical terms many of the difficult issues which may arise as death approaches.

Dworkin, Ronald. *Life's Dominion: An Argument About Abortion, Euthanasia and Individual Freedom* (New York: Vintage Books, 1994).

> This small book is an extended argument about the issues in the title. Dworkin is a professor of law and philosophy who has written about the American legal tradition and Constitutional law as well as divisive social issues.

"Euthanasia." American Medical Association Policy # 22.21, *http://www.ama-assn.org/appa/pf_new/pf_online?f_n=browse&doc=policyfiles/HnE/E-2.21*. Accessed 7/2/2008.

"Euthanasia in Holland." *http://euthanasia.cc/dutch.html*.

"Euthanasia in the Netherlands." International Task Force. *http://www.internationaltaskforce.org/fctholl.htm*.

Fagerlin, Angela and Carl E. Schneider, "Enough: The Failure of the Living Will," *The Hastings Center Report* 34, no. 2 (2004): 33.

Gillick, Muriel, "Rethinking the Role of Tube Feeding in Patients with Advanced Dementia." *New England Journal of Medicine*, 342.3 (20 Jan 2000): 206-210.

Grier, Katherine C. *Pets in America*. Chapel Hill: U of North Carolina P, 2006.

> A history of pet keeping in America, Grier focuses on the changing role of pets in family life, new standards of animal welfare, the problem presented by borderline pets like livestock pets, and the marketing of both animal and pet products.

Grollman, Earl A. "Ethical Wills: Values with the Valuables," *Frontline* (Summer, 2002): 1.

Hartwig, John. "Is There a Duty to Die?" *The Hastings Center Report* 27.2 (March-April 1997): 34-42.

Hendin, Herbert, M.D. *Seduced By Death: Doctors, Patients and the Dutch Cure*. New York: W.W. Norton & Co., 1997.

> Hendin, a psychiatrist, examines the practice of euthanasia in Holland, the first Western country to legalize it, and speculates on how the practice might work if legalized in the US. His book includes many interviews with Dutch doctors reflecting on their experiences providing euthanasia for their patients as well as information from the Dutch Royal Medical Society and Dutch courts.

"The Hippocratic Oath." History of Medicine Division, National Library of Medicine, National Institutes of Health. *http://www.nlm.nih.gov/hmd/greek/greek_oath.html*. Accessed 10 April 2011.

"Holland: Bending the Rules?" BBC News 28 Nov. 2000. *http://news.bbc.co.uk/1/hi/health/background_riefings/euthanasia/331270.st*. Accessed 10 April 2011.

"Hospice: A Service That Satisfies—But Is Unavailable to Many Dying Americans," *State Initiatives in End-of-Life Care* 17 (November, 2002).

"It's Over, Debbie." *Journal of the American Medical Association* 259.2 (8 Jan. 1988): 272.

Jennings, Bruce, Gregory E. Kaebnick, and Thomas H. Murray. "Improving End of Life Care: Why Has It Been So Difficult?" Special Hastings Center Report (Nov.-Dec. 2005): 1-61.

Jonsen, Albert R. "What Does Life Support Support?" *The Pharos* (Winter 1987): 4-7.

Kapalin, Melinda. "Gifts of Grace from Terminally-Ill Children: The Benefits of Children Writing Their Own Life Stories," Unpublished Master's capstone paper, Hiram, OH: Hiram College, 2006.

Keizer, Garret. "Life Everlasting: The religious right and the right to die." *http://www.harpers.org/archive/2005/02/0080411*, p. 6.

Kiernan, Stephen P. *Last Rights: Rescuing the End of Life from the Medical System*. New York: St. Martin's, 2006.

> According to journalist Kiernan, half of people who die in hospitals suffer from severe, untreated pain, only one example he claims shows the sub-standard care of the dying in the US. Too many patients and families experience a nightmare of hospitals, specialists, high-tech treatments and helplessness dealing with a medical system that means well but does not listen.

Kirsch, Michael, M.D. "Organ donations stirs life-or-death debate." *Cleveland Plain Dealer* 28 June 2003: E 3.

Kohn, Martin. "On Futility." *Bio-Quarterly* 8.2 (1999): 1-2.

Lerner, Barron H. "A Calculated Departure: For Someone in Good Health, Can Suicide Ever Be a Rational Choice?" *http://www.biopsychiatry.com/misc/suicide.html.6*.

Levine, Stephen. *A Year To Live: How to Live This Year As If It Were Your Last*. New York: Bell Tower, 1997.

> Most of us go to extraordinary lengths to ignore or deny the fact that eventually each of us will die. Levine claims that preparing for death is one of the most rational and rewarding acts of a lifetime. In this book he shares insights from his year of living as if it was his last.

> Joanne Lynn is one of the physician-founders of the new medical specialty of palliative care. Written expressly for patients and their families by experts from nursing, hospice, counseling and the arts, this book offers

important insights and practical information for those nearing the end of their lives.

Lynch, Thomas. "Good Grief." *AARP Magazine*, July/August 2005: 28-29.

Lynch, Thomas. "Good Grief: An Undertaker's Reflections." *The Christian Century* 26 July 2003.

Lynn, Joanne, M.D. and Joan Harrold, M.D. and The Center to Improve Care of the Dying. *Handbook for Mortals: Guidance for People Facing Serious Illness*. New York, Oxford UP, 1999.

McHugh, Paul R. "The Kevorkian Epidemic." *The American Scholar* 66 Dec., 1996: 15-27.

Nuland, Sherwin B., M.D. *How We Die: Reflections on Life's Final Chapter*. New York: Alfred A. Knopf, 1993.

> Surgeon and teacher Nuland focuses on the mechanisms by which we die, how stroke and heart attack, AIDS and Alzheimer's disease actually kill us. But he uses patient stories to share portraits of dying that help make clear the choices that can be made to allow each of us his or her own death.

Quill, Timothy E., M.D. *Caring for Patients at the End of Life: Facing an Uncertain Future Together* (Oxford: Oxford UP, 2001).

> Timothy Quill is a prominent physician in the area of palliative care as well as the plaintiff in *Vacco v. Quill*, a case ultimately decided by the US Supreme Court in 1997 which found that there was no constitutional guarantee of a "right to die."

Quill, Timothy E. "Death and Dignity: A Case of Individualized Decision Making." *New England Journal of Medicine* 324.10 (7 March 1991): 691-694.

Rachels, James. *The End of Life: Euthanasia and Morality* (Oxford: Oxford UP, 1986).

> A small but important book by philosopher Rachels who defends the practice of euthanasia.

Reich, Warren T. Editor in chief. *Encyclopedia of Bioethics*, 5 vol. New York: Macmillan Library Reference USA, 1995.

> A multi-volume work covering bioethics history and practice up to 1995.

Ruskin, Paul E. "Aging and Caring." *Journal of the American Medical Association* 278.16 (22 Oct. 1997): 1384.

Sachs, Greg A. "Sometimes Dying Still Stings," *Journal of the American Medical Association* 284. 19 (15 Nov. 2000): 2423.

Siegel, Barry. "A Debate Over Life After Death." *Los Angeles Times* 10 Feb 1997. *http://articles.latimes.com/1997-02-10/news/mn-27239_1_brain-death*. Accessed 10 April 11.

Singh, Kathleen Dowling. *The Grace in Dying: A Message of Hope, Comfort, and Spiritual Transformation*. San Francisco, HarperSanFrancisco, 1998.

> Singh proposes an essential unity among dying, contemplative practice and spiritual growth. This is not a book for those who are dying or their families but is meant to be studied by those who are currently well so they might begin spiritual growth which will be helpful when death becomes closer.

Smith, Wesley J. "Noxious Nitschke." *http://nationalreview.com/script/printpage.p?ref=/smithw/smith200411150826.asp*

Stolick, Matt. "Fostering True Hopes of Terminally Ill Patients." *BIO Quarterly* 17.2 (Summer 2006): 3-10.

Stolick, Matt. "Overcoming the tendency to Lie to Dying Patients." *BIO Quarterly* 2.2 (Summer 2000): 1-5.

Tolstoy, Leo. *The Death of Ivan Ilyich*. New York: Penguin Classics, 2008.

> A short novella dealing with the impact of denying impending death and how it isolates the dying from families.

Veatch, Robert M. *Death, Dying and the Biological Revolution: Our Last Quest for Responsibility*. New Haven: Yale UP, 1989.

> Although this is an older book, in it philosopher Veatch explores the philosophical, ethical, legal and public policy aspects of the biological revolution

which now allows medicine to prolong life for many years in ways never before possible. This volume is particularly strong on philosophical, ethical and public policy analysis.

Verhey, Allan. *The Christian Century,* April 19, 2005:9-15.

Webb, Marilyn. *The Good Death: The New American Search to Reshape the End of Life.* New York: Bantam Books, 1997.

> A wide-ranging work by a journalist examining how modern medical technology has led to struggles over end of life decisions that sometimes pit patient and family against hospitals and doctors, insurance companies, religious groups and the law. Organized around individual patient stories used as examples, this is an accessible book which also explores possibilities for achieving one's individual version of a good death.

Williams, Marjorie. "Death is not a matter of policy or control." *Cleveland Plain Dealer* Nov. 22, 1999.

"Withholding or Withdrawing Life-Sustaining Medical Treatment," American Medical Association Policy E-2.20. *http://www.ama-assn.org/ama/pub/about-ama/our-people/house-delegates/policyfinder.page.* Accessed July 12, 2006.

Zerwekh, Joyce V. "Dehydration: A Natural Analgesic When Death Is Imminent," *Critical Care Specialist* 1.1 (July-August 1993): 3.

Other Resources

Advance Care Planning. "Courage in Conversation: A Personal Guide." The Hospice of the Western Reserve, Cleveland, OH. *http://www.hospicewr.org*

Brock, Dan W. "Voluntary Active Euthanasia." *The Hastings Center Report* (March-April 1992): 10-22.

Lo, Bernard, M.D., Gordon Rubenfeld, M.D., M.Sc. "Palliative Sedation in Dying Patients." *Journal of the American Medical Association* 294.14 (12 Oct. 2005): 1810-1816.

Howell, Joseph H. and William F. Sale, eds. *Life Choices: A Hastings Center Introduction to Bioethics*, 2nd ed. Washington, D.C.: Georgetown UP, 2000.

> The two major bioethical think tanks in the US are the Kennedy Institute of Ethics and The Hastings Center. This is their introductory text on the broad field of bioethics. It contains a series of carefully chosen essays and readers might find section V, "Termination of Treatment," to be helpful as introductory material.

Jonsen, Albert R., Robert M. Veatch, and LeRoy Walters, eds. *Source Book in Bioethics: A Documentary History*. Washington, D.C.: Georgetown UP, 1998.

> A collection of important documents which have shaped the field of bioethics, including seminal legal cases and reports from presidential commissions.

Kass, Leon R. "Is There a Right to Die?" *The Hasting Center Report* (Jan.-Feb 1993): 34-43.

Kelly, David F. *Medical Care at the End of Life: A Catholic Perspective* (Washington, D.C.: Georgetown UP, 2006).

> Kelly, professor emeritus of theology and health care at Duquesne University, offers a Roman Catholic perspective on the difficult and painful issues which often arise at the end of life. His book is short and practical.

Quill, Timothy E. *A Midwife through the Dying Process: Stories of Healing and Hard Choices at the End of Life*. Baltimore: Johns Hopkins UP, 1996.

> In this book Quill uses stories about his patients to highlight the many choices for shaping the end of our lives using palliative care and hospice. It is fairly easy reading since the book is organized around stories.

Spiro, Howard M., Mary G. McCrea Curnen and Lee Palmer Wandel, eds. *Facing Death*. New Haven: Yale UP, 1996.

> A collection of essays by medical professionals, theologians, historians, anthropologists, literary scholars and pastors tell about personal experiences dealing with life's ending and how other cultures and religions perceive death and mourn their dead.

Steinbrook, Robert, M.D. and Bernard Lo, M.D. "Artificial Feeding— Solid Ground, Not a Slippery Slope." *New England Journal of Medicine* 318.5 (4 Feb 1988); 286-290.

Recordings

On Our Own Terms: Moyers on Dying.

> Originally broadcast on PBS September, 2000. 4 episodes on 4 videotapes; now also available on DVDs. PDF discussion guide available online at *http:// www.pbs.org/wnet/onourownterms/community/pdf/discussionguide.pdf.* Most public libraries have this series available to check out.

PREPARING FOR THE CONVERSATION

Defining your wishes for end of life care

It is important to give careful consideration for your choices in care. Use this worksheet to help you define those choices in preparation for your *"Courage in Conversation."*

1. My Quality of Life

I would like my doctor to try treatments that may restore an acceptable quality of life so that I may do what I feel is important and necessary. On a scale of 1 to 5, with 1 being very important and 5 not important to me, I rate these issues, which define my quality of life:

	(Please check one)
Being able to recognize my family and friends	① ② ③ ④ ⑤
Being able to communicate with them and knowing I am understood	① ② ③ ④ ⑤
Having the ability to think clearly	① ② ③ ④ ⑤
Being free from pain	① ② ③ ④ ⑤
Being free from symptoms most of the time (nausea, diarrhea, shortness of breath)	① ② ③ ④ ⑤
Being able to eat and drink	① ② ③ ④ ⑤
Being able to control my bladder and bowels	① ② ③ ④ ⑤
Being able to live in my own home	① ② ③ ④ ⑤

2. My Prognosis

If I was very ill and told there was little chance that I would live much longer, it is important that I be able to:

	(Please circle one)
Continue with all possible treatments in the hope that a miracle might happen to restore my health	Yes No Unsure
Be allowed to die with dignity and given medications to alleviate any pain or discomfort I might have	Yes No Unsure

If I were in a coma and my doctors thought there was little hope for regaining consciousness, I would like to:

	(Please circle one)
Be kept alive indefinitely in the hope that future medical advancements would restore my health	Yes No Unsure
Have all treatment discontinued, and no new treatment started	Yes No Unsure

Hospice of the Western Reserve, 300 East 185th St. Cleveland, Ohio 44119
Information 1-800-707-8922   Referrals 1-800-707-8921   www.hospicewr.org

3. Treatments

These are my choices on possible treatments that can be administered if
I should have a terminal illness, dementia or serious stroke or in a coma:

	(Please circle one)		
Surgery	Yes	No	Unsure
CPR to start my heart or breathing if either should stop	Yes	No	Unsure
Medicine for infections (antibiotics)	Yes	No	Unsure
Kidney dialysis	Yes	No	Unsure
A respirator or ventilator to breath for me	Yes	No	Unsure
Food or water through a tube in my vein, nose or stomach	Yes	No	Unsure
Blood transfusions	Yes	No	Unsure

4. The End of the Journey

My last days are an important time to say, "I love you" "Thank you" and "Goodbye." On a
scale of 1 to 5, with 1 being very important and 5 not important to me, I rate these issues,
which define how I would like to spend those days:

	(Please check one)				
At home	1	2	3	4	5
In a hospital	1	2	3	4	5
Surrounded by family and friends	1	2	3	4	5
Free from pain and discomfort	1	2	3	4	5
Being alert, even if I might be in pain	1	2	3	4	5
Having time with my pastor, rabbi, priest or other spiritual advisor	1	2	3	4	5
Having time to address forgiveness, gratitude and love	1	2	3	4	5

5. Notes Section

Now that you have completed this worksheet, which helps to define your choices for end of
life care, it is important to begin thinking about your own "Courage in Conversation."
By sharing your choices with the your loved ones you are giving clear direction to help
guide them through the variety of treatments and options.

You should share your wishes with the person you've chosen to be your health care
advocate as identified in your health care power of attorney document. It is also important
to talk with other loved ones and your trusted advisors (medical, legal and financial
professionals).

Index

A

Abandonment, medical, 13–16
Acceptable death, 97–98
Activities of daily living, dementia and, 25, 69
Adaptive techniques, 112
Addiction, 104–105
Adkins, Janet, 133
Advance directives, 19–38
  copies of, 36–37
  creating, work involved in, 28
  definition of, 19
  early planning of, 20, 161
  end-of-life decisions and, 30–31
  ethical wills and, 37–38, 114
  family conflict and, 33–34
  forms, 28, 161
  laws governing, 19
  as legal document, 28, 30–32
  proxies
    appointing, 31, 32–36, 37, 130, 148, 161
    forms, 19, 44
    importance of, 32, 148, 161
  refusing life-sustaining/life-saving treatments and, 90
  responsibilities of patient in, 27–28, 34
  revising, 36
  witnesses to, 28
  See also Durable power-of-attorney (DPA); End-of-life issues; Living wills
"Aging and Caring" (Ruskin), 127

Alsop, Stewart, 103–104, 106, 107
Alzheimer's disease, 12, 23, 133–134
  See also Dementia
American Board of Hospice and Palliative Care, 58
American Medical Association, 61, 70, 133
Amyotrophic lateral sclerosis (ALS), 13–14, 28, 29, 91, 134, 144–145, 149
Anxiety, 68, 100, 117–118
Appetite at end of life, 50, 69, 70–72
Aries, Philippe, 5–6, 8
Army of Bird-Defenders, 16
Aspiration pneumonia, 68–69, 79
Automated electrical defibrillators (AEDs)
Autonomy, 123–124, 130–131, 132, 140
Awake but unaware, 81–82

B

Baines, Barry, 114
Baroody, A. Joseph, 96–97
Bathing
  after death, 51–52
  bed baths, 25, 45, 47, 57, 127
BBC reports, 139–140
Beauchamp, Tom L., 86
Bed baths, 25, 45, 47, 57, 127
Bedsores, 44
Belgium, euthanasia in, 121, 143
Best interest standard, 148
Bible, 91

Bioethicists, 10–11, 73–75, 89, 93, 120, 135, 148, 162–163
Biographical completeness, 16–17
Black as color of mourning, 3–4
Block, Susan, 111, 113, 116
Bly, Mary, 2
Bowel movements, wiping after.
    See Toileting
Brett, Regina, 66
Bridge technology, 64, 70, 74, 84–85, 89
Brody, Howard, 65
Bush, George W., 74, 80
Butler, James C., xv
Butters, Nelson, 144–146
Byock, Ira, 136

C
Callahan, Daniel, 3, 6, 7–9, 17, 18, 25–26, 71–72, 78–79, 80–81, 89–94, 97–98, 100–101, 107–108, 122, 137–138, 147–150, 153, 155, 159
Callanan, Maggie, 54
Cancer
    dates of death in, predicting, 124
    depression and, 116–117
    hospice stay and, 56–57
    hunger/thirst and, 69
    medical abandonment and, 13
    nutritional state and, 84
    pain, 100, 102, 103–104, 131
    remission, 24
    resuscitation and, 153–154
    scare, 8, 165
    treatment, choosing, 22, 31, 152
    war on, 111, 150
Cardiac catheterization, 154
Cardiopulmonary resuscitation (CPR), 6, 21, 52, 65, 153–154
Caregiver, primary, 45
Catheters, Foley, 47, 155
Cecil Textbook of Medicine, 17

Chabot, Boudewijn, 141
Chaplains, 45, 57, 86, 108, 113
Cheyne-Stokes respirations, 49–50
CHF (Congestive Heart Failure), 22, 24, 40, 41
Children
    Dutch euthanasia and, 140
    dying, 10, 72–74, 98, 116
    grieving, 48, 52, 57
Christian Century, The (magazine), 76
Christian values, 75–80
Chronic obstructive pulmonary Disease (COPD), 22
Chronological age, 16–17
Church, 76–77
    See also Religious tradition/spiritual practices
Church Fathers, 61, 79
Clement of Alexandria, 61
Cleveland Plain Dealer (newspaper), 13, 66
Closure, achieving, 5, 118
Cobb, John B., Jr., 97
Commonweal (magazine), 77
Competent terminally ill patients, 44, 47, 132, 139–140, 163
Condolence, appropriate phrases of, 3
Congestive Heart Failure (CHF), 22, 24, 40, 41
Constipation, 107
Continuous positive airway pressure (CPAP), 40
Conversations. *See under* End-of-life issues
Coope, Christopher, 128–129
COPD (chronic obstructive pulmonary Disease), 22
Coping skills, 111–112
"Courage in Conversation: A Personal Guide to Advance Directives" (Hospice of the Western Reserve), 36

CPAP (continuous positive airway pressure), 40
CPR (cardiopulmonary resuscitation), 6, 21, 52, 65, 153–154
Crick, Nancy, 142
Cruzan, Nancy, 20, 70, 82–84, 161
Cryopreservation, 150
Cull, William, 2
Cure, hoping for, 15, 118–119
Cystic fibrosis, 151

D
Death
  advance planning for, 35, 160–161
  as an evil, 79–80
  brain death and ventilators, 72–73
  death-on-demand, 142–143
  with dignity, 20, 126–130, 134–135
  dream visits from loved ones before, 54–55
  as Great Enemy, 10–11, 16, 17, 18, 122, 162
  hearing and, 50
  imminent, signs of, 49–51
  merciful, 97, 106, 120
  as necessary and inevitable endpoint of medical care, 147–159
    acknowledging, elements to consider in, 151–155
    decision-making and, 148
    nature and, 148–151
    questions to ask with each serious illness, 155–158
    warfare metaphor and, 10–16, 67, 147–150, 159, 162
  peaceful, 8, 12, 15, 118–119
  sanctity of, 95–97
  tame, 5–6, 8
  witnessed, being shaped by, 163–164
"Death and Dignity: A Case of Individualized Decision Making" (Quill), 134

Death of Ivan Illyich, The (Tolstoy), 116
Death-on-demand, 142–143
"Death with Dignity" (Coope), 128
Deceased family members, visits from, 54–55
Decision-making
  best interest standard, 148
  living wills used to guide, 20
  moral, 92–93
  order of precedence for, 20
  surrogate, 148
Dehydration at end of life, 69, 70–72, 162
DeLay, Tom, 71
Delirium, 117–118
Dementia
  activities of daily living and, 25, 69
  difficulty with eating/drinking and, 69
  feeding tubes and, 12, 64, 68–70
  percent of persons with, 7–8, 22–23
  personal growth at end of life and, 115
  research on, 68
  See also Alzheimer's disease
Demoralization, 116–117
Denial
  end-of-life growth and, 113, 115–116
  of family, 113, 115–116
  as mental strategy for facing life-threatening illness, 112
  of patients, 112–113
Depression
  cancer and, 116–117
  end-of-life growth and, 117
  situational, 116–117, 124, 125, 131
  suicide and, 117, 125–126
Diapers, 155
Diarrhea, 69, 153
Dignity
  death with, 20, 126–130, 134–135
  definition of, 127
Do Not Resuscitate (DNR), 21–22, 65, 154, 165

DPA. *See* Durable power-of-attorney (DPA)
Dream visits from loved ones before
    death, 54–55
Drug-seeking behavior, 105
"Due Process of Euthanasia: The Living
    Will, a Proposal" (Kutner), 19
Durable power-of-attorney (DPA)
  appointing, 26, 32–33
  conversations with patient and, 26–27
  ethical wills and, 37–38, 114–115
  forms for creating, 36
  vs. living wills, 26
  proxies
    appointing, 31, 32–36, 37, 130,
      148, 161
    forms, 19, 44
    importance of, 32, 148, 161
  purpose of, 26
  responsibilities of, 26, 27
Dutch euthanasia, 138–144
  accepted indications for, 140
  children and, 140
  guidelines for patient killing and,
    erosion of, 141–143
  mixed reviews of, 143–144
  requirement of repeated requests
    for, 126
  senior citizens and, 140–141
  voluntary *vs.* involuntary, 120,
    139–140
Dutch Justice Ministry, 140
Dutch Pediatric Association, 140
Dutch Supreme Court, 141
Dworkin, Ronald, 62, 129
Dying
  before 21st century
    funeral customs and, 3–4, 5
    in home, 4
    infectious diseases and, 7
    mourning clothes and, 3–4
    preparing body for burial and, 4
    visitation and, 4–5

  in 21st century
    black as color of mourning and, 3–4
    choosing where and when to die,
      124, 126, 130, 136, 144, 164
      (*See also* Euthanasia/physician-
      assisted suicide)
    condolences and, expressing, 3
    distance between family members
      and, 7
    in home, 53–54
    in hospitals or nursing homes,
      6, 7–8
    medical abandonment and, 13–16
    medical language and, 9–16
    place of death within medical
      practice and, 17–18
    technology and, 6–7, 8
    unfamiliarity with dying and,
      1, 2–3
    visitation and, 4–5

E
Emphysema, 22
End of Life, The (Rachels), 106
End-of-life growth, 110–119
  anxiety/fear and, 68, 100, 117–118
  articulating meaning in his/her
    life, 113
  common themes in, 110
  communicating love for each other
    and, 110–111
  concern for one's family and, 111
  conversation and, 111, 113, 115–116
  coping skills and, 111–112
  delirium and, 117–118
  dementia and, 115
  denial and, 113, 115–116
  depression and, 117
  ethical wills/end-of-life letters and,
    114–115
  finding meaning to one's life and, 112
  hope and, 118–119

pain control and, 115
preconditions in, 115
psychiatric disorders and, 116–118
psychological integrity and, 111
religious tradition/spiritual practices
    and, 112–113
soundness of mind and, 115
End-of-life issues
conversations about
    between doctor and patient, 28–30
    between family and patient, 26–28,
        31, 35–36
    form for preparing for, 189–190
    growth at end of life and, 111, 113,
        115–116
    tools to help facilitate, 34–36
hospice guides for, 36
language and, 67–68
pain and suffering, 99–109
See also Advance directives; End-of-
    life growth
End-of-life letters, 114–115
Ethical wills, 37–38, 114–115
European Court of Human Rights, 143
Euthanasia/physician-assisted suicide,
    120–146
American Medical Association's
    position on, 61
autonomy and, 123–124, 130–131,
    132, 140
in Belgium, 121, 143
death with dignity and, 126–130,
    134–135
Declaration of Independence and,
    121–122
definition of, 86–87, 120, 120–121
direct killing *vs.* allowing to die and,
    149–150
Dutch (*See* Dutch euthanasia)
Final Exit and, 94, 134–135
financial consequences of illness and,
    125–126, 136

Hippocratic Oath and, 133
history of opposition to, 133
in Holland, 144
Kevorkian and, 94, 125, 133–134, 135
laws against, 131
legalizing
    opponents of, 135–136, 143, 144,
        145–146
    proponents of, 94, 106, 124–132,
        145–146
in Luxembourg, 143
moral legitimacy of, debate over,
    121–123
patient's need to be in control and,
    130–131
peaceful pill, 143
personhood and, 126
vs. physician-assisted suicide, 121
rational suicide and, 131–132
religion/spirituality and, 131, 135,
    137, 138, 142
suffering and
    spiritual, 107–109
    unbearable, 125
    unnecessary, 124–125
Evans, Susan L., xv
Extraordinary treatment, 20–21,
    91–92, 109

F
Faulkner, Charles, 2
Faulkner, William Harvey, 2
Fear, 68, 100, 117–118
Feeding tubes
    dementia and, 12, 64, 68–70
    as futile treatment, 71–72
    nutritional status and, 72, 84
    PEG tubes, 70
    problems associated with, 69
    removing, 76–77, 82–83
    as temporary bridge to restored
        health, 84–85

Final Exit (Hemlock Society), 94,
    134–135
Final Gifts (Callanan and Kelley), 54
Foley, Kathleen M., 56–57
Foley catheters, 47, 155
Four phases of hope, 118–119
Funeral customs, 3–4
Funeral directors, 52
Futile treatments, 64–74, 88, 154
    data and, 68
    Hippocratic Oath and, 65, 133
    in ICU, 67
    irretrievably dying patient and, recog-
        nizing, 67
    language and, 67–68
    mortality rates for surgeries and, 66
    sanctity of life and, 64–68, 72, 74, 88
    See also Life-sustaining/life-saving
        treatments

G
Gate control theory of pain, 105
Gauderer, Michael, 70
Genesis, 38, 61, 79–80
God
    miracles performed by, 72–73
    playing, 80, 92, 97
Goodbyes, 13, 106, 158
Great Enemy, death as, 10–11, 16, 17,
        18, 122, 162
Greer, George, 77
Grief
    depression and, 116–117
    faith and, 5
Growth at end of life. *See* End-of-life
    growth
Guides for end of life issues, 36

H
Haskins, C. C., 16
Hawkins, Anne Hunsaker, 14
Healer's Power, The (Brody), 65

Health care justice/injustice, 73–74
Healthcare power-of-attorney, 114, 161
    See also Durable power-of-attorney
        (DPA)
Health decline, patterns of, 23
Hearing, death and, 50
Heilbrun, Carolyn, 131–132
Hemlock Society, 94, 134
Hendin, Herbert, 141–142
Hippocrates, 133
Hippocratic Oath, 65, 133
Hippocratic School, 133
Hiram College, 10, 34, 55, 97, 160
Historical mourning test, 78
Holland, euthanasia in, 121, 126,
        138–144
Hope
    definitions of, 15, 118
    four phases of, 118–119
Hospice
    acute care *vs.* hospice care, 56–57
    attitudes of nurses/aides in, 47–48
    bathing after death and, 51–52
    cost of, coverage for, 46, 56, 57
    diet and, 45
    doctor's reluctance to discuss, 58–59
    evaluation of patient for entering,
        43–46
    guides for end of life issues, 36
    home assessment and, 44–45
    hospitalization required during, 60
    in-home care and, 46
    inpatient, 46, 60, 109
    knowledge of, 56
    length of stay in, median, 56–57
    medical equipment provided by,
        44–45, 47, 57
    medications and (*See* Medications)
    outliving hospice benefit, 56
    pain and (*See* Pain; Pain medications)
    palliative care and, 58–60
    paperwork after death and, 50, 57

patients referred to, for only a few
  days, 57
patient's understanding of, 46–47
primary caregivers and, 45
refusing, 56–57
rehearsing moment of death and, 52
removing body after death, 52
rescue squads and, 50
for those without terminal
  diagnosis, 56
when death occurs, 50
Hospice and Palliative Care Nursing
  Association, 58
Hospice of the Western Reserve, 36, 161
Hospital beds, 44, 47
Hoyer lifter, 44–45, 47
Hume, David, 92
Hunger at end of life, 50, 69, 70–72

I
Ice chips, 50, 69, 71, 72
ICU psychosis, 67
Imaginative tests
  historical mourning test, 78
  treatment invention test, 78–79
Imminent death, signs of, 49–51
Incontinence, 42
Indiana Law Journal, 19
Infectious diseases, 7
Inflammation, 100
Inpatient hospice, 46, 109
Insurance coverage for hospice, 46, 56
Intravenous fluids, 71
"It's Over, Debbie" (anonymous), 133

J
Jennings, Nancy, 2
Johnson, Huldah, 54
Jonsen, Albert H., 74–75
*Journal of the American Medical Associa-
  tion (JAMA),* 127, 133
Julian, 79

K
Kapalin, Melinda, 10
Kelley, Patricia, 54
Kevorkian, Jack, 94, 125, 133–134, 135
Kirsch, Michael, 75
Koran, 91
Kutner, Luis, 19

L
Lancet study, 139
Language
  definitions for critical terms and,
    86–87
  futility and other end-of-life issues
    and, 67–68
  in living wills, 20–22
  medical jargon, 9–10
  warfare metaphor, 10–16, 67,
    147–150, 159, 162
Lemon-glycerin swabs, 50, 69, 71, 72
Lerner, Barron, 131–132
Letters, end-of-life, 114–115
Liberty interest, 163
Life-challenged *vs.* terminal, 10
*Life's Dominion: An Argument about
  Abortion, Euthanasia and Individual
  Freedom* (Dworkin), 62
Lifespan, average, 2
Life-sustaining/life-saving treatments,
    63–75
  CPR orders and, 6, 21, 52, 65,
    153–154
  DNR orders and, 21–22, 65, 154, 165
  futile use of, 64, 74–75
  living wills and, 21
  nature and, 149–150
  non-theological approach and, 78–79
  religious traditions and, 75–78
  removing, 65–66, 73
  right to refuse, 90, 130, 163
  sanctity of life and, 61–98
  See also Feeding tubes; Ventilators

Liquid morphine, 48–49, 51, 105, 106
Living wills
  decision-making guided by, 20
  vs. DPA, 26
  first use of term, 19
  forms for creating, 36
  hypothetical choices and, 22
  language used in, 20–22
  laws enabling, 19–20
  limitations in applying, 20–26
  purpose of, 20
  remaining length of life and,
    overestimating, 22–25
  See also Advance directives
Locke, John, 121–122
Lou Gehrig's disease, 13–14, 28, 29, 91,
    134, 144–145, 149
Luxembourg, euthanasia in, 143
Lynch, Thomas, 5
Lynn, Joanne, 91

M
Maladaptive techniques, 112
Mathews, Chris, 97
McCarrick, Theodore, 77
McHugh, Paul, 116–117, 125, 144–146
Medical abandonment, 13–16
Medicare coverage for hospice, 46, 56
Medications
  assistance with, 25
  for delirium, 117–118
  goals of, 137–138
  under hospice care, 44–45
  in hospice evaluation, 43, 44
  See also Pain medications
Medicide, 94
Medicine-as-warfare metaphor, 10–16,
    67, 162
Mental strategies for facing life-threatening
    illness, 112
Merciful death, 97, 106, 120
Mercy killing, 120

See also Euthanasia/physician-assisted
    suicide
Miracles, 65, 68, 72–73, 88
Moon, Rachel, 2
Moral dilemmas
  in euthanasia/physician-assisted
    suicide, 121–123
  moral culpability *vs.* physical causality
    and, 90–91
  moral decision-making and, 92–93
  moral obligations and, 65, 74–80
  Netherlands and, morality in, 138
  in relieving suffering, 100–101
  sanctity of life and, 85–98, 153
"Morality of Euthanasia, The"
    (Rachels), 106
Morphine, liquid, 48–49, 51, 105, 106
Morse, Hannah, 2
Mourning clothes, 3–4
Mouth swabs, 50, 69, 71, 72
Moyers, Bill, 34

N
Nagel, Thomas, 129
Nasogastric feeding tubes. *See*
    Feeding tubes
Natural rights, 121–122
Nature, 148–151
Nazis' "Final Solution," 136, 141
Negative right, 163
Netherlands, morality in, 138
Netty, 141–142
New England Journal of Medicine, 134
New York Review of Books, 129
Nitschke, Philip, 142–143
Nozick, Robert, 129

O
Oijen, Wilfred van, 144
Oncologist, definition of, 13
On Our Own Terms (PBS series),
    34–35

Ordinary *vs.* extraordinary treatment, 20–21, 91–92, 109
Oregon, physician-assisted suicide legislation in, 121, 139, 143

P

Pain, 99–109
  definition of, 100
  growth at end of life and, 115
  poorly treated or uncontrolled, 102–103, 109, 158, 161–162, 163
  research on, 102–106
  vs. suffering, 99–100, 163
  See also Pain medications
Pain medications
  aggressive measures in, 109
  liquid morphine, 48–49, 51, 105, 106
  side effects of, 107
  terminal sedation, 109, 117–118
Paley Lecture, 74–75
Palliative care
  access to, 136
  definition of, 58
  See also Hospice
Patient-Controlled Analgesia (PCA), 102, 106
Peaceful death, 8, 12, 15, 118–119
Peaceful pill, 143
PEG tubes, 70
Pelagius, 79
Permanent Vegetative State (PVS), 79, 81–82, 83
Personhood, 126, 128
Phillips, Derek, 138
Physical causality *vs.* moral culpability, 90–91
Physician-assisted suicide. *See* Euthanasia/physician-assisted suicide
"Piece of My Mind, A" (*JAMA* column), 127
Planning ahead, 160–161

  See also Advance directives; End-of-life issues
Plato, 65
Playing God, 92, 97
Pneumonia, 55, 63, 85
  aspiration, 68–69, 79
Ponsky, Jeff, 70
Presence of "someone not alive," 54–55
Primary caregiver, 45
Prime Time Live (TV series), 144
Protestant Christian Elderly Society, 140–141
Proxy
  appointing, 31, 32–36, 37, 130, 148, 161
  forms, 19, 44
  importance of, 32, 148, 161
Psychiatric disorders, 116–118
  See also Depression

Q

Quasi support, 75
Quill, Timothy, 58, 134–135
Quinlan, Karen Ann, 20, 161

R

Rachels, James, 93, 106
Rapid breathing, 51
Rawls, John, 129
Reeve, Christopher, 64
Reflux (backing up), 69
Refusal
  of hospice care, 56–57
  of life-sustaining/life-saving treatments, 90, 130, 163
Religious tradition/spiritual practices
  end-of-life growth and, 112–113
  ethical wills and, 37–38, 114–115
  euthanasia/physician-assisted suicide and, 131, 135, 137, 138, 142
  spiritual suffering and, 107–109
  suicide and, 131

Religious tradition/spiritual practices
   (*continued*)
  understanding of place of death in
   human life and, 151–152
  See also Sanctity of life
Remmelink Report, 139–140
Republic, The (Plato), 65
Research
  on dying children, 10
  on feeding tubes, 68–72
  on hospice/palliative care, funding
   for, 136
  on likelihood/odds in a given
   situation, 68
  on pain, 102–106
  warfare metaphor in, 11
Resuscitation, 6, 21, 52, 65, 153–154
Royal Dutch Medical Association, 139
Rules, according to Buckley, 160–164
  for being shaped by witnessed deaths,
   163–164
  for death not being optional, 160
  for dehydration and suffering, 162
  for documenting end-of-life
   desires, 161
  for pain control, 161–162
  for pain *vs.* suffering, 163
  for planning ahead, 160–161
  for refusing life-sustaining/life-saving
   treatments, 163
  for warfare metaphor, 161
  for withholding/withdrawing
   treatment, 162–163
Ruskin, Paul, 127

S
Sachs, Greg, 60
St. Augustine, 79
St. Nicholas (magazine), 16
Sanctity of death, 95–97
Sanctity of life, 61–98
  Christian values and, 75–80

church and, 76–77
death as an evil and, 79–80
futile treatments and, 64–68, 72,
  74, 88
history of medicine and, 64–65
life-support technology and, 61–98
likelihood/odds in a given situation
  and, 68
moral dilemmas and, 85–89
moral obligations and, 65, 74–80
in non-religious sense, 62
non-theological approach and, 78–79
religious values and, 75–80
sanctity of death and, 95–97
technology for life-extension and,
  62–64
translations of, 61–62
Saunders, Cecily, 56
Saw-tooth downward pattern, 23, 42
Scanlon, Thomas, 129
Schiavo, Terri, 20, 66, 70–71, 74, 76,
  77, 80–84, 123
*Seduced by Death: Doctors, Patients and
  the Dutch Cure* (Hendin), 142
Self-deliverance, 94, 134
Self-governance. *See* Autonomy
Seven Rules for Dating My Daughter
  (sitcom), 160
Sheets, custom-made, 44
Show codes, 153–154
Simple/ordinary *vs.* complex/extraordinary
  medical procedures, 91–92
Situational depression. *See* Depression
Skin breakdown, 47, 69
Sleep apnea, 40, 41
Sloan-Kettering Medical Center, 31
Slow code, 154
Smith, Wesley, 142–143
"Sometimes Dying Still Stings"
  (Sachs), 60
Soundness of mind, 115
Spiritual counselors and ministers, 108

Spiritual guides, 108
Spiritual practices. *See* Religious
    tradition/spiritual practices
Spiritual suffering, 94, 100, 107–109
Starvation at end of life, 69, 70–72
Stephen Ministry, 53
Stolick, Matthew, 15, 118–119
Suffering, 99–109
    dehydration and, 69, 70–72, 162
    euthanasia/physician-assisted
        suicide and
        spiritual, 107–109
        unbearable, 125
        unnecessary, 124–125
    vs. pain, 99–100, 163
    relieving, moral dilemmas in,
        100–101
    spiritual, 94, 100, 107–109
Suicide
    depression and, 117, 125–126
    Final Exit and, 94, 134–135
    legality of, 131
    See also Euthanasia/physician-assisted
        suicide
Summerfield, Elizabeth, 2
SUPPORT study, 24
Surgeries, mortality rates for, 66
Surrogate decision-making, 148

T
Tachyphylaxis, 105
Talmud, 91
Tame death, 5–6, 8
Technological brinkmanship, 89–90,
    122–123
Terminal illness/terminally ill patients
    appetite and thirst changes in, 50, 69,
        70–72, 162
    children, 10, 72–74, 98, 116
    competent, 44, 47, 132, 139–140, 163
    euthanasia/physician-assisted suicide
        and, 124, 139–140, 143
    four phases of hope during, 118–119
    indignities of, 129
    life-challenged *vs.*, 10
    living wills and, 22
    psychiatric disorders in, 116–118
    See also Cancer
Terminal sedation, 109, 117–118
Terri's Law, 82
Thielicke, Helmit, 96–97
Thirst at end of life, 50, 69, 70–72, 162
Thomson, Judith Jarvis, 129
Thought experiments. *See* Imaginative
        tests
Toileting, 25, 126, 127, 129
Tolstoy, Leo, 116
To refuse to act, 81, 93, 94
Treatment invention test, 78–79
Trial of therapy, 89
Troubled Dream of Life, The (Callahan),
        3, 17

U
U.S. Living Will Registry, 36
U.S. Supreme Court legislation
    euthanasia/physician-assisted
        suicide, 143
    Nancy Cruzan case, 83
    right to refuse life-sustaining/life-
        saving treatments, 163
    Terri Schiavo case, 82
Urinary tract infection (UTI), 25, 29, 42,
        47, 78

V
Vanderbilt, Commodore, 7
Vanderbilt, George Washington, 7
Ventilators
    brain death and, 72–73
    care for a patient on, 28, 63
    decision to turn off, 72–73, 85,
        91, 145
    definition of, 20

Ventilators (*continued*)
  living wills and, 20–21
  long-term dependence on,
    63–64
  as a temporary bridge to restored
    health, 63, 91
Verhey, Allen, 76
Versluys, Zier, 140
Vitalistic view of life, 151–152

W
Walters, LeRoy, 86
Warfare metaphor, 10–16, 67, 147–150,
    159, 162

Washington *Post,* 131
Weisman, Avery, 112
Wendel, Cees van, 144
Wetting the bed, 42
Wheelchairs, 47
Williams, Marjorie, 130–131
"Withholding or Withdrawing Life-
    Prolonging Medical Treatment"
    (AMA), 70
Witnesses to verify signature, 28
Wolf, Susan, 135–136

Z
Zylicz, Ben, 126